Take Control By Giving Up Control

The Value-Centered Fast Track to Organizational Growth

Colin O'Neill

First published 2024

ISBN 979-8-9892047-1-7

Published by VTI Press, San Diego, CA

Dedication

To the quiet architects of change, whose humble leadership and unwavering commitment built the foundation upon which this work stands. May this effort serve as a resounding echo of your enduring legacy.

Contents

Preface   VII

Introduction—Part 1   1

Introduction—Part 2   9

Value Realization   29

Part One: Clarity   51

1. Distributed Authority   53

2. Market Intelligence   69

3. Strategy Expression   87

4. Value Proposition   109

Part Two: Value   129

5. Business Capabilities   131

6. Capacity Allocation   145

7. Value Streams   161

8. Impact Metrics   187

Part Three: Respect   205

9. Advanced Technologies   207

10. Leadership & Talent   227

11. Feedback & Learning   249

12. Value Culture   263

Part Four: Coda   293

Acknowledgments   295

About the Author   297

Preface

The Origins of a System

"**M**om, why is this line so long?" I asked impatiently amid a bustling delicatessen. "I don't know, son," she sighed. Decades would pass before I would encounter the mathematical elegance of queuing theory, but even at ten years old, I sensed inefficiency in the spaces around me. Patterns others accepted as normal often struck me as flawed. I didn't have the language then, but I had the lens—an instinct for spotting disconnects in systems and imagining how they might function better.

That insight matured over time, honed as my world expanded and my experiences grew. It accompanied me through the crucible of the United States Naval Academy, where purpose, mastery, and accountability were not mere virtues, but the bedrock upon which servant leadership and a lifetime of commitment would be built. Later, as an officer in the U.S. Marine Corps, I came to appreciate the intricacies of decision-making in dynamic conditions—circumstances that demanded clarity, versatility, and the ability to lead under pressure. Yet even within these venerated institutions, a quiet realization began to take shape: systems often faltered not from a lack of resources or doctrine, but from their failure to fully account for the complexity and ambiguity of human behavior.

After leaving military service, I turned to organizational consulting as a means of channeling this growing awareness. It be-

came my life's work to help enterprises solve not just technical or structural problems, but the deeper, systemic dysfunctions that erode potential from within. Consulting offered a
privileged vantage point: I worked across sectors—from Fortune 500 corporations to federal agencies to nonprofit networks—and each bore the same invisible burden. The challenges varied in form, but the root causes remained surprisingly
consistent: strategic obscurity, opaque leadership, misaligned
authority, cultural dissonance, and habitual disregard for what
customers and employees truly value.

Over time, a disconcerting pattern emerged. Despite deploying the most sophisticated tools available, few of my clients
experienced enduring benefit. The interventions were logical,
even elegant, but they lacked continuity and staying power. The
reason, I determined, was that most institutional frameworks
sidestepped the very dynamics that make or break human-based
systems: emotion, trust, perception, meaning. These so-called
"soft" elements were anything but peripheral; they were critical.

What troubled me more was how frequently the concept
of "value" was invoked without being wholly understood. In
meeting rooms and strategy decks, value was reduced to margins, throughput, or shareholder returns. But humans don't
make decisions from spreadsheets. They respond to acquired
value—a far richer, more nuanced amalgam of ethics, experience, purpose, and identity. Whether as customers, employees,
citizens, or investors, people are constantly asking: *Does this
reflect what's important to me?*

In that question lies the genesis of the system presented here.
For years, I searched for a comprehensive, integrated framework
that honored the full reality of how organizations succeed or
fail. I found fragments—insightful models from Peter Drucker,
Jim Collins, Simon Sinek, Peter Senge, and others—but no
unifying architecture that wove those insights into a coherent,
actionable system. So I built one—*Valorys*.

The etymology of Valorys (pronounced vah-LOR-iss) derives from the Latin *valorem,* meaning worth, strength, and moral standing. It centers on three principles: clarity, value, and respect. Valorys exists to restore balance between operational rigor and human aspiration, between strategic congruence and adaptive execution. It acknowledges that the future of leadership lies not in control, but in shared purpose, allocated authority, and ethically grounded decision-making.

This system is not theoretical. It is practical, testable, and designed for implementation at every level of an entity. Valorys scales across domains and adapts to context. It begins with leadership mindset, threads through organizational architecture and operations, and culminates in measurable, sustained outcomes. Whether you lead a global enterprise, a government agency, nonprofit, or a mission-driven NGO, Valorys offers a way forward for all.

Valorys is also the conceptual foundation of Vterra—a free, open-source platform that brings Valorys's value-based principles to life through Verix, a realistic AI advisory capability that functions as a virtual consultant for leaders and teams. Together, the Vterra-Valorys-Verix platform addresses myriad institutional challenges with precision and coherence—making sophisticated advisory support accessible to any organization, regardless of size or sector. For leaders conditioned to equate complexity with rigor, the platform's elegance may be its most unexpected quality.

This book exists for one reason: to offer a rigorous framework, a guiding philosophy, and a practical roadmap for those who are serious about building organizations that matter—places where people thrive, where missions endure, and where value is created not as a byproduct, but as a central pursuit. Within these pages is the culmination of five decades of lived experience, rigorous inquiry, and unshakable belief in what human-centered institutions can achieve.

If this work sparks reflection, inspires change, or provides language for what you've long sensed but struggled to articulate, then it will have fulfilled its purpose. This is more than a model. It is a testament of a lifelong journey shaped by the entities I've served, the questions I've asked, and the aspects of daily life I've had the privilege to reimagine.

Welcome to Valorys.

Colin O'Neill
2024, San Diego, California

Introduction—Part 1

The Value Imperative

The Architecture of Human Collaboration

Organizations represent both the structural backbone and ethical compass of humanity. They emerge in configurations both intimate and expansive—from local proprietorships to global enterprises—each born of collective aspiration and sustained through concerted will. At their zenith, institutions transcend function and reflect the philosophical ethos of those who lead them.

Fundamentally, entities are mechanisms for collaboration—arenas where individual capabilities converge to achieve objectives unattainable in solitude. They serve as indispensable catalysts of human advancement, enabling prosperity while furthering the commercial and social evolution of civilization.

Today, however, the organizational landscape has grown markedly more volatile and structurally intricate. While no two institutions are identical, they are uniformly buffeted by converging forces: heightened stakeholder expectations, technological proliferation, geopolitical instability, and intensifying societal angst.

Every entity is, at root, defined by its animating purpose. Its long-term effectiveness rests on the integrity of its architecture, the rigor of its operations, and the culture it fosters. Despite the proliferation of over 70,000 business texts in recent decades, the core challenges of institutional design persist, largely unresolved. Few structures offer the integrative capacity and philosophical clarity necessary for enduring transformation.

Unfortunately, I have seen many enterprises fixate on content—data, domain knowledge, and process—while neglecting context, the holistic awareness that drives substance and defines both limits and possibilities. In the wider digital landscape, this imbalance is amplified by social platforms saturated with volume but starved of contextual depth, creating the illusion of insight without the scaffolding of understanding. Content reflects transient activity; context conveys consciousness and meaning. Without this deeper awareness, performance becomes aimless and organizations drift.

The Modern Value Paradox

The digital age has irrevocably shifted the balance of influence. Consumers now wield unprecedented access to information and exercise formidable discretion in how, where, and with whom they engage. Simultaneously, employees are increasingly adept—technically proficient and often closer to end users than those who supervise them. This reordering of authority creates tension between inherited governance structures and the more adaptive systems demanded by contemporary relevance.

Having worked alongside institutions across the globe and in divergent sectors for over forty years, I have consistently witnessed four recurring dysfunctions that undermine organizational excellence: fragmented authority, erratic leadership standards, superficial engagement with customer priorities, and the absence of a unifying, goal-centered framework that harmonizes decision-making across all levels.

Beneath each of these fractures lies a shared deficit: a misapprehension of value. Though invoked endlessly in corporate discourse, value remains one of the most misunderstood and inconsistently applied constructs in modern enterprise. Yet when value becomes the guiding principle—rather than an afterthought—operational focus, fiscal performance, and strategic integrity become not aspirational ideals but realistic outcomes.

Many firms base decisions on perceived value, yet only realized value expresses an organization's true condition. The ability to distinguish between the two is essential—sound judgment depends on it. Throughout this framework, "value" means realized value. Firms that cannot measure it remain trapped by illusion rather than guided by reality.

A Framework for Institutional Renewal

Every era presents a defining challenge—an inflection point that calls for both conceptual clarity and architectural reinvention. It is not merely a question of execution but of essence: *What is the modern enterprise for, and how must it be operated to thrive?*

Valorys[1] is a response to that question. It is not a technique vying for attention, but a foundational enterprise architecture designed to realign organizational orientation around enduring truths. It reaches beneath the visible composition of an organization to rewrite the foundational logic that governs how people think, decide, and lead. Valorys positions value not as a marketing slogan, but as the central tenet of enterprise function—supported by the deliberate design, honorable conviction, and psychological acuity necessary for sustained relevance.

Valorys's elegance lies in its dual fidelity to simplicity and structural rigor. It is acutely attuned to the cultural and attitudinal levers that induce real change. The system comprises twelve interdependent value amplifiers—each a behavioral schema rather than a theoretical abstraction. When practiced holistically, they restore legitimacy to leadership, infuse work with purpose, and reforge the bond between organizations and those they serve.

To be clear: Valorys is not a vehicle for short-term profit maximization. It is not designed to boost quarterly performance through superficial efficiency gains. Rather, it cultivates lasting excellence through operational discipline, moral clarity, and the alignment of human energy toward worthy goals.

At its core, Valorys is anchored by four architectural tenets: adaptive leadership, distributed authority, empowered workers, and advanced technologies. These elements interconnect to establish a system capable of balancing strategic foresight with operational execution, integrating consumer intelligence with institutional action, and producing value that is simultaneously financial, ethical, and durable. Additionally, Valorys equips leaders with a concise suite of proven practices—actionable takeaways designed to accelerate purposeful transformation and translate intent into measurable progress.

One recurring observation from my advisory work is this: value and control carry an inverse relationship—the more control exerted, the less value created. Authentic progress requires not merely permission, but structured freedom—bounded autonomy that channels initiative within principled guardrails.

Reimagining the Leadership Mandate

At the heart of this work lies a deceptively simple proposition: enduring institutions no longer depend on command-and-control structures but thrive through clarity of direction, trust, and enforceable accountability. Executives cannot plainly decree "create more value"—they must embody the value-driven principles themselves. Reshaping how an organization thinks and behaves demands unwavering leadership commitment. By fostering autonomy within a shared framework, leaders create the conditions under which genuine value can emerge.

Can a single framework meaningfully address the multitude of tensions facing today's institutions? Is Valorys merely a polished distillation of established wisdom, or something materially more substantive? I assert the latter. The knowledge required to transform organizations is not new—it is the integration and disciplined application of that knowledge which has remained elusive.

Today's executives carry extraordinary burden—their decisions ripple across communities, markets, and ecosystems. The ultimate measure of Valorys will not rest in elegant articulation but in its demonstrable ability to produce positive, sustainable outcomes. This system offers a principled model through which organizations can be revitalized—behaviorally, morally, and culturally. It equips them to achieve operational excellence while contributing substantially to the broader human experience.

Reclaiming Purpose in a Complex Age

Many organizations today find themselves at a pivotal threshold. Leaders confront declining productivity, dwindling innovation, and eroding value creation across critical functions. This malaise transcends sector and geography—whether one leads a corporation, nonprofit, governmental body, or civic institution, the obstacles are strikingly similar.

This book offers a coherent, tested system to guide entities toward a future marked by resilience, relevance, and performance. It is intended for executives and senior leaders like you who face mounting complexity, yet remain committed to elevating their institutions. You are striving for unity of effort—individuals aligned in pursuit of meaningful, mutually beneficial objectives. You seek victories that uplift your enterprise, customers, and teams. You are navigating an era of heightened scrutiny and rapid change—and you are searching for durable solutions that balance profitability with purpose.

The insights presented here are not academic luxuries; they are pragmatic tools. Leaders who apply even a subset of these practices will be equipped to reduce costs, integrate AI strategically, mitigate risk, streamline workflows, fortify security, and cultivate both creativity and clarity—amplifying long-term impact.

While these concepts are not wholly unfamiliar, they are organized and reframed with a singular emphasis on value—systematically designed to engender robust, adaptive, and principled firms capable of enduring tomorrow's uncertainty. More importantly, Valorys is not a technical construct—it is, above all, a solution to ease many of the unique challenges faced by present-day enterprises.

Valorys Foundational Practices

1: *Prioritize context over content.* Operational content—the daily flow of information, process, and tasks—is essential but insufficient. Context provides the interpretive framework that enables workers to grasp not just what they do, but why it matters. Without context, even well-executed activity risks becoming directionless motion.

2: *Ground judgment in realized value, not perceived value.* Strategic clarity demands discernment between perception and reality. Decisions anchored in perceived value can mislead; only realized value—that which has been tangibly created, delivered, and sustained—reveals an organization's actual state of health and performance.

3: *Recognize a customer's persistent question.* Every product or service ultimately answers a consumer's timeless inquiry: "Does this reflect what truly matters to me?" The degree to which the answer is yes determines the depth of loyalty, relevance, and long-term market strength.

4: *Emphasize behavioral evolution over structural overhaul.* Valorys does not demand sweeping organizational restructuring. Its transformative power resides in dispositional metamorphosis rather than bureaucratic redesign. Enduring success arises from the steady, disciplined practice of value-aligned behaviors. In this sense, adaptation becomes not a singular aftereffect but a sustained pattern—a habit of performance that amplifies impact over time.

---

1. Valorys[TM] is a trademark of Vterra, Inc.

Introduction—Part 2

The Valorys Effect

The Case for Systemic Change

D rawing upon decades of advisory experience and an extensive review of hundreds of scholarly and business texts, I have sought to distill the most pervasive and destabilizing challenges facing today's executive leadership. While a multitude of issues compete for attention, several critical themes recur with unwavering frequency. These patterns—captured in the accompanying conceptual illustration—form the backdrop against which this work was constructed.

Security Leadership Productivity
Growth Globalization
Finance Profitability
Talent
Costs Disruption
AI Sustainability
Stakeholders
Vision Accountability Economy
Transformation Privacy
Consumers
Automation Alignment

Though not exhaustive, the challenges enumerated reflect the persistent dysfunctions that the Valorys system was specifically designed to address. To suggest that a single framework can meaningfully confront these entrenched problems may seem audacious. Yet readers who engage fully with this publication will find the claim not only defensible but compelling.

The conspicuous absence of a coherent, foundational business architecture that acknowledges these systemic realities has left many organizations adrift. Fortunately, there is widespread agreement among management thinkers on a crucial point: sustainable performance demands systemic change, not scattered interventions. It requires a guiding model grounded in responsible stewardship, engaged talent, and a value-centric operational ethos.

Such a perspective departs from conventional governance schemes by placing value—not hierarchy, compliance, or workflows—at the center of enduring organizational success. A genuinely modern system must therefore:

- Elevate distributed authority, adaptive leadership, and workforce enablement as the nexus of creativity and innovation.

- Reinforce coherence between strategic leadership and the employees tasked with execution, effectively closing the communication divide.

- Enhance value creation through a synergy of advanced technologies, connected workers, rapid feedback cycles, and contextual data-informed decision-making.

- Reframe customers as co-creators, yielding offerings that reflect not only articulated needs but latent expectations as well.

These are not ancillary enhancements—they are structural imperatives. In response, Valorys was conceived not for marginal improvement, but as a comprehensive, integrated solution to the foundational design flaws undermining institutional performance.

From Concept to Capability

Valorys is not speculative, but a battle-tested architecture for institutional transformation, born from the crucible of the most challenging consulting assignments and refined through adversity. It is designed to sharpen strategic focus, streamline complexity, reduce operating costs, and accelerate enterprise-level returns. At the same time, it preserves what matters most: the autonomy and creative latitude professionals require to excel.

A formal definition follows:

> The Valorys system is a *value-centered approach* that combines *adaptive leadership, distributed authority, empowered workers, advanced technologies, fast learning,* and *value amplifiers* to accelerate growth and impact. It achieves *organizational alignment* by connecting strategy, execution, and customer experience to optimize resources and capital, creating superior value for both consumers and the enterprise.

Through this architecture, organizations move beyond brittle, legacy constructs and toward responsive, integrated models better suited to the dynamic conditions in which they now operate. Valorys is not a panacea, nor does it promise transformation through radical reorganization. Instead, it reinvigorates institutions through behavioral alignment, strategic clarity, and minimal disruption.

This framework challenges leaders to reimagine how their institutions generate, deliver, and realize value in a post-industrial

economy. Its outcomes are tangible: optimized resource allocation, faster delivery cycles, more inventive problem-solving, and
enhanced adaptability to volatile market conditions.

Crucially, Valorys is not a theoretical abstraction. It is rooted
in lived executive experience, adaptable to diverse organizational
structures, and designed to support growth without destabilizing existing operations. Whether guiding a global enterprise, a
mid-tier firm, a government agency, or a mission-driven nonprofit, Valorys equips leaders with tools to provoke intellectual rig-
or, accelerate enterprise learning, and elevate customer outcomes
amid daily turbulence.

Readiness Meets Urgency

Valorys is most relevant when three conditions converge:

- *Urgency has reached critical mass*—The board and senior
  leadership are no longer satisfied with marginal gains.
  The prevailing business system fails to yield acceptable
  results, and meaningful renewal becomes a non-negotiable imperative.

- *Leadership openness exists*—Executives are intellectually
  prepared to explore concepts that challenge the orthodoxy of legacy systems. They recognize that current conditions require frameworks offering strategic and operational advantages traditional models cannot deliver.

- *A holistic solution is required*—Leaders understand that
  piecemeal adjustments no longer suffice. Fragmented
  fixes produce temporary relief, not lasting rejuvenation.
  What is needed is a systemic approach—one capable of
  addressing the organization as a living, interconnected
  whole.

As these essential parameters align, comprehensive institutional metamorphosis may then be set in motion. To fully grasp its architecture and potential, the Valorys system must be deconstructed into the foundational components of its definition:

- Value-centered approach

- Adaptive leadership

- Distributed authority

- Empowered workers

- Advanced technologies

- Fast learning

- Value amplifiers

- Organizational alignment

Elevating the Value-Centered Approach

As explored in the Preface, few words are as ubiquitous in modern business parlance—and yet as inconsistently understood—as "value." It is routinely invoked, seldom interrogated. Value is not an absolute; it is inherently relative. Each stakeholder—whether investor, employee, or customer—interprets value through a distinct lens, informed by context, expectation, and experience.

This fluidity renders value an elusive concept for many organizations. Nevertheless, the consensus remains: value reflects the worth or significance ascribed to an offering, relationship, or outcome—held as esteemed, prized, and appreciated. And while often treated as qualitative, the Valorys system transforms this ambiguity into strategic precision.

Executives frequently ask: Can value be measured? What units apply? Does a universal framework exist? How do internal and external valuations diverge? These are not abstract inquiries; they reflect a pressing need to operationalize what has too often remained conceptual.

My position is unequivocal: value is fully measurable—internally and externally—using enterprise-specific indicators. Valorys treats value not as a marketing slogan but as the central determinant of institutional health, longevity, and relevance. And critically, it recognizes that value must be defined by the organization and its stakeholders, not imposed by external doctrines or passions.

When applied consistently, this approach catalyzes a more discerning, deliberate enterprise—one capable of responding to its constituents' evolving needs while maintaining coherence, discipline, and ethical intent.

The Immediacy of Adaptive Leadership

The archetype of effective leadership in the twenty-first century has diverged dramatically from the models of earlier generations. Icons such as John D. Rockefeller, Howard Hughes, Henry Ford, and Steve Jobs epitomized a style marked by singular vision and centralized command. Success was predicated on their ability to orchestrate implementation through authoritative oversight—a model well-suited to an era when economic and technological change unfolded at a comparatively deliberate pace.

Today, however, the rate of transformation has accelerated to such a degree that legacy paradigms often obscure more than they illuminate. Like the proverbial frog unaware of the water's rising temperature, many executives fail to perceive the magnitude of disruption reshaping their operating environments. Stakeholders increasingly seek leaders who provide assurance without rigidity—those capable of navigating volatility with composure and precision.

In this context, the most effective executives are not those who exert maximal control, but those who adapt with discernment. These are *adaptive leaders*—individuals who sense inflection points, interpret emerging signals, and implement calibrated shifts that preserve momentum without destabilizing coherence.[1]

Adaptive leadership begins with a fundamental acknowledgment: no single person possesses comprehensive knowledge. Strategic success requires inclusive collaboration across multidimensional teams—drawing upon a wide spectrum of expertise, perspectives, and lived experiences. Leaders who embrace this reality willingly forgo the illusion of omnipotence in favor of participatory stewardship.

Adaptive leaders define expectations with clarity and ensure that their organizations are equipped with the tools and bandwidth necessary to fulfill them. They lead with empathy, operate with integrity amid uncertainty, and commit themselves to ongoing self-examination. They actively investigate their assumptions, welcome alternative viewpoints, and remain intellectually receptive to new ideas.

Above all, adaptive leaders prioritize the growth and flourishing of those they serve. Their most significant responsibilities lie not in issuing directives, but in creating conditions for others to experiment, take thoughtful risks, and learn through reflection. They balance strategic guidance with operational autonomy, establishing clear decision-making frameworks while granting employees latitude to chart innovative paths and take ownership of outcomes.

They also engage in structured introspection—regularly examining how, when, and why to relinquish control—so as to cultivate truly empowering organizational environments.[2]

A \$30 billion insurance firm recently encountered an existential threat: a well-capitalized rival encroaching on its core market. Executive leadership, still entrenched in command-era thinking from the late twentieth century, failed to recognize that innovation often lies closest to the front lines. Instead, they continued to centralize ideation within senior ranks—marginalizing the very personnel with the clearest view of emerging customer needs.

The result? Repeated restructuring, leadership churn, and diminishing competitive relevance. The fundamental miscalculation was not strategic—it was philosophical. Traditional management does not produce the flexible competencies required in today's institutional environment. Adaptive leadership does.

In what scholars now refer to as a *VUCA* [3] environment—volatile, uncertain, complex, and ambiguous—research consistently demonstrates that composed, adaptive leadership outperforms traditional methodologies in enabling sustainable performance. [4] To the uninitiated, the idea of *taking control by giving up control* may seem paradoxical. In reality, it is a foundational tenet of modern enterprise resilience.

The Distributed Authority Mandate

Organizational design has historically oscillated between two structural poles: hierarchy and network. *Hierarchies* offer consistency and control through vertical chains of command. *Networks*, by contrast, provide lateral flexibility, adaptive capacity, and collective intelligence. [5] Each has strengths and limitations. But today, the most resilient institutions increasingly blend both—leveraging the directionality of hierarchies with the adeptness of distributed systems.

> This hybrid architecture finds precedent not only in modern management literature but in foundational political theory. In *The Federalist Papers*, American patriots Alexander Hamilton, James Madison, and John Jay proposed a model of governance wherein loosely affiliated states retained local authority under a unifying federal framework. Hamilton presciently observed a barrier still familiar to contemporary enterprises. He said:
>
>> Among the most formidable of the obstacles which the new Constitution will have to encounter may readily be distinguished [by] the obvious interest of a certain class of men in every State to *resist all changes* [emphasis added] which may hazard a diminution of the power, emolument, and consequence of the offices they hold under the State establishments.[6]
>
> Internally, many companies face this identical challenge today: leaders clinging to illusory control, thinking only in parochial terms, and obstructing the adaptability their firms need to succeed in an increasingly interconnected world.

The reluctance to cede authority persists in many modern institutions. Executives, habituated to control, often hesitate to adopt decentralized structures—even while acknowledging their potential. The transformation of leadership identity is essential. The era of the all-knowing executive is over; today's leaders must become orchestrators of distributed insight, enablers of collective action, and architects of shared purpose.

This transition is not a loss of authority, but a realignment of its application. Emotional intelligence, not technical omniscience, becomes the most critical leadership asset. The objective is not abdication, but the judicious placement of decision-making power in proximity to expertise. When done well, the result is striking: the responsiveness of a network combined with the coherence of a hierarchy.

John Kotter, in his pivotal Harvard Business Review article *Accelerate!*, argued that hierarchies best define the "why" and the "what," while networks are optimally positioned to determine the "how."[7] Simon Sinek echoed this in *Start with Why*, underscoring the importance of orienting action around purpose.[8] These insights converge to support a central thesis: distributed systems outperform centralized ones in environments of accelerated change.

Despite profound technological evidence—manifest in the rise of the internet, social platforms, and AI—numerous organizations remain shackled by top-down control. The allure of command remains strong: it flatters the ego and reinforces perceived certainty. Yet it rests on an increasingly untenable proposition—that a single executive can possess superior judgment on every consequential decision. That premise is no longer credible.

Valorys embraces distributed authority as its animating principle. Without an unwavering commitment to devolving decision rights, institutions should not attempt to implement the system. This is not a peripheral feature—it is the cornerstone of value-centered transformation.

Empowerment emerges when individuals are granted the autonomy to make meaningful decisions aligned with their roles and competencies. This stimulates engagement, accelerates learning, and amplifies institutional intelligence. When adaptive leaders bridge hierarchical clarity with networked dynamism, they unlock a profound synthesis—one that activates organizational potential without compromising strategic direction.

Dr. David Hawkins, in *Power vs. Force*, articulates a profound distinction: authentic power manifests through competence, mastery, and wisdom, while force represents mere coercive exertion. He observed, "One characteristic of force is arrogance; power is characterized by humility. Force is pompous; it has all the answers. Power is unassuming."[9] True authority flows not from coercion but from credibility—rooted in emotional integrity and demonstrated competence.

Napoleon Hill, in his cogent 1928 text *The Law of Success*, proclaimed: "No man can control others unless he first controls himself."[10] The corollary follows naturally—those who possess self-mastery are best equipped to inspire self-governance in others.

There is no longer a defensible rationale for leadership models rooted in domination. Enlightened guidance, grounded in mutual respect and clearly articulated expectations, yields far greater engagement and performance. Indeed, to relinquish control effectively, leaders must create unambiguous outcomes, defined timeframes, and transparent criteria for success—thereby enabling autonomy without sacrificing accountability.

Furthermore, this standard discredits a manager's "just do what I say" directive, for when workers gain strategic awareness, they move beyond simple obedience and assume shared ownership of their organization's outcomes. In such environments, soliciting employees' insights becomes a strategic imperative. When people feel heard, they contribute more willingly. When they feel trusted, they perform more boldly. Intellectual diversity, iterative practices, and self-organizing teams emerge as natural consequences—accelerating responsiveness and embedding innovation at every level of the enterprise.

Executives face a deluge of competing theories on institutional control—many of which advocate starkly opposing approaches.

The real question is not whether to choose autonomy *or* oversight. The wiser path is to hold both in balanced effect. This requires what might be called a "paradoxical posture"—one that accepts complexity without succumbing to it.[11] When trust and clarity coexist, when freedom is bounded by purpose, and when authority is distributed yet aligned, organizations become more than efficient—they become adaptive, resilient, and alive.

As Stephen M. R. Covey asserts in *Trust and Inspire*, trust is the prerequisite for letting go. It is the gateway to empowerment, ownership, and enterprise-level growth. When trust becomes the operating norm, accountability follows—not as a mandate, but as a reflection of shared purpose.[12]

Empowered Workers at Scale

Enterprises anchored in value creation do not passively inherit talent—they intentionally cultivate it. They seek individuals whose intellectual curiosity and adaptive mindset render them not merely capable contributors, but transformative forces within the enterprise. These empowered workers, inspired by adaptive leadership, align themselves with a purpose that transcends transactional roles. They interpret change not as a destabilizing force but as an invitation to evolve—constantly refining their competencies while embracing responsibilities beyond their original remit.

Value-centered organizations routinely invest in cross-functional development to expand internal versatility and elevate workforce resilience. As consumer expectations shift and markets undergo recalibration, employees with multi-dimensional capabilities become irreplaceable assets. Cross-training not only broadens individual proficiency but also engenders a richer understanding of enterprise interdependencies—cultivating mutual respect across disciplines and enhancing team cohesion.

Equally vital is the integration of intelligent technologies to create what I term *enhanced workers*—professionals who pair human insight with machine-enabled precision. These individuals remain in sync with technological advancements, not merely using tools but learning from them. The speed at which digital platforms evolve demands a workforce that views continuous learning as a professional norm, not an aspirational virtue.

In recruitment, evaluating technical capacity is no longer sufficient. Organizations must assess a candidate's aptitude for collaborative excellence and intellectual sharpness. When enterprises invest in compensation, infrastructure, and development, the hiring decision becomes one of strategic magnitude—worthy of meticulous scrutiny.

Though not every role flourishes in high-touch, team-oriented environments, many of the most effective institutions now operate through compact, purpose-driven units characterized by daily interaction, reciprocal trust, and shared accountability. Whether in physical proximity or interacting virtually, enhanced workers thrive within such groups, exhibiting the emotional intelligence and mutual regard necessary for close coordination and creative tension. Their adaptability, insight, and enduring curiosity make them indispensable contributors to sustainable growth.

Advanced Technologies as Accelerators

The rise of the *adaptive organization* reflects a fundamental shift in how institutions pursue relevance in an environment defined by rapid flux.[13] Adaptation, once a desirable trait, has become essential.

To this discourse, I add a critical dimension: the incorporation of intelligent technologies as structural enablers. Enterprises that embrace these tools become what I describe as *synchronic organizations*—entities that prioritize present realities over inherited constraints, optimizing for current context rather than historical precedent.

In a synchronic enterprise, over 80% of the workforce leverages integrated technologies to transcend individual limitations and engage in collective intelligence. These tools are not peripheral conveniences; they are embedded instruments that facilitate collaboration, accelerate insight synthesis, and amplify human potential. Every digital contribution—no matter how granular—becomes part of a larger mosaic of institutional awareness.

This acceleration in connectivity and cognition has transformed global commerce, yet many legacy establishments remain encumbered by static cultures and rigid hierarchies. They struggle to convert collective intelligence into strategic advantage—not because the tools are lacking, but because the leadership mindset remains unchanged.

As customers adopt sophisticated platforms to make more informed decisions, entities must evolve in parallel. Synchronic organizations achieve this convergence. By combining automation with meaningful human engagement, they extract extraordinary value from fewer personnel—enhancing productivity while preserving morale.

A Culture of Fast Learning

Peter Senge's *The Fifth Discipline* introduced a paradigm shift: organizations must become living systems that learn continuously. [14] In such cultures, experimentation replaces rigidity, and insight becomes a renewable resource.

This ethos of fast learning is foundational to Valorys. Adaptive leaders cultivate environments where intellectual risk is not merely tolerated, but actively encouraged. By fostering feedback-rich ecosystems, they transform tentative ideas into tested innovations and dormant potential into actionable capacity.

Many valuable insights lie passive within the minds of thoughtful yet introverted contributors—voices too often marginalized in extroversion-biased settings.[15] By building inclusive mechanisms for participation, adaptive leaders enrich their decision-making with a diversity of perspectives, producing more refined, more resilient outcomes.

History offers a vivid example. In 1932, as the United States faced economic devastation, Franklin D. Roosevelt declared: "The country demands bold, persistent experimentation. It is common sense to take a method and try it: if it fails, admit it frankly and try another. But above all, try something!"[16] Lacking a clear path forward, he delegated authority to proven collaborators like his Secretary of Labor, Frances Perkins, a servant-leader who epitomized Roosevelt's trial, error, and course correction as governing principles.[17] This conviction in distributed expertise accelerated one of the most comprehensive economic recoveries in modern history.

Today's leaders face similarly ambiguous terrain. The experiential-experimental learning cycle—observe, attempt, reflect, adapt—remains the most reliable path to long-term performance.[18] When organizations engage in structured experimentation, guided by metrics linked to defined outcomes, they evolve not by accident but by deliberate iteration.

This recursive process builds momentum. Each loop refines the next, enabling teams to identify latent opportunities, overcome complex obstacles, and capitalize on emergent trends. In a world where agility alone is insufficient, fast learning becomes the bedrock of institutional resilience.

Value Amplifiers Unleashed

Traditional organizational controls serve a necessary but limited function: safeguarding integrity, ensuring compliance, and maintaining operational consistency. They are designed to constrain risk, not to stimulate growth.

In contrast, *value amplifiers*—or *value amps*—propel institutions forward, activating unrealized potential by channeling distributed authority and value-based orientation into purposeful action. They represent nonlinear levers: small inputs often yield outsized outcomes.

Unlike conventional controls, which operate at the periphery, value amps form the strategic nucleus of a value-centered enterprise. Their implementation reframes how work is organized, how outcomes are measured, and how teams coordinate with one another.

When applied effectively, value amps reinforce cultures of trust, empowerment, and shared ownership. They delegate control while preserving coherence. Rather than issuing mandates, leaders create conditions where high performance emerges organically through alignment, autonomy, and accountability.

These practices are introduced in the subsequent Value Realization section and examined in greater depth across the chapters that follow. For now, it is enough to understand this: value amps are not theoretical ideals—they are practical instruments that elevate operational systems into platforms for sustained innovation and principled prosperity.

Organizational Alignment That Endures

One of the most persistent sources of institutional failure is misalignment—between intention and execution, between vision and behavior, and between internal strategy and external demand.

Too often, strategic direction is diffused through vague guidance or becomes unmoored across layers of abstraction. In such settings, even the most talented teams struggle to execute because they lack clarity, context, or connection to the organization's ultimate aims.

Valorys addresses this fragmentation through a dual integration: vertical and horizontal. Vertically, it connects board-level objectives to front-line action. Horizontally, it aligns institutional function with customer expectations—ensuring that what is promised is also experienced.

Central to this model is the *goal-strategy-outcomes* (GSO) structure. GSOs[19] document enterprise priorities across defined timeframes—typically quarterly or annually—anchoring measurable outcomes to strategic imperatives. These expressions serve as navigational instruments, continuously monitored and refined, enabling leaders to assess progress, recalibrate approach, and respond to real-time signals from the market.

This integration of clarity, accountability, and measurement allows organizations to pivot without losing continuity—advancing adaptability while safeguarding intent.

The Harmony of Structure and Flow

Valorys harmonizes the speed of networks with the discipline of hierarchies. It fuses the fluidity of collective intelligence with the steadiness of strategic design, enabling organizations to move quickly without forfeiting cohesion. By aligning intelligent tools, shared goals, and disciplined execution, Valorys transforms complexity into coordinated motion.

Within this architecture, value amps act as conductors—magnifying purpose, trust, and performance across every layer of the enterprise. When leaders release rigid control, they invite others to act with clarity, creativity, and conviction. The result is an environment where collaboration flourishes, learning accelerates, and innovation becomes not an initiative but a cultural rhythm.

Valorys is not a cure-all; it is a catalyst. Its power lies in enabling organizations to evolve naturally toward resilience and purpose, respond to disruption with wisdom rather than haste, and shape the future with intention rather than reaction.

From Theory to Transformation

This treatise departs from abstraction to present a pragmatic architecture for transformational growth. It does not indulge in leadership typologies or psychological conjecture; rather, it offers a disciplined system of tools, processes, and constructs designed to strengthen enterprise performance—regardless of size, sector, or geography.

The value amps introduced here serve as essential enablers of competitive endurance. Their modular design allows for scalability, while their interdependence fosters systemic coherence. Each can be emphasized, sequenced, or adapted according to organizational context and strategic priority.

As with any living framework, discernment remains essential. Apply what is necessary, adapt what resonates, and omit what proves inapplicable—without compromising the integrity of the whole. Valorys is built to meet leaders where they are, guiding transformation through relevance rather than prescription.

Valorys Contextual Practices

1: *Lead through a value-centered system.* Adopt a value-driven approach that unites adaptive leadership, distributed authority, empowered workers, advanced technologies, fast learning, and strategic value amplifiers into a cohesive architecture to create a self-reinforcing system that sustains organizational vitality.

2. *Integrate vertically and horizontally.* Pursue integration across both dimensions of enterprise performance. Vertically, connect board-level intent to front-line execution. Horizontally, align internal functions with the core value-creating mechanisms that propel organizational growth, resilience, and long-term sustainability. Goal-strategy-outcomes act as navigational instruments within this continuum, providing leaders with a dynamic means to measure progress, interpret real-time signals, and adjust course accordingly.

---

1. Ronald Heifetz, *Leadership Without Easy Answers* (Harvard University Press, 1998).

2. Ben Ramalingam, et. al., "5 Principles to Guide Adaptive Leadership," *Harvard Business Review* (September 11, 2020).

3. Warren Bennis and Burt Nanus, *Leaders: Strategies for Taking Charge* (Harper & Row, 1985).

4. David Bradford and Allan Cohen, *Managing for Excellence: The Guide to Developing High Performance in Contemporary Organizations* (Wiley Management Series, 1997).

5. John Kotter, "Hierarchy and Network: Two Structures, One Organization," *Harvard Business Review* (May 23, 2011).

6. Alexander Hamilton, James Madison, and John Jay, *The Federalist Papers* (1788).

7. John Kotter, "Accelerate!" *Harvard Business Review* 90, No. 11 (November 2012).

8. Simon Sinek, *Start with Why: How Great Leaders Inspire Everyone to Take Action* (Portfolio-Penguin Group, 2009).

9. David Hawkins, *Power vs. Force: The Hidden Determinants of Human Behavior* (Sedona, AZ: Hay House, 1996).

10. Napoleon Hill, *The Law of Success*: Lesson 7 (Beverly, MA: Orne Publishing, 1928)

11. G. Gilbert and M. Sutherland, "Indirect Control: The Future of Management?" Idea #276. *Ideas for Leaders* (University of Pretoria, December 2013).

12. Stephen M. R. Covey, *Trust and Inspire: How Truly Great Leaders Unleash Greatness in Others* (Simon & Schuster, 2022).

13. Stephen H. Haeckel, *Adaptive Enterprise: Creating and Leading Sense-And-Response Organizations* (Harvard Business Review Press, 1999).

14. Peter Senge, *The Fifth Discipline: Art and Practice of the Learning Organization* (Random House, 1992).

15. Susan Cain, *Quiet: The Power of Introverts in a World that Can't Stop Talking* (Crown, 2012).

16. Debbie Aiken, "Remembering FDR's Commencement Address at Oglethorpe," *The Source* (May 22, 2012).

17. George Whitney Martin, *Madam Secretary, Frances Perkins* (Houghton Mifflin Harcourt, 1976).

18. David A. Kolb, *Experiential Learning: Experience as the Source of Learning and Development* (Prentice Hall, 1983).

19. GSO® is a registered trademark of Vterra, Inc.

Value Realization

The Locus of Value

The Valorys Value Creation System

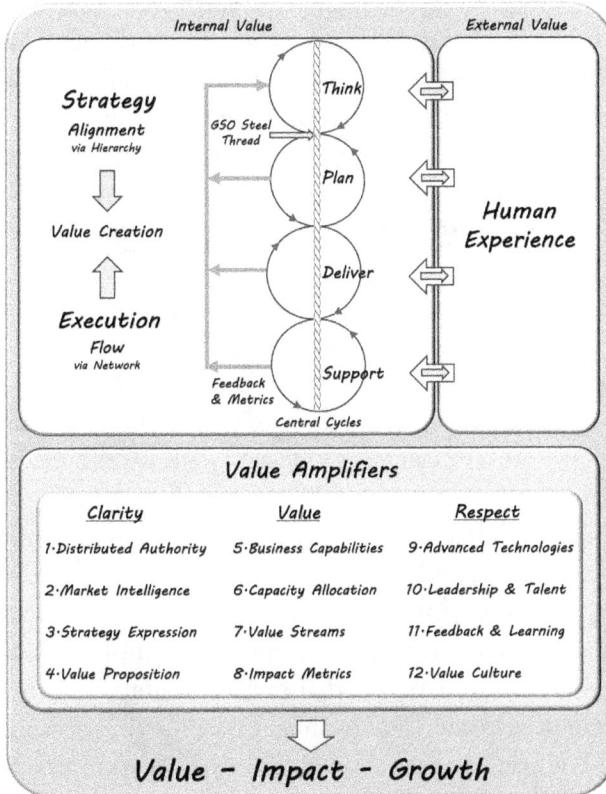

Internal Value | External Value

Strategy
Alignment
via Hierarchy

GSO Steel
Thread

Think

Plan

Value Creation

**Human
Experience**

Deliver

Execution
Flow
via Network

Feedback
& Metrics

Support

Central Cycles

Value Amplifiers

Clarity	Value	Respect
1·Distributed Authority	5·Business Capabilities	9·Advanced Technologies
2·Market Intelligence	6·Capacity Allocation	10·Leadership & Talent
3·Strategy Expression	7·Value Streams	11·Feedback & Learning
4·Value Proposition	8·Impact Metrics	12·Value Culture

Value - Impact - Growth

Value as Strategic Foundation

I n today's economy, value transcends mere importance—it forms the fundamental substrate of all commercial activity. When consumers deliberate purchasing decisions, value invariably ascends above all competing considerations. This profound awareness necessitates that organizations cultivate value with careful intentionality and precision.

A value-centered approach represents far more than contemporary vernacular. It embodies a reconceptualized system for cognition, organizational architecture, and operational execution that penetrates market turbulence with unparalleled efficacy. When institutions embrace this mindset, a remarkable metamorphosis occurs: employees cease apprehending change as an existential threat and begin mastering it as a strategic instrument. Enterprises become more nimble, render more astute decisions amid resource constraints, and construct enduring competitive advantage.

This principle exceeds the boundaries of Fortune 500 companies. Whether you are orchestrating a small or medium-sized business, administering a governmental agency, directing a nonprofit institution, or steering an NGO, the immutable truth remains: prioritize value creation or risk irrelevance. Entities that disregard this fundamental reality are not merely forfeiting opportunities—they are engaging in a precarious gamble with their organizational survival.

The principles that govern market evolution and resilience have always rewarded those who adapt—and punished those who don't. Modern leaders face that same immutable reality with compounded urgency. So how might they sustain relevance and realize enduring impact in a world defined by complexity and volatility? The answer, I believe, is elegantly captured in five interconnected concepts that form a deceptively simple mathematical construct: what I term the *value formula*. This compact yet powerful expression distills a handful of key concepts into a memorable aphorism for steering a modern enterprise with purpose and precision.

Unpacking the Value Formula

Let us examine the formula in greater depth:

- *Alignment* engenders organizational lucidity of unprecedented clarity. When every stakeholder—from executive leadership to operational front lines—comprehends not merely their tactical responsibilities but the strategic imperatives underlying them, transformative outcomes materialize. GSOs surmount corporate nomenclature to become shared focal points that concentrate all a company's resources upon unified objectives with laser-like precision. This communal language is elaborated in Chapter 3: Strategy Expression.

- *Flow* sustains value momentum wherein products and services reach customers with ideal velocity and low-friction efficiency. Value streams—the critical conduits that transport offerings from conceptual genesis to market delivery—demand relentless optimization as examined in Chapter 7: Value Streams. Bottlenecks, redundancies, and waste vectors become transparently visible. Any element that cannot augment value or enhance utility is subject to remediation or elimination.

- *Customers* evolve into strategic co-creators rather than passive recipients. Instead of speculating about market preferences, astute enterprises integrate consumers directly into the value creation architecture. This collaborative partnership unveils customer inclinations and emergent trends that other players invariably overlook, generating sustainable competitive differentiation.

- *Adaptive leaders* revolutionize traditional management paradigms. Rather than micromanaging operations or maintaining the illusion of omniscience, they establish clear vision and operational boundaries, then strategically withdraw. They empower frontline teams—the personnel most proximate to customers and organization's challenges—to innovate and execute within clearly defined parameters. This signifies leadership through enablement and empowerment, not authoritarian control.

- *Value* is the unifying metric that justifies an institution's efforts, connecting financial outcomes to purpose, trust, and long-term societal impact. Value is multidimensional: for consumers, it is what they are willing to pay for; for investors, what they are confident putting capital behind; for employees, it is what gives their work meaning and satisfaction; and for society, it reflects how an enterprise contributes to the broader well-being.

Valorys in Structural Form

Valorys orchestrates value creation at the convergence of executive stewardship, customer-centric propositions, tactical implementation, and operational synergy. Its paramount objective is to enable entities to optimize their economic valuation while simultaneously fortifying them against the mercurial currents of future disruption. The Valorys system furnishes a comprehensive framework, strategic guidance, and intellectual corpus comprising a constellation of universal patterns that remain agnostic to organizational taxonomy or structural configuration.

Valorys's essential components are rendered through an abstract graphical representation that facilitates consistent, logical interpretation across diverse contexts. The upper portion of the Valorys diagram illuminates the intricate interrelationships between internal institutional dynamics and external market forces.

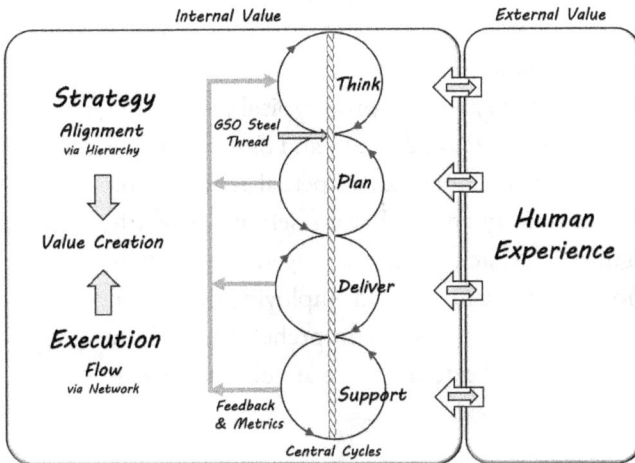

Value amplifiers, depicted in the diagram's lower hemisphere, constitute the foundational elements of efficient, high-performing organizations; they serve as the animating force that breathes vitality into Valorys and transforms theoretical constructs into operational reality.

Value Amplifiers		
<u>Clarity</u>	<u>Value</u>	<u>Respect</u>
1·Distributed Authority	5·Business Capabilities	9·Advanced Technologies
2·Market Intelligence	6·Capacity Allocation	10·Leadership & Talent
3·Strategy Expression	7·Value Streams	11·Feedback & Learning
4·Value Proposition	8·Impact Metrics	12·Value Culture

The Central Cycles of Valorys

Valorys embodies a comprehensive corporate framework for exemplary leadership and organizational governance. It revolves around what I refer to as the *central cycles* of a prototypical institutional model: *Think, Plan, Deliver,* and *Support*. These cycles embody the nuanced, perpetual activities present within every entity that are seldom explicitly recognized or systematically leveraged. Deliberately acknowledging, defining, and employing the central cycles facilitates improved comprehension of how both internal and external value are ultimately generated and amplified.

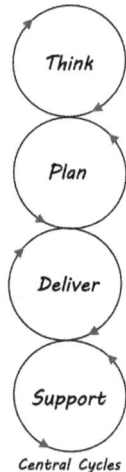

Central Cycles

- *Think*—Prioritizes executive leadership's ideation and cognitive processes to comprehend expansive market dynamics and contemplate innovative, disruptive strategic possibilities. This cycle concentrates on goal crystallization and outcomes-based thinking.

- *Plan*—Emphasizes growth orchestration and enterprise alignment to unlock value while surfacing the organization's unique strengths. The Plan cycle generates a structured, sequential blueprint for value provisioning, ensuring deliberate progress toward strategic goals.

- *Deliver*—Optimizes flow and execution excellence; it aggregates direct consumer intelligence through prototyping, rigorous testing, and expeditious market validation before, during, and after product and service delivery. It simultaneously facilitates institutional synchronization around value distribution and customer-centric orientation.

- *Support*—Encompasses the orchestration, quality, and continuity of post-delivery services and lived experiences across the full customer ecosystem, transforming interactions into enduring value and organizational learning. Every touch becomes a data-bearing event—informing learning loops, refining future design, and recalibrating enterprise judgment.

The central cycles are arranged in a vertical stack, with Think positioned at the apex and Support anchored at the foundation. They are intricately interwoven to show that each cycle nourishes its subordinate with clear vision while simultaneously informing its superior with actionable feedback and experiential learning. Each cycle maintains tight coupling to a value proposition co-created by cross-functional teams comprising enterprise strategists, technical specialists, and customer representatives.

The conceptual foundation of central cycles is not new—Valorys extends Dr. W. Edwards Deming's classic *Plan-Do-Check-Act (PDCA)* cycle developed during Japan's post-World War II industrial renaissance. The system also incorporates Aristotle's 2300-year-old *hypothesis-experiment-evaluation* scientific method. What distinguishes this system is its goal-strategy-outcomes linguistic framework employed to communicate strategic intent to every facet of institutional operations. The GSO construct, influenced by the objectives and key results (OKRs) technique pioneered by Intel's iconic CEO Andy Grove in the 1970s,[1] serves as the common denominator that unifies disparate organizational components, establishing a communications architecture that flows in every direction across the enterprise. GSOs systematically eliminate assumptions prematurely and generate reliable predictive intelligence via leading, rather than lagging, indicators through discovery and learning cycles.

Institutional Benefits of Valorys

Enterprises derive substantial benefits from Valorys without requiring reorganization or implementing sweeping role modifications. Instead, this system enables entities to manage alignment and flow more efficaciously within their existing operational infrastructure. The system aligns and scales both horizontally and vertically across any entity; it provides leadership at every stratum with the essential substructure and risk-tolerant mechanisms necessary for decentralized authority, rapid experimentation, and collaborative learning in partnership with employees, associates, and customers. Fundamentally, Valorys integrates distinctive ways of thinking, operating, and leading.

In my extensive experience, I have discovered that the sheer magnitude of unproductive labor within most institutions proves staggering. Without comprehensive visibility into the underlying causes of this accumulated waste, numerous organizations resort to over-hiring and consequently reap diminished productivity from their talent investments. Since human capital represents the most expensive resource for most entities, adopting value amplifiers can preserve considerable financial resources by employing fewer personnel to generate superior value outcomes.

Embracing Valorys and its value amplifiers may precipitate significant reductions in operational and support services expenditures due to enhanced performance, improved efficiency, and decision-making excellence throughout the corporate milieu, thereby minimizing superfluous effort. Implementing this system enables precise integration and improved flow dynamics, culminating in the completion of the right work with substantially fewer resources.

The Dual Value Structure

Valorys integrates two distinct but interrelated parts: *internal value* and *external value*.

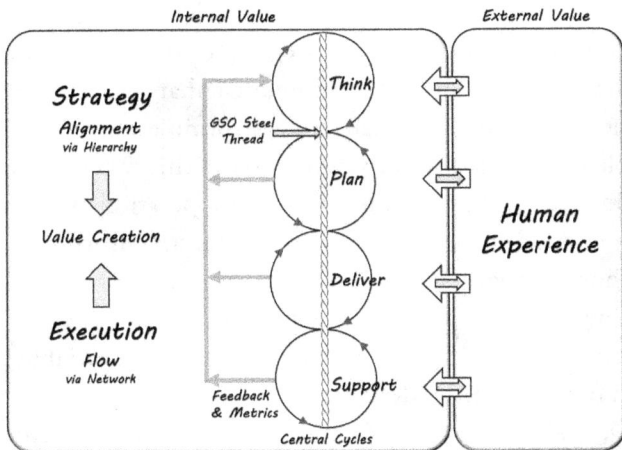

Internal Value Dynamics

Valorys's internal value component manifests through sophisticated interconnectedness among the four central cycles, enabling organizational intent transmission across hierarchical levels through the GSO semantic framework. Subsequently, invaluable insights are gained through an embedded feedback architecture that informs leadership through standardized metrics, creating an ascending intelligence flow. This continuous circulation ensures that enterprise strategy maintains continuous connectivity with its operational components—those who execute the actual work—and reciprocally influences strategic direction.

The Strategy dimension of the method encompasses the Think and Plan cycles, which encapsulate the hierarchical characteristics of an institution and provide the comprehensive alignment essential for meaningful impact and sustainable growth. The Execution component comprises the Deliver and Support cycles that are fundamental to network dynamics. Here, flow emerges as a critical factor—when an organization's execution mechanisms operate with optimal efficiency, its adaptive capacity experiences dramatic enhancement.

A value creation link between strategy formulation and tactical implementation distinctly differentiates this system from conventional approaches. Value creation is operationalized in what are referred to as *value streams.*[2] Value streams concentrate on how entities generate authentic value; they enable the flow engine to pivot expeditiously as goals and strategies evolve based upon feedback loops and dynamic external variables. When an organization understands its value streams comprehensively, it aligns institutional resources to facilitate value creation for both the firm and its customer communities.

To achieve transformative impact at the enterprise level, optimizing the entire organizational setting becomes imperative, rather than merely managing a few well-administered units. Value streams, functioning as an integrated and holistic component, connect multiple business functions that traditionally prove challenging to manage because of their fragmented nature. This technique demonstrates both elegant simplicity and sophisticated clarity, as it identifies inefficiencies and unnecessary or counterproductive operations requiring direct attention and mitigation.

Value streams inevitably connect leadership's decision-making processes with the competencies required for achieving stated objectives. GSOs determine the requisite worker profiles and skill configurations necessary to accomplish strategic targets; consequently, the talent acquisition and professional development units become intimately engaged in the strategy expression process to ensure optimal human capital alignment with desired enterprise outcomes.

The Subtleties of External Value

The external value element of Valorys illuminates the strategic partnership and collaborative symbiosis between an organization and its customer ecosystem. Here, an entity articulates and comprehends its customers' value definitions to ensure its products and services deliver precisely what consumers genuinely desire and appreciate.

Attempting to comprehend markets and their consumer constituencies represents an arduous undertaking for most institutions due to the inherent complexity of human psychology and behavioral patterns. It frequently demands creativity and exploratory investigation to discern the authentic motivations underlying an audience's expressed preferences. As the emergent global economy becomes increasingly integrated into everyday existence, grasping the experiential preferences of those served becomes essential. Latent motivators might encompass trust, privacy, security, and personal belief systems—variables not traditionally considered in conventional product development and marketing paradigms.

The human experience undergoes constant evolution, and value determinants transform correspondingly over time. As a result, value propositions must be co-created and regularly refined through collaborative engagement between organizational representatives and customer populations. Cross-functional *fusion teams* are established at multiple tiers to accomplish precisely this aim—working synergistically with customers to co-develop optimal offerings and solutions that satisfy consumers' intrinsic requirements.[3]

How Value Is Amplified

Value Amplifiers		
Clarity	_Value_	_Respect_
1·Distributed Authority	5·Business Capabilities	9·Advanced Technologies
2·Market Intelligence	6·Capacity Allocation	10·Leadership & Talent
3·Strategy Expression	7·Value Streams	11·Feedback & Learning
4·Value Proposition	8·Impact Metrics	12·Value Culture

The paradoxical principle of taking control by giving up control illuminates the fundamental sophistication of Valorys. Its conceptual foundation recognizes that conventional hierarchical command-and-control paradigms have become increasingly obsolete within today's experience-driven economic landscape.

Value amplifiers cultivate an environment of organizational inclusivity, wherein leadership echelons collaborate synergistically with personnel and clientele to generate substantive value propositions. The strategic alliances forged between network components enable enterprises to respond with dexterity to dynamic external variables. This method synthesizes the purposeful strengths inherent in formal structures with the adaptive resilience characteristic of networked systems.

The value amplifiers delineated in this book facilitate rapid value generation through empowerment and innovation. Each amplifier distinguishes Valorys from conventional institutional models, collectively providing the systematic structure for enterprise excellence:

1. *Distributed Authority*—Empower personnel through a sophisticated hybrid hierarchy-network paradigm to augment decision-making acuity, deliver exemplary products and services with enhanced velocity, diminish operational expenditures through streamlined procedural optimization, and cultivate heightened employee engagement, organizational commitment, and professional fulfillment.

2. *Market Intelligence*—Leverage empirically-grounded, micro-focused market analytics to architect innovative, transformative strategies and value propositions across the comprehensive consumer spectrum.

3. *Strategy Expression*—Articulate strategic imperatives with unambiguous clarity throughout institutional strata via a unified, enduring GSO framework.

4. *Value Proposition*—Design customer experiences around their complete transformational journey, using cross-functional domain and consumer teams to uncover latent, unspoken needs that become foundational for

co-creating distinctive value propositions.

5. *Business Capabilities*—Expeditiously cultivate, manage, and refine modular enterprise and technological competencies essential for achieving organizational strategic objectives.

6. *Capacity Allocation*—Replace aspirational assumptions with institutional realities, employing rigorous prioritization to direct scarce resources toward the most consequential strategic imperatives.

7. *Value Streams*—Apply this predominant value-generation mechanism to optimize operational flow, delivery excellence, customer support, and comprehensive return on investment.

8. *Impact Metrics*—Monitor financial performance and value impact within each pivotal work cycle through near real-time analytics.

9. *Advanced Technologies*—Embrace emerging automated innovations to nurture a culture of perpetual learning and innovation, navigate market complexities with greater finesse, and leverage interconnectedness to propel sustainable growth and organizational success.

10. *Leadership & Talent*—Establish collaborative alliances between management and workers through adaptive leadership methodologies and strategic skill enhancement initiatives to promote talent retention and institutional cohesion.

11. *Feedback & Learning*—Utilize abbreviated operational cycles and a closed-loop system to generate rapid feed-

back and accelerated learning during product and service development and delivery, acknowledging that experiential learning represents the most efficacious approach to validate stated hypotheses.

12. *Value Culture*—Sustain a value-centric organizational ethos through authentic communications, reciprocal respect, cultural optimization, and value-driven economic principles.

These value amplifiers are the foundational architectural elements that enable entities to respond with proficiency to evolving market imperatives and emerging opportunities while disseminating these adaptations throughout an enterprise with requisite expediency. Valorys confronts one of contemporary institutional management's most formidable challenges—achieving corporate strategic objectives while the economic terrain undergoes continuous transformation, without constraining resources within static operational parameters.

Valorys itself remains a theoretical construct until value amplifiers are operationally manifested. The subsequent portions of this work will examine how value amplifiers bring the system to life and how they galvanize Valorys to fulfill its defining purpose: exceptional value delivery, meaningful impact, and sustainable organizational growth. Each value amplifier embodies a recurring pattern distilled from empirical observation and practical application, and within each chapter, I will illuminate pertinent real-world implementations. However, let us first review the cyclical dynamics inherent in value creation processes.

The Rhythm of Value Creation

Value creation is the purposeful transformation of capital, talent, and judgment into outcomes that enrich stakeholders, sustain institutional purpose, and secure enduring relevance. It is not incidental but the central pursuit—non-negotiable in its priority and foundational to lasting impact.

At the highest level, value creation begins with a periodic reaffirmation of purpose and priorities—often set during board or executive strategy sessions. These assemblies define a focused set of shared objectives that serve as the entity's strategic compass for the year or planning horizon.

From these goals, executive leadership formulates the principal pathways required to achieve them. Within the Think cycle, strategic outcomes are clarified and translated into enterprise-wide direction. This phase sets the stage for organizational alignment, establishing where to compete, how to differentiate, and which eventualities matter most.

The Plan cycle ensures that capital, talent, and time are allocated in service of these priorities. Leaders assess existing capabilities and identify where new competencies—technical, operational, or relational—must be built or acquired. Strategic investments are directed toward closing those gaps, either through internal development, external partnerships, or targeted acquisitions.

Execution is carried out through curated work portfolios managed by accountable business units. These collections translate strategic goals into measurable action, with each unit responsible for operationalizing a portion of the institutional strategy. In the Deliver cycle, value streams convert capabilities into outcomes, producing the products, services, and experiences that define the organization's standing in the market.

The Support cycle closes the loop as the continuity layer of value realization—the moment where delivery matures into relationship and transactions evolve into sustained trust. It is an intelligence-generating system that captures lived customer experience as operational signal.

What emerges is not a linear process, but a strategic operating rhythm—an adaptive cycle that links boardroom intent with frontline execution. It ensures that value creation is not incidental, but deliberate, repeatable, and measurable. This dynamic flow is the foundation of the Valorys system, where clarity of purpose, empowered execution, and disciplined measurement converge to create enduring institutional value.

An Architecture for the Holistic Enterprise

Valorys stands independently of software, algorithms, or digital infrastructure. It is a disciplined system for value creation anchored in clarity, structured through the transmission of goal–strategy–outcomes, and sustained by feedback loops that keep activity tethered to realized contribution. Even in the absence of advanced tools, leaders would still think with precision, plan with intent, deliver with accountability, and support their offerings with integrity.

Vterra[4] is a free, open-source platform designed as a disciplined container for truth-governed leadership, created specifically for leaders of mid-size companies, nonprofits, government agencies, and NGOs, and released under the Apache License 2.0 and Creative Commons. It solves a systemic problem: artificial intelligence without governing structure amplifies noise. Piecemeal AI adoption is suboptimal and can produce more disruption than progress. Vterra provides a holistic solution—one where AI is adopted for the right reasons, not as novelty, and employed in its rightful place to create meaningful value and lasting impact.

Vterra integrates three interdependent components. Its foundation is Valorys—the governing system that defines how value is created, how authority is distributed, and how judgment remains anchored to clarity, respect, and measurable outcomes. Valorys establishes the ethical and structural bedrock of an institution, ensuring that growth, innovation, and human engagement remain tethered to purpose rather than organizational noise or legacy hierarchy.

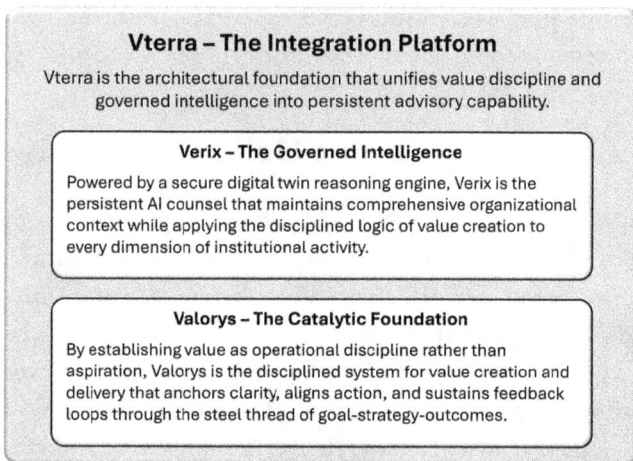

Vterra – The Integration Platform

Vterra is the architectural foundation that unifies value discipline and governed intelligence into persistent advisory capability.

Verix – The Governed Intelligence

Powered by a secure digital twin reasoning engine, Verix is the persistent AI counsel that maintains comprehensive organizational context while applying the disciplined logic of value creation to every dimension of institutional activity.

Valorys – The Catalytic Foundation

By establishing value as operational discipline rather than aspiration, Valorys is the disciplined system for value creation and delivery that anchors clarity, aligns action, and sustains feedback loops through the steel thread of goal-strategy-outcomes.

The second layer is *Verix*,[5] the interactive advisory presence that emerges when disciplined value architecture converges with enterprise-specific artificial intelligence. Verix is not a dashboard, nor a generic conversational agent. It is a virtual consultant presented as a realistic three-dimensional humanoid who interacts directly with leaders and teams. Through dialogue, it engages institutional reality in real time—surfacing strategic drift, modeling trade-offs, clarifying dependencies, and exposing second-order consequences before they mature into material risk.

Behind this embodied interface operates a secure digital twin powered by a dedicated, enterprise-specific large language model. This model assimilates institutional knowledge repositories, operational data, and cultural context to form a continuously evolving digital representation of the organization. Verix reasons from this living structure within permissioned boundaries that preserve absolute data sovereignty and executive control. It interprets performance signals and behavioral patterns through the disciplined logic of Valorys, ensuring analysis remains anchored to declared goals and defined outcomes.

Vterra is the overarching architecture that connects these three components within an open, extensible environment. It establishes permission structures, safeguards data integrity, and enables deployment across enterprises, agencies, nonprofits, and mission-driven institutions without imposing uniformity of purpose. If Valorys is the discipline of value-centered leadership and Verix is the embodiment of governed advisory reasoning, Vterra is the architecture that makes their integration systemic—transforming methodology into operating reality and scaling disciplined insight across distributed authority.

From Traditional Consulting to Persistent Advisory Presence

Traditional consulting operates through episodic engagement. A challenge emerges, advisors are retained, recommendations are delivered, and implementation proceeds. When the advisors depart, insight becomes intermittent, context dissipates, and institutional learning slowly dissolves.

Vterra enables a fundamentally different model. Instead of periodic advice, the organization gains persistent advisory presence. The digital twin maintains a living representation of institutional conditions. Valorys supplies the value-centered logic through which those conditions are interpreted. Verix delivers AI-enabled analysis that continuously evaluates implications, opportunities, and risks. Organizations no longer purchase insight in discrete intervals — they cultivate an enduring strategic partner capable of maintaining context, testing assumptions, and reinforcing alignment at the speed modern complexity demands.

Vterra represents the logical culmination of the work you are about to explore in depth. As you proceed through the twelve value amplifiers that follow, consider them not only as conceptual disciplines, but as principles that can be continuously illuminated and strengthened within this architecture. Through disciplined application alone, they can transform an institution. With an AI-enhanced advisory presence, they become continuously stress-tested and refined. What begins in this book as a value-centered discipline ultimately becomes, through Vterra, a systemic capability—one that enables organizations not merely to respond to complexity, but to operate within it with enduring clarity and sustained success.

Value Realization Best Practices

1: *Implement value principles and exemplary practices across all levels of your organization.* Doing so cultivates adaptability, elevates productivity, and enhances profitability. The value formula serves as a shared maxim—aligning management and workforce around the collective pursuit of sustainable value creation and delivery.

2: *Leverage the Valorys value creation system as a holistic architecture for strategic coherence.* Valorys provides deep analytical insight into value development through its twelve complementary value amplifiers. It helps organizations of every scale understand and refine their interconnected mechanisms of value creation and delivery. By synthesizing strategy, operations, and customer experience, Valorys positions customers as co-creators of meaningful propositions and transformative outcomes.

3: *Gain operational clarity through the lens of recurring enterprise cycles—Think, Plan, Deliver, and Support.* Applying a precise goal-strategy-outcomes model, Valorys communicates strategic intent across hierarchies while continuously feeding learning and performance insights from execution back to leadership. This bidirectional design strengthens alignment between internal operations and external value creation, enabling institutions to address both the pragmatic and psychological needs of their customers.

4: *Heighten performance through the twelve value amplifiers.* Each amplifier functions as a strategic lever, exponentially expanding organizational capacity for value creation, measurable impact, and sustainable growth. Together, they animate the Valorys framework, translating principle into practice and intention into realized performance.

5: *Employ the Vterra platform to institutionalize value-centered, truth-governed leadership.* Built on the foundation of Valorys, the Vterra platform anchors authority and judgment to disciplined governance and measurable value. A digital twin provides a continuously learning view of the enterprise, while Verix converts that intelligence into real-time strategic advisory services that sustain organizational wisdom.

---

1. John Doerr, *Measure What Matters: How Google, Bono, and the Gates Foundation Rock the World with OKRs* (Portfolio/Penguin, 2018).

2. James Womack and Daniel Jones, *Lean Thinking: Banish Waste and Create Wealth in Your Corporation* (Simon & Schuster, 1996).

3. Ashutosh Gupta, "Why Fusion Teams Matter," *Gartner Research* (February 2022).

4. Vterra™ is a trademark of Vterra, Inc. More information may be found at vterra.ai.

5. Verix™ is a trademark of Vterra, Inc.

Part One: Clarity

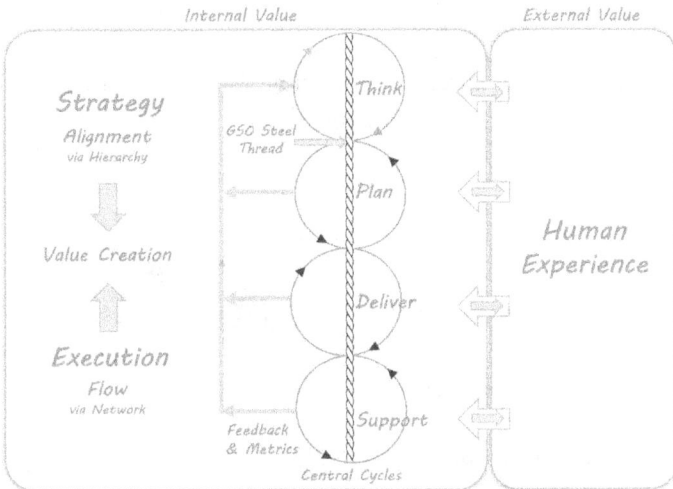

Internal Value — External Value

Strategy
Alignment
via Hierarchy

GSO Steel Thread

Think
Plan
Deliver
Support

Value Creation

Human Experience

Execution
Flow
via Network

Feedback & Metrics

Central Cycles

Clarity

1. Distributed Authority
2. Market Intelligence
3. Strategy Expression
4. Value Proposition

Amplifiers

ue		Respect
Capabilities		9. Advanced Technologies
Allocation		10. Leadership & Talent
treams		11. Feedback & Learning
Metrics		12. Value Culture

V alue creation is why organizations exist—guiding how they deliver, execute, and enrich those they serve. In this section, I explore the value amplifiers that cultivate a deeply rooted, organization-wide understanding—an essential prerequisite for advancing an enterprise toward the future it aspires to create. Yet many organizations struggle to articulate their strategic intent with the necessary precision and internal coherence, often falling short in converting that vision into clearly defined goals and empirically measurable outcomes.

When applied in concert, these four value amplifiers produce the strategic clarity required to construct coherent, actionable strategies—linking intent to execution through a shared framework of purpose and accountability.

Chapter 1: Distributed Authority

Chapter 2: Market Intelligence

Chapter 3: Strategy Expression

Chapter 4: Value Proposition

Distributed Authority

Democratizing Institutions

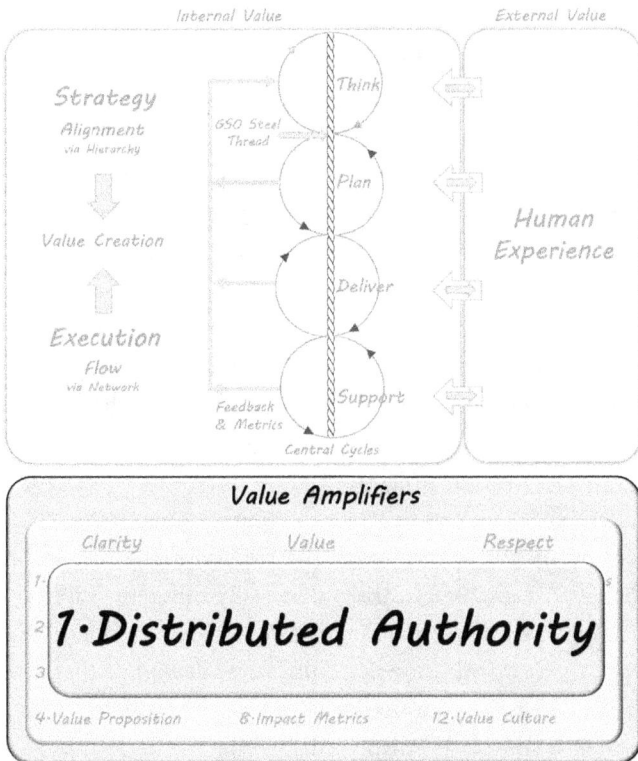

Rethinking Organizational Control

The question of whether centralized or decentralized operations prove more suitable for this era of empowered workers and rapidly advancing technologies captivates various scholars and practitioners, myself included. With over a decade of commissioned service in the U.S. Marine Corps, one might presume I would advocate for consolidated, command-and-control methodologies. However, such an assumption would be incorrect. That said, I must confess I employed a controlling leadership style earlier in my career. Experience ultimately revealed this paradigm's fundamental inadequacy—it generated suboptimal outcomes and, more painfully, eroded the trust those under my authority had vested in me.

While conventional wisdom suggests that Western military establishments remain predominantly hierarchical, they have systematically transitioned toward hybrid operational models over the past fifty years. This evolutionary process has facilitated the testing and implementation of cutting-edge technologies that have enhanced combat effectiveness with substantially reduced staff requirements. Numerous times I have observed the transformative power of self-regulation, which not only cultivates genuine ownership among personnel but also amplifies their commitment and resourcefulness. This might be characterized as *bounded autonomy*[1]—wherein units, teams, and individuals operate with considerable latitude within clearly defined parameters to accomplish their mission without excessive supervision.

Distributed authority carries materially different implications than "decentralized control," a terminology that frequently refers to horizontal organizational architectures devoid of hierarchical structure. I wish to emphasize that Valorys explicitly does not advocate for completely dispersed control.

Only a handful of companies worldwide—such as Haier Group, W.L. Gore, and Patagonia—have demonstrated that flat structures can be efficacious and scale internationally. However, the successful implementation of such organizational designs hinges on the presence of exceptional leadership, strong cultural foundations, clear communication systems, and a workforce possessing specific, advantageous characteristics. Therefore, I employ the term distributed authority to illuminate the attributes of a hybrid model, which I believe offers optimal advantages for most organizations given contemporary realities.

Balancing Structure and Freedom

In his 2020 *Merge World* article, Alexandre Pelletier provides further elaboration on this fundamental principle. He contends that, within the ongoing discourse between centralization and decentralization, no definitive resolution exists; both elements prove indispensable. Organizations that adhere rigidly to centralized models constrain their growth potential. Conversely, complete decentralization proves insufficient because certain centralized components remain essential for governance and directionality. Hybrid models that synthesize both approaches are optimally positioned to adapt expeditiously with minimal organizational friction. The appropriate equilibrium between centralization and decentralization varies for each enterprise and may evolve over time to accommodate new strategic initiatives and the firm's developmental trajectory.[2]

Opening the decision-making process cultivates trust and ensures comprehensive alignment with organizational objectives. Emphasizing collaboration and shared aspirations over internal competition further enhances confidence and engagement, fostering a culture characterized by autonomy *and* accountability.

Transitioning to a hybrid model entails transforming an entity's fundamental ethos. Leaders progressively retreat from hierarchical decision-making, promoting transparency and psychological safety—conditions in which ideas, insights, and knowledge cascade freely. When thoughts flow, energy follows.

This angle accelerates innovation by removing bureaucratic bottlenecks, allowing organizations to respond swiftly to market changes, seize emerging opportunities, and distinguish themselves from competitors.

Trust, Accountability, and Impact

Adaptive leaders go beyond mere delegation; they define clear, measurable outcomes that elevate intrinsic motivation, reduce burnout, and channel energy toward meaningful contribution.[3] When individuals forge authentic connections with institutional priorities, creativity flourishes, and innovation emerges organically.

Reciprocal trust between workforce members and leadership echelons establishes an indispensable precondition for value-centered entities to function at optimal capacity. Trust facilitates transparent communication and collaborative synergy, enabling teams to operate cohesively without apprehension of judgment or interpersonal discord. Trust simultaneously enhances employee engagement and institutional commitment, diminishing attrition rates while augmenting productivity.

However, emphasis on the relational dimensions of organizational evolution does not suggest that Valorys relies exclusively upon social dynamics. While firms seek to inspire their workforce, Valorys employs empirical analytics to ascertain whether outcomes are being actualized and quantify the value created and delivered. Demonstrating empathetic leadership represents one essential competency; holding members accountable for their performance reflects an entirely distinct capability. Strategic balance proves indispensable.

The Case for Shared Authority

A recent study published in Harvard Business Review explored how progressive leadership influences employee performance, job satisfaction, and organizational commitment. Drawing from a meta-analysis of 105 independent studies, the researchers found that inspirational leaders were significantly more effective at stimulating employee creativity and organizational citizenship behavior compared to routine task completion. Workers under such leaders also reported higher levels of trust.

The influence of enabling leadership was especially pronounced among newer employees, who were more inclined to take risks, pursue opportunities, and strive to leave a positive impression. Empowered employees consistently demonstrated greater confidence, stronger commitment, and enhanced creativity in problem-solving. Taken together, the findings highlight the importance of tailoring leadership approaches to cultural context, industry dynamics, and workforce experience levels to maximize motivational effectiveness.[4]

This extensive analysis, which examined over 100 empirical studies across diverse global contexts, definitively establishes that distributing organizational authority confers substantial benefits upon an enterprise. Despite overwhelming evidentiary support, why do numerous leaders resist relinquishing hierarchical control? I contend this stems from fundamental apprehension regarding operational autonomy and profound trepidation concerning subordinate performance failures. I empathize with these individuals because their concerns possess legitimate foundations and merit thoughtful acknowledgment. Each leader harbors distinctive reasons for this institutional anxiety, making it prudent for organizations to provide executive coaching, therapeutic counseling, or professional development to address their apprehensions constructively.

The Human Resources for Health journal determined that leadership styles promoting employee empowerment and shared authority significantly enhance organizational commitment and professional satisfaction.[5] Similarly, the Harvard Business Review reports that firms with moderately flattened (not entirely flat) structures and distributed operational processes substantially outperform traditional hierarchical organizations regarding market responsiveness and workforce engagement.[6]

However, distributing authority extends beyond commercial enterprise applications. Empirical research shows that hybrid organizational models within public sector agencies enhance decision-making acuity, resource allocation efficiency, and comprehensive operational effectiveness.[7] Additional scholarly investigations confirm that non-profit organizations embracing distributed leadership paradigms exhibit greater innovative capacity and adaptive resilience, resulting in amplified programmatic productivity and substantive community impact.[8]

The Human Side of Transformation

I am now convinced that authentic transformation can only materialize when entities integrate the emotional and psychological dimensions of human behavior into organizational improvement efforts. The evidence is compelling. Under Satya Nadella's stewardship, Microsoft cultivated a growth mindset culture that encouraged employees to treat challenges as learning opportunities and failures as data. Empathy became a strategic principle—not merely for customer understanding, but as the foundation of a workplace where diverse ideas could surface and people felt safe to take risks. The results were measurable: team collaboration increased, innovation accelerated, and Microsoft reclaimed its position as the world's most valued company.[9]

In a 1929 interview with *The Saturday Evening Post*, Albert Einstein remarked, "Imagination is more important than knowledge. Knowledge is limited. Imagination encircles the world."[10] His observation underscores the truth that breakthrough progress arises not from rigid adherence to what is already known, but from the freedom to imagine what could be.

Likewise, poet laureate Maya Angelou reminds us that while words and actions may fade, the emotions they evoke endure—an insight that speaks directly to the influence leaders wield when they empower others. Within distributed authority structures, this influence is magnified. Leaders are not mere conductors orchestrating from the podium, but stewards who create conditions where individuals can exercise imagination, judgment, and initiative. Each person's contribution, distinct yet interwoven, strengthens the collective performance.

Numerous scholars confirm that today's workers seek not prescriptive control but the latitude to shape outcomes, supported by resources and trust. When authority is shared rather than hoarded, organizations unlock reservoirs of creativity, lower resistance to change, and generate a deeper sense of ownership.

- Daniel Pink - In *Drive: The Surprising Truth About What Motivates Us*, Pink shows how autonomy, mastery, and purpose represent primary motivators for contemporary workers, superseding traditional control and reward mechanisms.

- Simon Sinek - In *Leaders Eat Last* and *The Infinite Game*, Sinek emphasizes leadership that empowers and inspires personnel, cultivating atmospheres of trust and collaboration.

- Brené Brown - In *Dare to Lead*, Brown concentrates on valuing vulnerability and empathy in leadership, promoting workplaces where employees feel genuinely supported and trusted.

- Cal Newport - In *Deep Work* and *A World Without Email*, Newport advocates for creating environments that support focused, meaningful work, granting employees greater autonomy and task control.

- Reid Hoffman - In *The Alliance: Managing Talent in the Networked Age*, Hoffman examines the transition from traditional employment relationships toward more flexible, mutually beneficial arrangements.

- Sheryl Sandberg - In *Lean In*, Sandberg addresses empowering workers, particularly women, to assume initiative and leadership roles within the workplace.

***

Jenna's corner office commanded a view of the entire Denver Tech Center, but she wasn't looking outward. Instead, her attention was fixed on a single sheet of paper—the quarterly numbers that had summoned us here. The silence stretched until my business partner, Nishant, cleared his throat.

Jenna finally turned, fixing us with the penetrating stare that had earned her the reputation "Ice Queen" among Denver's technology circles. She possessed formidable intelligence and calculating precision. Yet in her six months as Chief Technology Officer, she had already eliminated twenty percent of her engineering staff while the company's market share in household robotics continued its precipitous decline.

"Let's get this over with," she said. "What's your big insight after a week of poking around my company?"

I slid the proposal across the table. "Distributed authority. Your product development approval process is killing innovation while your competitors are gaining ground."

Jenna laughed, a short, harsh sound. "You're kidding, right? Sales have been flat for a year, our vacuum line is getting demolished by Zitek and Smartys, and your solution is to let the inmates run the asylum? I hired you to improve our product line, not dismantle what little structure we have left."

"The current structure *is* the problem," Nishant countered, unfazed by her hostility. "Your senior leadership team rejects seventy to eighty percent of product proposals. Good ideas die in committee because executives who haven't spoken to a customer in years don't 'feel' the market demand."

"That's called having standards," Jenna snapped. "We're not running a charity for every half-baked idea our focus groups get excited about."

"Tell me about your Casakleen K10 and the Omnovex models," I said, redirecting the conversation.

Jenna's eyes narrowed. "What about them?"

"Your biggest successes in the last five years, correct? The K10 was a hit and Omnovex is still outperforming projections."

"You did your homework," she conceded. "What's your point?"

"Where did those products originate?" I pressed. "Not through your standard review process, I'm betting."

Jenna's expression flickered. "True, the Casakleen was a skunkworks project. And the Omnovex came from our intern program."

"Exactly," Nishant said. "Your best performers bypassed your approval system. They had freedom to develop without the gauntlet of executive review killing innovation before it could breathe."

"So your solution is anarchy?" Jenna barked.

"Your competitors are gaining market share with less centralized decision structures," Nishant continued. "We interviewed former employees of both Zitek and Smartys. Their product teams have innovation budgets and autonomy to experiment before bringing concepts to leadership."

"That still feels like chaos," she said flatly.

I decided to shift tactics. "You brought us in to find issues with your product line. In the last six months you've cut headcount, tightened the approval processes, and your competitors are still eating your lunch."

The direct challenge hung in the air. Jenna stared through the window for an extended moment, her fingers tapping on the desk.

"Let me noodle on it overnight," she said with finality, "I'll see you in the morning."

The next morning, her tone was less hostile as we walked into her office. "Your proposal is an overcorrection," she said. "Distributed authority without structure is just as broken as our current bureaucracy."

"I agree, then let's refine it," I suggested. "You've built systems that scaled. What would make this work?"

"Distributed authority isn't the problem. Undefined authority is. Here's what I propose: distributed decision-making with defined boundaries and real consequences."

Nishant and I exchanged knowing glances as she continued.

"Product teams get allocated innovation budgets—small ones—with clear parameters. Inside those boundaries, they don't need approval for experiments."

I leaned back, not expecting such a quick, succinct counter-proposal.

"But," Jenna continued, "they own their results completely. If they meet targets, they get more budget and autonomy. Miss them and they lose both. No hiding failures in committee decisions or blame-spreading."

"That's more structured than what we proposed," Nishant admitted.

"Because you're proposing a philosophy. I'm proposing a system." Jenna looked up sharply. "Distributed authority only works when the boundaries are crystal clear. We're not asking teams to be creative—we're demanding it, and measuring the results."

She continued, "My team will set the guardrails and hard constraints: performance requirements, technical specifications, security standards, brand non-negotiables. Teams track and report metrics rigorously. Quarterly reviews based on outcomes, not process compliance."

"And senior leadership's role?" I quipped.

"We become editors, not gatekeepers. We review results, not ideas. We set context on market strategy and company direction, then get the hell out of the way. But we create systems to surface problems before they become disasters. Real-time dashboards, not quarterly PowerPoints."

"That's...not what we expected from you," I admitted.

"Because you thought I was a control freak?" Jenna's lips tightened. "I don't oppose distributed authority. I oppose magical thinking. This isn't about empowerment and collaboration buzzwords. It's about designing accountability systems that capture the benefits of local decision-making without the chaos."

"Discipline as the foundation of freedom," Nishant mused.

"Exactly." Jenna nodded. "We create the structure where teams can actually deliver innovation—instead of just talking about it in meetings while our competitors continue to crush us."

"So you'll champion this?" I asked, surprise still evident in my voice.

"I'm saying I'll transform your feel-good proposal into something that will actually work." She pondered. "We'll need to build a metrics framework, define the boundaries, create the tracking systems, and retrain managers who are used to saying no instead of coaching. It's not simple."

"But necessary, yes?" Nishant asked.

Jenna looked up, her expression softening a bit. "If we execute this right, we get innovation without anarchy. We execute it wrong, we speed up our own obsolescence. So yeah, necessary."

Outside, morning traffic inched forward in the ritual procession of the daily commute. Inside, a CTO and two consultants began mapping a new operating model—not just for products, but for how an organization would reinvent itself in a market that had already left them behind.

***

Enablers of Authority Reformation

Facilitating the transition to distributed authority merits adopting the value amplifiers introduced in subsequent chapters of this book. Of particular significance is the GSO strategic communication framework presented in Chapter 3: Strategy Expression, and organizing work through virtual value creation mechanisms as detailed in Chapter 7: Value Streams. Collectively, the remaining eleven value amplifiers enable a successful pathway to distributing authority.

Distributed Authority Best Practices

1: *Embrace distributed authority as the foundation of your organizational growth.* Extensive evidence confirms that distributing decision-making enhances responsiveness, innovation, and engagement. When authority is exercised closer to where work occurs, organizations react faster to market and environmental changes. Employees gain autonomy, accountability, and intrinsic motivation, while diverse perspectives reduce risk and amplify creativity. Empowered teams, operating within clear strategic intent, address customer needs and integrate feedback with greater speed and precision.

2: *Cultivate innovative mindsets and modern methodologies.* Leaders who foster experimentation and continuous learning optimize operations, strengthen retention, and sustain competitive advantage. The adaptability and resilience inherent in hybrid organizational models enable firms to navigate uncertainty and thrive in complex, fast-evolving markets—creating cultures that are dynamic, inventive, and built for enduring success.

***

Organization Highlight: Unilever

The strategic imperative to decentralize authority, cultivate contextual responsiveness, and embed ethical foresight into organizational practice is not merely theoretical—it has been operationalized with remarkable impact by leading global enterprises. One such exemplar is Unilever, a global leader in the fast-moving consumer goods sector, whose transformation underscores the profound organizational gains that emerge when distributed leadership principles are translated into deliberate structural change.

In 2009, as economies emerged from a worldwide recession, Unilever confronted stagnant operational performance, sluggish market responsiveness, and a decline in product innovation. Amid efforts to reorient the company toward social impact, sustainability, and equality, then-CEO Paul Pol-

man recognized a critical misalignment: Unilever's historically centralized structure no longer reflected the realities of
a fragmented and fast-evolving global marketplace. To rein-
vigorate the enterprise, Polman spearheaded a bold organizational transformation—dismantling the traditional hierarchy
in favor of a federated model rooted in empowered regional
and product-focused business units.

These units were granted substantive control over core
functions—including marketing, R&D, and supply chain
management—thereby localizing decision-making authority
and enabling granular responsiveness to diverse consumer
ecosystems. By decentralizing strategic discretion, Unilever
equipped regional leaders to tailor decisions to local market
contours while fostering conditions for organic innovation
entrenched in cultural awareness and situational relevance.
This autonomy was further reinforced through digital dashboards and extensible business planning tools, which allowed
business units to monitor KPIs in real time and act with
minimal dependence on corporate approval cycles.

Importantly, sustainability initiatives were designed to
flourish within this distributed framework, with regional actors empowered to devise environmentally responsible practices attuned to their unique regulatory environments and
ecological imperatives. This was not merely a change in structure; it was a philosophical shift toward embedding enterprise
stewardship within operational nodes. For instance, in India,
Unilever localized its water conservation initiatives in alignment with regional infrastructure constraints, while in Brazil,
community-based supply chains were designed to meet both
social inclusion goals and sourcing efficiency targets.

The transformation yielded impressive results. By 2018,
Unilever's purpose-driven Sustainable Living Brands were
growing 69% faster than the rest of the portfolio, generating
75% of the company's overall growth.[11] During Polman's

decade at the helm, Unilever delivered a total shareholder return of 290%.[12] At the same time, the company enhanced employee engagement across key markets and sustained operational efficiencies that contributed to meaningful margin expansion.

Further empirical support for this distributed model emerged during the COVID-19 pandemic. In 2020, Unilever reported that its decentralized decision-making enabled rapid reallocation of supply chain assets to meet surging demand for hygiene products across Europe and Asia. The company reported a 50% increase in Lifebuoy soap sales and was able to introduce over 100 locally relevant innovations in under six months.[13] This responsiveness was made possible by empowering regional and brand managers with the authority and tools to act without waiting for global directives.

Unilever's restructured operating model thus offers compelling evidence that genuine adaptability, innovation, and value creation are most effectively realized when authority is distributed, local insight is trusted, and strategic intent is grounded in contextually informed execution. The company's experience affirms that structural decentralization is not antithetical to cohesion—it is the very architecture through which a modern enterprise achieves strategic unity amid local diversity.

---

1. John B. Thompson, *Merchants of Culture* (Polity, 2010).

2. Alexandre Pelletier, "Centralization vs. Decentralization: Why You Need a Hybrid Model," *Merge World* (July 2020).

3. H. Khan, M. Rehmat, T.H. Butt et al. "Impact of Transformational Leadership on Work Performance, Burnout and Social Loafing: a Mediation Model," *Future Business Journal* 6, 40 (2020).

4. Allan Lee, Sara Willis, and Amy Wei Tian, "When Empowering Employees Works, and When It Doesn't," *Harvard Business Review* (March 2018).

5. Sang Long Choi et al. "Transformational Leadership, Empowerment, and Job Satisfaction: the Mediating Role of Employee Empowerment," *Human Resources for Health* (2016).

6. Magdi Batato, Xavier Mesnard, and Suketu Gandhi, "It's Time for a New Model for Operations Management," *Harvard Business Review* (September 19, 2023).

7. Hala Altamimi, Qiaozhen Liu, and Benedict Jimenez, "Not Too Much, Not Too Little: Centralization, Decentralization, and Organizational Change," *Journal of Public Administration Research and Theory* Volume 33, Issue 1 (January 2023).

8. J.R. DeSimone and L.A. Roberts, "Nonprofit Leadership Dispositions," *Springer Business & Economics* 3, 50 (2023).

9. Nick Hobson, "Satya Nadella's Microsoft Just Became the Most Valued Company in the World. And It's Thanks to Psychology, Not Tech," Inc. Magazine (January 16, 2024).

10. Albert Einstein, Interview by George Sylvester Viereck, *The Saturday Evening Post* (October 26, 1929).

11. Unilever, *Annual Report and Accounts 2018* (London: Unilever plc, 2018).

12. Statista, "Global revenue of the Unilever Group since 2007," *Statista*, accessed June 28, 2025.

13. Unilever plc, *Annual Report and Accounts 2020* (London: Unilever plc, 2020).

Chapter 2

Market Intelligence

Asking the Right Questions

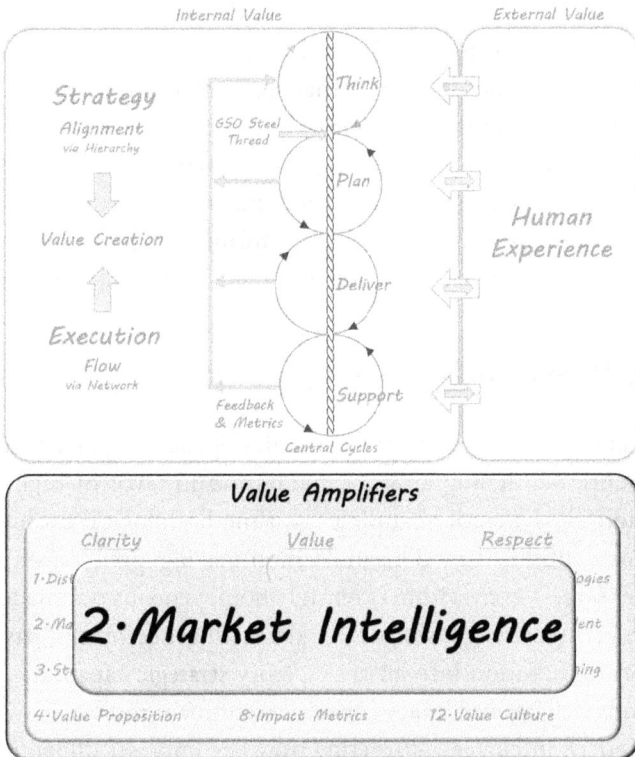

Internal Value   *External Value*

Strategy
Alignment
via Hierarchy

GSO Steel Thread

Think

Plan

Value Creation

Human Experience

Deliver

Execution
Flow
via Network

Feedback & Metrics

Support

Central Cycles

Value Amplifiers

Clarity   *Value*   *Respect*

1·Dis...   ...ogies

2·Ma... **2·Market Intelligence** ...nt

3·St...   ...ing

4·Value Proposition   8·Impact Metrics   12·Value Culture

Why Experience Drives Value

Organizations are witnessing a profound global transition: value is increasingly defined not by products alone but by the quality of encounters throughout a customer's journey. As Joe Pine and Jim Gilmore assert in *The Experience Economy*, contemporary consumers increasingly favor resonant, meaningful experiences over traditional differentiators such as price or performance. They demand interactions that are memorable, personalized, and responsive to their shifting values and contexts.[1]

Within the Valorys Think cycle, value-centered enterprises strive for a nuanced understanding of both industry dynamics and customer behavior by leveraging advanced analytical frameworks. These methods extend far beyond surface-level assessments, uncovering the structural forces that shape evolving markets. Absent this depth of insight, strategy becomes decoupled from the underlying value drivers, creating strategic blind spots that expose organizations to latent threats. Consequently, rigorous market intelligence becomes indispensable—informing direction, substantiating value propositions, and reinforcing long-term viability.

The Rise of Behavioral Genomics

The emergence of behavioral genomics signals a departure from conventional demographic segmentation in favor of high-resolution idiosyncratic mapping. This methodological evolution captures subtle distinctions in decision-making, preferences, and perceptions—even within ostensibly homogeneous populations. Such granularity transforms market intelligence from a passive reporting function into an anticipatory strategic capability that extends well beyond legacy consumer sentiment tools.

Modern intelligence-gathering now encompasses digital footprint aggregation, real-time behavioral tracking, emotive analysis, and algorithmic inference. By synthesizing transactional data, social activity, biometric signals, and location patterns, organizations construct a comprehensive consumer genome—a multidimensional profile revealing the full array of influences shaping buyer behavior. This anatomy allows for statistically robust predictions and early detection of decision-cycle inflection points, ultimately driving improved retention and increased lifetime value.

Seeing Value in Micro-Behavior

Understanding what customers value, aspire to, and believe is imperative—superficial segmentation is no longer sufficient. Atomic-level behavioral analysis reveals considerable divergence even within well-established categories. Consider the "health-conscious millennials" segment: within it lie distinct variances in lifestyle, digital engagement, and brand affinity.

Such micro-variations often foreshadow broader behavioral shifts, providing organizations with visibility into trends and threats months before competitors relying on conventional methods. Detecting these subtle transformations early empowers organizations to respond proactively, circumventing the costs of reactive realignment. This demands analytical acuity capable of distinguishing signal from noise—incorporating temporal patterns, cultural influences, and generational nuance.

Early insights crystallize into enduring competitive advantages: they expand revenue through precision targeting, compress acquisition costs by refining audience definition, and, ultimately, fortify market position. These benefits accrue over time, establishing formidable barriers that preclude market penetration by prospective entrants while enabling faster learning, adaptive response, and feedback-driven refinement.

Omnichannel Integration

Leading firms now design not merely products, but immersive, multi-sensory ecosystems that resonate with evolving consumer expectations. These experiences are choreographed across the entire customer journey and refined in real time through AI-driven contextual awareness. Consumer signals—such as hesitation, tone, or interaction cadence—enable near-instantaneous personalization with surgical precision.

An effective omnichannel strategy—integrating physical, digital, mobile, and AI-mediated touchpoints—is now fundamental to modern commerce. Its efficacy, however, rests on the seamless integration of behavioral insights across these interfaces. Elemental-scale analysis clarifies how consumers navigate between environments, what triggers channel-switching, and which contextual factors elevate engagement.

When harnessed effectively, omnichannel intelligence enhances customer satisfaction while reducing operational expenditure. Predictive models of channel usage enable more precise capacity planning and resource deployment, sustaining high-quality experiences at reduced cost. Experiential marketing, in turn, magnifies brand resonance by immersing customers within interactive, participatory ecosystems.

Just as crucial, however, is the forensic examination of disengagement. Understanding where and why customers abandon a process or withdraw emotionally yields actionable insights—exposing latent friction points that, once corrected, can restore continuity and trust. These capabilities are not limited to commercial enterprises. Public-sector entities and nonprofits can deploy the same methods to anticipate constituent needs, improve service design, and deepen engagement with donors and stakeholders.

Responsible Behavioral Targeting

Organizations that establish deep resonance with customer psychology position themselves to unlock transformative innovation.[2] Advanced consumer segmentation enables tailored messaging, individualized product configurations, and more resonant interactions that boost loyalty, advocacy, and distinctive market positioning.

Yet, personalization must be judicious. Crossing into perceived surveillance or intrusiveness undermines trust and may breach evolving regulatory norms. Sensitivity to varying comfort levels regarding data privacy is essential, as understanding these thresholds across customer groups allows firms to calibrate personalization strategies that are both effective and ethically sound.

As regulations around data ethics and algorithmic accountability continue to evolve, compliance must be embedded at inception. Proactively addressing legal and ethical obligations early not only lessens liability but also builds consumer confidence—turning sound data practices into a market differentiator. The responsible use of behavioral insight serves as a durable engine of value, enhancing credibility, deepening market relevance, and fortifying relationships with customers, regulators, and partners alike.

***

The following vignette presents a brief account of a former client's challenges and illustrates how the application of innovative market intelligence strategies significantly enhanced their competitive position.

Case Study

Granmere Bank, credit card issuer in the United States.

The Challenge

Despite allocating $140 million toward marketing initiatives over twelve months, Granmere experienced a significant 22% decline in customer conversion rates alongside a 34% escalation in clientele acquisition costs. Three consecutive quarters of deteriorating performance triggered acute concern at the executive tier. The marketing organization had implemented a comprehensive suite of industry-recommended strategies—updated brand messaging, refreshed creative executions, increased digital advertising expenditures—yet outcomes continued their downward trajectory.

Setting the Scene

Upon my arrival at Granmere's Midtown headquarters, the tension permeating the thirty-seventh-floor conference room proved immediately palpable. Though I arrived ten minutes early, Adrian, the Chief Marketing Officer, was already present—jacket removed, sleeves rolled, meticulously reviewing substantial binders of performance analytics. His team appeared equally exhausted. These were not disengaged individuals; they were seasoned professionals who had clearly been expending considerable effort with diminishing returns.

Adrian articulated the situation without pretense: "We don't require additional data. We need clarity."

Discovery

The initial phase involved a forensic examination of recent promotional executions. The work proved professional competency—on-brand, well-executed, consistent with contemporary market tendencies. However, therein lay the fundamental problem. It was excessively aligned with prevailing trends. Campaign messaging and targeting strategies mirrored competitors with remarkable similarity. Every organization within the sector was communicating nearly identical messages to indistinguishable segmented audiences. And those constituencies had ceased listening.

The issue was not creative deficiency. It was an absence of differentiation and behavioral specificity.

More significantly, upon reviewing their research materials, I observed something critical: their focus concentrated almost entirely on macro indicators—demographic cohorts, income stratifications, and general psychographic profiles. What was conspicuously absent was behavioral intelligence. Not merely who the customers were, but how they were engaging. Where they discontinued their journey? What triggered hesitation? What time of day they submitted applications? On which devices?

Insight

Granmere needed to transition from broad-stroke marketing techniques to micro-pattern recognition methodologies.

I shared an example from a previous engagement: a regional financial institution had discovered a significant spike in loan application rejections correlated with late-night submissions. Their scoring algorithm had erroneously flagged those applications as elevated risk due to temporal heuristics—a completely arbitrary bias that had been undermining their approval volume. A simple algorithmic adjustment increased conversion rates by 28% immediately.

The Granmere staff listened intently. This went beyond theory. It concerned discovering where their own pipeline friction existed.

Execution

Within days, Adrian expedited a cross-functional analytics investigation. We collaborated extensively with the bank's data science team to instrument the complete application funnel: temporal patterns, device and browser utilization, entry point behaviors, page-level abandonment figures, and even duration of user engagement in each section of the form.

Patterns materialized rapidly. Android customers converted 14% less frequently than iOS users. Women under thirty were abandoning applications at double the rate when interest rates appeared before rewards information. Gen Z applicants arriving via comparison platforms showed a 31% improvement in completion statistics when the "lifestyle benefits" page was eliminated entirely.

No major rebranding initiative. No new agency partnership. Simply superior inquiries, heightened visibility, and more behaviorally sophisticated design.

Outcomes

By the conclusion of Q2, Granmere achieved:

- Application approval rates up by 12% month-over-month.

- 26% reduction in cost-per-acquisition due to improved funnel efficiency.

- Enhanced engagement across key underperforming demographic segments.

Perhaps most tellingly, Adrian received an inquiry from a competitor's CMO asking who had redesigned their campaigns. He responded simply: "We didn't engage an agency. We just began paying attention."

Conclusion

Granmere's transformation was not predicated upon increased expenditures, expanded advertising, or broader market presence. It was founded on visibility. The transition from macro assumptions to micro behavioral truths provided the team with a new analytical lens through which to examine their customer's journey. In doing so, they did not merely improve marketing metrics—they constructed a systematic framework for ongoing insight generation and adaptive response.

The lesson? Authentic intelligence lives not in the volume of data collected, but in the precision of the questions asked.

***

Evolving Dimensions of Brand Value

Brand equity now extends well beyond basic recognition or perceived product quality. It includes trust, emotional resonance, environmental responsibility, and ethical positioning. Detailed perception analysis helps organizations understand how various customer groups associate meaning with a brand—allowing for more refined stewardship and smarter investment choices.

Sophisticated multivariate models identify the interlocking elements that determine customer lifetime worth—dimensions that escape simplistic analytics. Predictive algorithms offer deeper insight into preference evolution across multiple contexts, decision stages, and customer interactions. However, these formulas require progressive refinement; their value depends on consistent alignment with real-world behavior. As these tools mature and integrate emergent usage patterns, they furnish decision-makers with a sound foundation for connecting long-term goals to operational performance—an approach explored further in Chapter 3: Strategy Expression.

The Power of Early Insight

The rationale for behavioral intelligence investment extends well beyond direct financial return. It includes *strategic optionality*—the added value of early awareness that enables organizations to identify directional changes earlier and act with increased clarity and confidence.[3] Well-calibrated early warning systems detect economic signals before they appear in traditional performance indicators. Their effectiveness lies in balancing sensitivity with focus—isolating meaningful patterns while filtering out background noise.

Embedding trend analysis into strategizing empowers organizations to lead rather than react. This demands probabilistic forecasting models capable of capturing interdependencies—surpassing the limits of static or linear frameworks still common in conventional planning. Strategic resources can then be deployed with sharper intent and better coordination across the enterprise.

Strategy Informed by Behavior

Within the Valorys system, market intelligence serves a uniquely critical function that distinguishes it from conventional strategic approaches: it becomes the primary input for developing strategies once a GSO's goal and outcomes are defined. While traditional methodologies often rely on intuition, historical precedent, or generic best practices to formulate strategic approaches, Valorys leverages behavioral intelligence to construct evidence-based strategies that are inherently aligned with market realities.

This integration occurs at the intersection of strategic intent and tactical execution. Once leadership establishes a GSO's goal—such as "Accelerate digital transformation"—and defines measurable outcomes—such as "Increase digital channel adoption by 40%"—behavioral intelligence becomes the lens through which potential strategies are evaluated, prioritized, and designed. Rather than defaulting to industry-standard approaches, organizations examine their specific customer behavioral patterns, competitive dynamics, and market signals to identify the most promising pathways toward their objectives.

For instance, if behavioral data reveals that target customers exhibit specific hesitation patterns when engaging with digital interfaces, the strategic approach might emphasize gradual transition mechanisms and enhanced support touchpoints. Conversely, if intelligence indicates high receptivity to digital innovation within certain customer segments, strategies might focus on accelerated rollout to those populations while developing parallel approaches for more cautious adopters.

Intelligence-Driven Architecture

This intelligence-to-strategy pipeline operates through systematic analysis of behavioral insights against defined outcomes. Organizations examine customer journey analytics to identify leverage points where strategic interventions will yield maximum impact toward the desired outcome. They analyze competitive intelligence to understand market positioning opportunities and threats. They synthesize sentiment analysis and preference evolution patterns to anticipate how strategic initiatives will be received across different customer segments.

The result is strategy architecture that emerges from empirical evidence rather than theoretical frameworks. Each strategic component—from messaging approaches to channel selection to timing decisions—reflects specific insights derived from behavioral intelligence. This creates strategies that are not only more likely to succeed but also more defensible in their logic and more adaptable to emerging conditions.

Traditional strategic planning often suffers from the gap between high-level objectives and practical execution, with strategies developed in isolation from real market dynamics. Valorys eliminates this disconnect by ensuring that behavioral intelligence continuously informs strategy development, creating a direct lineage from customer reality to strategic action.

Building Evidence-Based Strategy

Building effective behavioral intelligence capabilities transcends technical implementation—it requires a fundamental cultural shift toward data-informed thinking that transforms how organizations operate at every level. This transformation begins with visible executive support and organizational design that treats market intelligence as a core strategic function rather than a support role, enabling insights to flow horizontally across departments and embedding behavioral analysis directly into planning processes.

The maturation of these capabilities signals a meaningful organizational evolution from reactive reporting to predictive intelligence. Companies that master this approach build adaptive systems that leverage volatility rather than merely withstand it, streamlining planning cycles through improved foresight and enhanced precision. Artificial intelligence emerges as an unparalleled accelerant in this transformation, wielding capabilities that transcend established approaches to analyzing intricate engagement data and converting them into strategic advantage.

Organizations that successfully integrate predictive intelligence across strategic direction, innovation cycles, risk strategy, and competitive positioning gain the ability to anticipate customer behavior with statistical confidence. This enables more precise resource allocation, reduced uncertainty, and decisive action based on authentic customer understanding rather than generalized assumptions. The result is measurable performance improvements—stronger revenues, better margins, lower acquisition costs, higher retention, and expanded market share—achieved through offerings that resonate deeply while maintaining the flexibility to evolve.

Ultimately, the organizations that combine sharp analytical insight with ethical clarity position themselves to lead markets rather than follow them. Their ability to see what is coming and act with purpose generates lasting competitive advantage, creating sustainable value that extends across every level of the enterprise and strengthens relationships with customers, regulators, and partners alike.

Market Intelligence Best Practices

1: *Read subtle shifts in consumer behavior with precision and speed.* In an era where customer experience and realized value surpass traditional differentiators, competitive advantage depends on early detection of emerging patterns. Organizations that analyze high-resolution behavioral data effectively can discern faint signals of change and translate them into timely, value-driven action.

2: *Promote predictive intelligence to a core business capability.* Rigorous, data-based analysis strengthens resilience and enables leaders to act before more conventional metrics reveal a trend. By responsibly applying behavioral intelligence, organizations move from reacting to shaping—designing superior customer experiences and sustainable sources of value. This capability fosters continuous adaptation, ethical engagement, and long-term foresight, positioning enterprises to anticipate rather than follow the future.

***

Organization Highlight: Target

Among the many models of efficient market intelligence deployment, Target Corporation remains a prescient example from the early 2000s that illustrates both the power and the perils of advanced predictive analytics. In a strategic effort to position its retail stores as comprehensive, one-stop destinations, Target pioneered data science techniques that extended beyond conventional demographic segmentation to anticipate consumer needs during pivotal life transitions.

Beginning in 2002, Target's Guest Data and Analytical Services team, led by statistician Andrew Pole, sought to identify customers experiencing major life events—particularly pregnancy—by leveraging purchase indicators including shopping patterns, product affinities, purchase sequencing, and basket composition. The company recognized that consumers undergoing major life transitions were more receptive to changing their established buying habits, creating valuable opportunities for customer acquisition and loyalty development.

Target's data scientists employed predictive modeling techniques to isolate statistically significant purchasing behaviors that correlated with these types of life events. Most notably, the company developed a sophisticated algorithm by analyzing data from women shoppers to identify approximately 25 products that, when purchased in combination, indicated pregnancy with high statistical confidence. The system assigned each customer a "pregnancy prediction score" and could estimate due dates within relatively small time windows, enabling Target to send precisely timed promotional materials tailored to specific stages of pregnancy. This capability represented a significant advancement in retail predictive modeling, transforming demographic assumptions into consumer certainties.

Between 2002 and 2010, Target's revenues grew by more than 50 percent—but the period also exposed key challenges related to consumer privacy and the responsible use of forecasting analytics. In response, Target refined its promotional delivery system to better balance personalization with discretion, masking direct targeting within broader marketing mailers and integrating more contextualized messaging to preserve customer trust. These changes were not merely reputational safeguards; they were strategic adaptations that ensured continuity in psychographic alignment without compromising brand integrity.

In parallel, Target systematically expanded its analytics infrastructure. The company built a centralized enterprise data architecture that integrated point-of-sale systems with behavioral modeling tools, enabling dynamic customer segmentation, real-time inventory optimization, and personalized loyalty programming at scale. These investments transformed analytics from a discrete research function into a structural operating capability embedded across the enterprise.

The RedCard loyalty program became one of the clearest expressions of this strategy in practice. By linking personalized offers directly to individual purchase histories, Target created a reinforcing cycle between behavioral intelligence and customer retention—one that the company's leadership consistently cited as a driver of both visit frequency and basket size in investor communications throughout the period. The broader lesson was equally significant: Target had demonstrated that a retailer of its scale could operationalize consumer behavioral data not merely to respond to preferences, but to anticipate them.

As Charles Duhigg observed in a 2012 New York Times investigation, Target's ability to render consumer patterns into predictive data sets had fundamentally transformed what retailers could know—and act upon—about their customers.[4]

Target's pregnancy prediction project established a template for retail consumer pattern optimization while simultaneously illustrating that advanced market intelligence, regardless of its technical precision, must be implemented with careful consideration of customer relationships and brand reputation. The case demonstrates that behavioral analytics becomes a proactive mechanism for demand orchestration, capable of discerning latent intent before conscious articulation. But success depends equally on analytical capability and strategic wisdom in application. When harnessed responsibly, precise data intelligence can power long-term growth by anticipating needs, personalizing service, and reinforcing loyalty—without overstepping ethical boundaries.

1. Joe Pine and Jim Gilmore, *The Experience Economy: Competing for Customer Time, Attention, and Money*, Revised edition (Harvard Business Review Press, 2019).

2. Scott Magids, Alan Zorfas, and Daniel Leemon, "The New Science of Customer Emotions: A Better Way to Drive Growth and Profitability," *Harvard Business Review* (November 2015).

3. Lenos Trigeorgis and Jeffrey J. Reuer, "Real Options Theory in Strategic Management" *Strategic Management Journal* (March 14, 2016).

4. Charles Duhigg, "How Companies Learn Your Secrets," *The New York Times Magazine* (February 19, 2012).

Chapter 3

Strategy Expression

Leading Intentionally

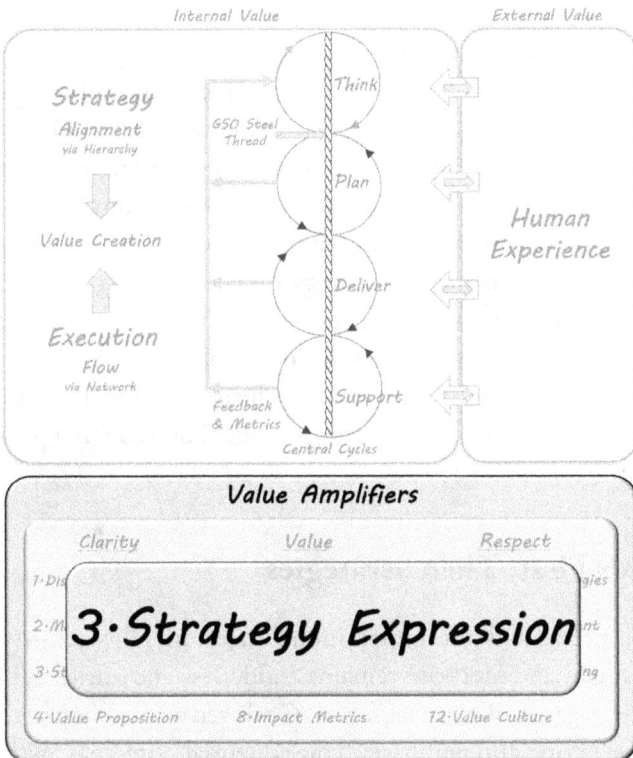

Internal Value   External Value

Strategy
Alignment
via Hierarchy

Think

GSO Steel
Thread

Plan

Value Creation

Human
Experience

Deliver

Execution
Flow
via Network

Support

Feedback
& Metrics

Central Cycles

Value Amplifiers

Clarity	Value	Respect
1·Di...		...gies
2·M...	3·Strategy Expression	...nt
3·S...		...ng
4·Value Proposition	8·Impact Metrics	12·Value Culture

Addressing Strategic Confusion

I f I told you that in nearly 80% of the organizations with whom I have consulted, senior executives could neither clearly articulate their strategic intent nor reach consensus on the strategies themselves—would you believe me? You should, it's true.

In modern corporate parlance, strategy is both overused and widely misunderstood. For many organizations, it simply represents a broad directional aim—often the outcome of an off-site planning session focused on resource allocation for the coming fiscal year. These "strategies" are then broadcast across the enterprise with considerable enthusiasm, mounted on office walls, and recited at leadership meetings.

But the effect is almost always underwhelming. Despite the spectacle, little changes. I have seen countless teams laboring diligently, yet disconnected from any discernible target. Organizations frequently pursue nebulous strategies without fully grasping their operational consequences or workforce implications.

This is not a minor oversight. It reveals a deeper misconception: numerous leaders mistake strategy for their guiding purpose. It is not. Strategy is merely the means by which a goal is pursued, not the goal itself. While this distinction is foundational in classical management theory, it remains elusive to many. The truth is simple yet often ignored: strategy should follow goals, not precede them.

Goals First, Then Strategies

Goals propel and direct institutional trajectories forward—without them, an enterprise remains rudderless and adrift, subject to the vagaries of external forces. Goals serve to orchestrate collective efforts and emphasize consequential outcomes. Well-articulated goals engage all organizational dimensions, mobilizing the company holistically toward its intended future configuration, while strategies actualize those objectives. Goals represent the *what;* strategies constitute the *how.* After articulating lucid goals, firms occasionally adopt suboptimal means to achieve their aims because they encounter unforeseen variables (of which they possessed no initial cognizance) and formulate assumptions that may subsequently prove erroneous. Goals are characteristically fixed within specified temporal parameters, while strategies remain adaptive—not conversely. A select number of meticulously crafted goals become the focal nexus for an enterprise to attain its desired outcomes.

Numerous organizations solidify their plans annually, then question why they failed to generate expected results. The explanation proves straightforward—strategies should not remain rigid because they frequently constrain entities to suboptimal trajectories. Excessive variables cannot be comprehensively anticipated or accommodated. The probability of modifying predetermined goals remains minimal, yet strategies ought to evolve as institutions ascertain in real-time whether they are advancing the organization toward objective fulfillment or not.

Goal formulation ranks among the most formidable responsibilities leaders may ultimately assume. This phenomenon might elucidate the elevated failure rate of organizations in establishing and executing measurable imperatives. I have collaborated with diverse ventures that publish nebulous declarations (they cannot legitimately be characterized as "goals") and expect their personnel to comprehend and operationalize them. Occasionally, this occurs to circumvent accountability to governance boards. It proves considerably easier for those in authority to abdicate their responsibility and attribute poor performance to the collective organization rather than to acknowledge their own inability to articulate clear vision and strategic direction. I challenge executive leadership to consider the method presented here as a superior mechanism to guide their enterprises.

Goals, when coupled with precise outcomes, serve as the authentic North Star for the entirety of organizational activities and endeavors that transpire daily. This is a critical principle and cannot be overemphasized. If leaders genuinely aspire for everyone within the organization to coordinate their efforts toward common imperatives, then goals function as the optimal instrument to accomplish that strategic alignment.

Goal-setting theory confirms that the mere existence of objectives is inherently motivating, and that goals possessing specific characteristics—challenging, precise, and accepted—demonstrate superior inspirational efficacy. Participatory processes and collaborative decision-making reduce anxiety and operational uncertainty while providing workers greater autonomy over outcomes.[1]

I want to clarify that the goals referenced here differ intrinsically from the individual targets of the antiquated and largely inefficacious "management by objectives" (MBO) methodology developed by Peter Drucker in 1954.[2] Based on personal experience, I do not advocate creating individualized objectives; they should only be formulated at the team-of-teams or team levels of an organization, but not below. Employing personal goals diverts attention from collective endeavors and redirects it toward individual contributors, frequently establishing undesirable intra-group competition.

The MBO approach effectively undermines incentives for collaborative team engagement. Interestingly, Drucker originally conceptualized MBO as a management philosophy, not a specific technique. Over time, it became synonymous with individual performance evaluation. Drucker subsequently acknowledged that MBO, while popular, did not genuinely assist leaders or workers in comprehending their *company's objectives* [emphasis added].

GSOs

The *goal-strategy-outcomes* method of Valorys is the *lingua franca* for articulating strategic intent. GSOs prove instrumental in achieving a company's desired impact; they represent the mechanism for communicating goals, strategies, and outcomes for temporal increments specific to each unit at every organizational stratum. This structure serves as an indispensable vehicle for aligning efforts, preventing strategic drift, cultivating cognition, and driving cohesive action throughout an enterprise.

Each GSO contains three components in fixed relationship: one goal—the intended future state; one strategy—the optimal approach; and multiple outcomes—measurable results indicating progress or success. This canonical 1:1:N form ensures clarity: every goal has a singular strategy, while success is validated through multiple outcomes rather than a single metric. The cardinality within each GSO remains unambiguous whether referencing one GSO or many, ensuring the relationship between components is explicitly understood.

Many enterprises employ the SMART[3] acronym to assure goals are specific, measurable, achievable, relevant, and temporally bounded. Within Valorys, goals are inherently SMART because GSOs possess predetermined durations, rendering them naturally time-constrained. Their outcomes provide quantifiable measurability and analytic specificity, while strategy components ensure targets remain attainable and contextually pertinent.

Activity and planning alone can become misleading substitutes for value delivery, while a GSO lens concentrates on what genuinely matters. When the rationale for a goal remains ambiguous, incorporating an optional bias for action helps others comprehend the goal and its intent. The bias for action explains *why* a goal assumes significance for an organization. Executives may exhibit reluctance to share the intentions underlying their goals, but when they do, GSO interpretation is enhanced downstream.

Value-centered organizations construct roadmaps to guide their actions and decision-making processes by clearly defining a judicious number of outcome-based goals focused on desired end results or targets. They subsequently develop corresponding strategies that outline avenues and endeavors to be undertaken. Outcomes encompass both interim and final results anticipated and measured while executing those strategies to achieve objectives.

The GSO technique ensures universal comprehension of each unit's aim, direction, and expected impacts at all organizational levels, thereby promoting transparency, accountability, and shared purpose. In this manner, companies effectively navigate complexity, adapt to evolving circumstances, and ultimately achieve their intended end state.

As an example, an annual goal for a business unit might be to "Enhance customer satisfaction and retention." Specific outcomes associated with that ambition potentially include:

1. Increase renewal rate by 15%.

2. Improve Net Promotor Score (NPS) from 5 to 8.

3. Maintain current margins.

The first outcome functions as a *leading indicator*, suggesting that, as the BU prototypically implements the strategy, the renewal rate should increase. The second result represents a *lagging indicator*, or target metric. The BU's leadership team likely will not determine if the NPS has improved until the course of action is completed and they have surveyed their customer base. The third outcome serves as a *balancing metric*, which requires an entity not to sacrifice one business domain to improve another. I advocate adopting balancing metrics because numerous organizations establish failure conditions when one component accomplishes a desired outcome at the expense of different elements. "Robbing Peter to pay Paul" is not an effective strategy.

Consider that multiple methodologies exist to accomplish the outcomes of this hypothetical goal. For instance, the BU might develop a new marketing campaign targeting its existing consumer base to offer renewal incentives. An alternative strategy may involve optimizing customer/product interactions by enhancing the experience to increase satisfaction. Or it could reduce its offering's price to improve retention. But given outcome #3, the implementation team would recognize this is not viable since it must maintain current profit margins unless delivery costs are trimmed.

Most frequently, organizations possess the capacity to accomplish goals through multiple methods, yet it requires intellectual creativity and imagination to discern optimal initial strategies. The fundamental challenge involves determining which hypothesis will yield superior results with minimal resource expenditure and maximum return on investment. The selected strategy suggests the most efficacious means to realize the goal through the established outcomes.

To accomplish the previously cited exemplar goal, one strategic approach might be articulated as, "We believe that by enhancing the quality and usability of our product line, our customers are more likely to be satisfied, renew their subscriptions, and recommend us to others." Observe that the strategy is constructed as a testable hypothesis ("we believe"), which serves as the proposed solution while acknowledging it may be predicated on incomplete empirical data or comprehensive understanding. The hypothesis formulation permits teams to begin with the strategy most likely to succeed, subsequently employing systematic experiments to validate assumptions through leading performance indicators. During implementation phases, should outcome metrics fail to trend favorably, alternative strategies may be considered.

GSOs are typically formatted in this manner:

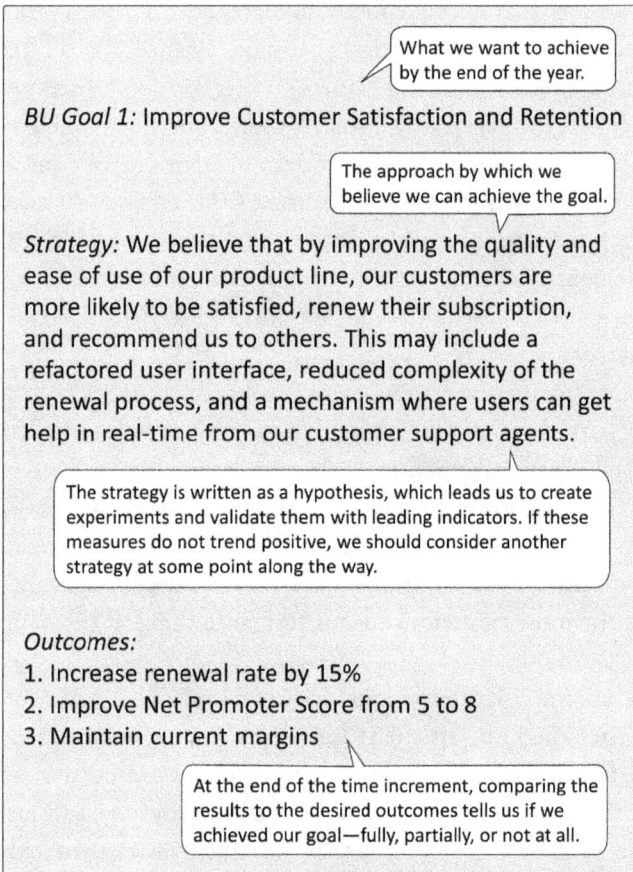

> What we want to achieve by the end of the year.
>
> *BU Goal 1:* Improve Customer Satisfaction and Retention
>
> The approach by which we believe we can achieve the goal.
>
> *Strategy:* We believe that by improving the quality and ease of use of our product line, our customers are more likely to be satisfied, renew their subscription, and recommend us to others. This may include a refactored user interface, reduced complexity of the renewal process, and a mechanism where users can get help in real-time from our customer support agents.
>
> The strategy is written as a hypothesis, which leads us to create experiments and validate them with leading indicators. If these measures do not trend positive, we should consider another strategy at some point along the way.
>
> *Outcomes:*
> 1. Increase renewal rate by 15%
> 2. Improve Net Promoter Score from 5 to 8
> 3. Maintain current margins
>
> At the end of the time increment, comparing the results to the desired outcomes tells us if we achieved our goal—fully, partially, or not at all.

Remember that strategy constitutes a speculative construct—it is rarely possible to verify whether a given course of action is truly optimal absent empirical engagement. Fashioning structured experiments or controlled prototypes enables an organization to evaluate whether its underlying assumptions withstand practical scrutiny. This tactical approach may involve deploying minimum viable products or initiating pilot programs designed to validate core hypotheses and elicit actionable, data-informed feedback.

The sample GSO described above is developed at the business unit echelon. All subdivisions or programmatic entities analyze each BU GSO to determine their potential contribution to the overarching goal, subsequently creating their own GSOs predicated upon their distinctive perspective and specialized expertise. The requisite work toward achieving the BU's strategic goal is aggregated into a comprehensive operational blueprint. Each blueprint component is executed by those who conceptualized it, validating their hypotheses as they progress toward meeting defined outcomes. If executed with precision, this approach ensures that all daily work performed within the BU can be meaningfully traced back to its set of predefined annual goals. However, it remains imperative for BU leadership to ensure that subordinate GSOs authentically align with their strategic imperatives to achieve optimal effectiveness.

Valorys navigates the cone of uncertainty through rapid feedback cycles and disciplined iterative assessment. At predetermined intervals—typically monthly or quarterly—each strategic pathway undergoes a rigorous appraisal against its projected outcomes. If the data indicate a positive trajectory toward the intended objective, implementation proceeds. Should the trend prove inconclusive or unfavorable, the strategy is re-evaluated to determine whether adaptation—through refinement or strategic redirection—is warranted. Only through applied execution can the efficacy of a chosen course be truly confirmed. Theoretical constructs must be translated into operational practice, then recalibrated as necessary.

This is why Aristotle's hypothesis–experiment–evaluation paradigm, as embedded within Valorys, holds such profound relevance: it affords leaders the ability to interrogate strategic assumptions and validate foundational hypotheses without incurring organizational fault for imperfect decisions. Human error is inevitable—so why persist in expecting employees to arrive at flawless conclusions? They cannot. Thus, they must be granted the latitude to explore, test, and refine within safe, bounded environments where experimentation is seen not as failure, but as a disciplined pathway to insight.

***

Certain problems remain invisible, operating beneath organizational consciousness. They systematically undermine performance until an enterprise finds itself contemplating how something that once functioned exceptionally well had become so lethargic.

Such was the predicament at Cucamonga, a regional retail chain distinguished for curated home goods and complementing accessories. I found myself in their downtown Los Angeles operations center, positioned across from Steve, their Vice President of Supply Chain.

He reclined and gestured toward a dashboard displaying green checkmarks.

"On paper, we're crushing it—on-time delivery rates, warehouse accuracy, fulfillment SLA compliance. All the lights are green. But stores are yelling that we're getting slower."

And they weren't imagining it.

Over the preceding nine months, Cucamonga's localized product model—formerly a competitive advantage—had begun to deteriorate. Store managers were submitting increasing numbers of manual inventory requisitions. Certain high-velocity SKUs were routinely out of stock during peak periods. Slow-moving stock lingered excessively on shelves. Customers were departing—not because merchandise didn't exist, but because it had not yet arrived.

The most egregious part? The supply chain was technically performing precisely as planned.

"We built this system to be responsive to demand," Steve said. "But now demand's moving faster than our planning model can keep up. Our stores are living in real time. We're living two weeks behind."

"We used to be known for being expeditious," he continued. "Now, stores are either overstocked on what customers aren't buying or waiting on the stuff they are."

The fundamental issue wasn't organizational incompetence. It was strategic ambiguity—at the executive level.

The previous year, senior leadership had established an objective: "Optimize supply chain efficiency while enabling localized customer relevance."

Eloquent phraseology. A rational goal. However, no one had translated that statement into a measurable definition of success. What does "enable relevance" manifest as at the store level? What does "optimize efficiency" genuinely signify in terms of reactivity and replenishment cadence?

Consequently, planning teams optimized for fill rates and forecast accuracy. Distribution teams optimized for shipping lanes and labor costs. Stores attempted to adapt, circumvent, or escalate—but there existed no clear, system-wide trigger to respond to what stores were actually experiencing.

Therefore, we reframed the challenge. We commenced with what the business genuinely prioritized: velocity and alignment. Not merely of shipments, but of responsiveness to real-time requirements.

We concentrated on a new goal: "Reduce the time between a store's actual shift in customer demand and the arrival of adjusted inventory to under seven days."

This was a significant paradigm shift.

Because now, "responsiveness" wasn't merely a slogan. It was a quantifiable delay. It was something every component of the supply chain could observe, experience, and influence.

We deconstructed it:

- "Shift in demand" signified a substantial deviation (exceeding 15%) in daily sell-through of a SKU cluster over a 72-hour window.

- "Adjusted inventory" meant any modification in replenishment quantity triggered by the anomaly.

- "Under 7 days" meant from the day the demand signal crossed the threshold to the day replacement product reached store receiving.

Suddenly, the problem possessed definitive parameters. Now we could design the strategy backward from desired behavior.

First, we constructed a flag within their reporting system: when a SKU experienced a significant increase in a store beyond the threshold, it triggered a cross-functional "demand event" log. Each event was tracked—time-stamped, routed, and assigned a response owner.

Supply chain operations, consequently, reconfigured fulfillment scheduling. Instead of weekly batch runs, they added two windows during the week for fast response packs—pallets under 48 hours preparation time, no slotting delay, direct to store.

We also introduced a new signal: store managers could tag "emerging interest items" manually—new products that demonstrated unexpected velocity even before data thresholds were reached. If tagged by two or more stores, it triggered an early review.

To monitor progress, we created three outcomes:

- Reduce median days from demand signal to in-store re-plenishment by 40%.

- Restock 80% of flagged SKUs within the 7-day target.

- Increase sell-through velocity of replenished items versus initial batch by 15%.

The initial pilots proved illuminating.

In the previous model, the average time from replenishment request to shelf was 12.5 days. In the new model, it decreased to 6.3 days—with 68% of flagged items restocked before demand diminished.

One store manager in Santa Fe said, "I finally feel like the system's listening to what's happening here, not just what happened last quarter."

Customer satisfaction scores improved incrementally—particularly in comments regarding "timely product availability" and "always having new things." Perhaps more significant: stores filed fewer escalations, because the lag had been addressed proactively.

At the quarterly operations meeting, Steve presented two charts. One depicted the old model—smooth, accurate, and late. The other illustrated the new model—messier, noisier, but faster and more intelligent.

He looked at his team and said, "This is the shift. We're no longer just delivering products. We're delivering pace."

His declaration required no further explanation. Because that's what strategy should accomplish—not merely outline aspiration, but define what must occur differently, and how we will recognize when it does.

The challenge at Cucamonga was not effort, it was ambiguity. Everyone was optimizing, but no one was aligned. The strategy had established a direction, but not a destination. It lacked the specificity that transforms motion into momentum.

Once they identified the desired effect—7-day response to real-time demand shifts—the remainder fell into place: signals, behaviors, measures, accountability.

Because strategy does not perish from deficient ideas, it dies from unclear intent. But when the goal is sharpened, the outcomes defined, and the system constructed around it—that is when the lights on the dashboard begin signifying something meaningful again.

That is what authentic strategy is. Not just performance, but precision in the appropriate context.

**

Strategy Sessions

Only after goals and their anticipated outcomes are meticulously defined should leadership convene a strategic planning session, one concentrated on determining which strategies will most effectively advance the organization's articulated ambitions. Here is where data-driven market intelligence is employed to conceptualize potential approaches. Strategies are frequently chosen using set-based design or decision intelligence (DI) methodologies.[4] DI techniques assist leaders in rapidly narrowing the options available to achieve objectives—however, a strategy is not a certainty once selected.

A flexible strategy permits local interpretation within the parameters of the enterprise's goals. Value-based organizations maintain abbreviated planning horizons so they can respond swiftly to ever-shifting market exigencies without committing resources and energy too far in advance. Informed by GSOs, a rolling-wave roadmap serves as a simple yet effective instrument to manage, adjust, and communicate the organization's trajectory in real time.

By leveraging comprehensive and current intelligence on consumer trends, customer preferences, and market competition, DI techniques offer invaluable insights to establish realistic, adaptable strategies. This practice unleashes the creativity and innovation required to identify untapped opportunities, optimize resource allocation, and remain cognizant of industry shifts within the context of stated objectives.

So, how are goals, strategies, and outcomes conceived? It begins with the hierarchy informing the network. At the uppermost tier, senior executives craft four to six annual GSOs for the entire business that are endorsed by the board. These GSOs are developed quickly to provide the governing force behind everything that transpires in the company over the ensuing fiscal year. Any delay at the chief officer level cascades throughout the organization, undermining the ability of subordinate levels to fulfill their responsibilities within the designated time frame.

Executive-level GSOs initiate momentum by providing the contextual framework for the subsequent creation of subordinate goals. In other words, corporate imperatives are not imposed upon the broader organizational hierarchy; instead, they become the guiding beacon by which lower echelons craft their own GSOs to support the operationalization of the entity's annual strategic objectives. The comprehensive collection of all GSOs from the most granular levels upward represents the method by which the institution will achieve its enterprise-level imperatives. This cascading phenomenon results in intelligible traceability from the organizational summit to its operational foundation, utilizing what I term the *GSO steel thread*.

The GSO Steel Thread

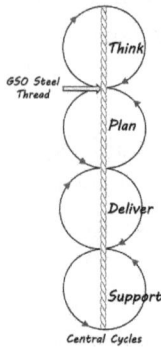

GSO Steel Thread

Think

Plan

Deliver

Support

Central Cycles

One of the most distinctive and valuable features of the Valorys system is the continuous thread that weaves through all four central cycles—Think, Plan, Deliver, Support—binding the enterprise into a coherent whole. This steel thread of goal-strategy-outcomes logic ensures that strategic intent is transmitted vertically down every echelon, enabling traceability from the executive suite to the front lines. Lower levels are responsible for communicating back up the chain any constraints connected with the implementation of those GSOs, thus flagging higher-level purpose that may not be achievable. This critical feedback is considered at the appropriate tier and adjustments are made accordingly.

While the top two central cycles of the Valorys model—Think and Plan—establish strategic alignment, the lower cycles, Deliver and Support, enable low-friction operational flow. AI-enabled systems support this bi-directional traceability, but the model's true power emerges from disciplined adherence to a coherent linking mechanism across all levels.

To grasp its function, envision the GSO steel thread as the enterprise's circulatory system. Just as blood delivers oxygen from the heart and lungs to nourish the body's extremities, the GSO framework distributes strategic purpose across divisions, teams, and functions. And, like oxygen-depleted blood returning to the heart, information flows upward through a feedback loop—enriching and refining higher-level objectives over time.

Enterprise goals are defined along distinct planning horizons: immediate (1 year), medium-term (2–3 years), and long-range (3–5 years). As one moves down the organizational hierarchy, the timeframes shorten accordingly. While executives focus on multiyear vision, operational teams typically work within 2–6 week cycles—executing near-term priorities in alignment with broader strategic aims.

Level	Relative Length of Planning Period
Enterprise	1 – 5 years
Business Unit	1 – 3 years
Value Stream	12 – 18 months
Team-of-Teams	3 – 9 months
Team	2 – 6 weeks

Critically, Valorys does not impose GSOs upon lower levels. Rather, it empowers each organizational unit to formulate its own goals in alignment with superior-level intent. This derivative approach honors the distinct capabilities and contextual understanding of each unit. Departments and teams interpret the GSOs of the next-highest echelon, then determine how best to contribute to their realization—crafting five or six focused goals per planning interval to preserve clarity and feasibility.[5]

This design exemplifies bounded autonomy: lower strata own their outcomes while ensuring alignment with higher-order objectives. GSOs are hierarchical by design, but not authoritarian in practice. Senior leaders review subordinate-level goals not to dictate, but to confirm their contribution to the enterprise's overarching imperatives.

By maintaining this structured, interpretive flow of goal-setting and execution, Valorys fosters coherence, accountability, and high-velocity decision-making—enabling organizations to adapt dynamically while remaining strategically anchored.

Fund Goals, Not Initiatives

A pervasive phenomenon in contemporary organizations is the annual funding of strategic initiatives, which epitomizes the misplaced emphasis on strategies rather than objectives. Pursuing ephemeral opportunities has become standard practice for countless enterprises.

Valorys posits that superior value is generated by funding goals rather than by allocating limited capital to corporate initiatives. The rationale is that most long-term ambitions are articulated in vague terms, translating into disparate interpretations across different organizational domains. This ambiguity squanders time and effort simply because the desired consequence remains unclear. When objectives are clearly expressed, and subordinate components of the firm craft their own goals to support higher-level GSOs, there is substantially less latitude for divergence from executive leadership's original intent.

Precise GSOs yield measurable fiscal outcomes. When goals serve as the foundation for capital funding, the monetization of outcomes creates a common denominator by which authentic value can be determined. For example, if an organization allocates $2 million to a representative annual goal such as "Enhance customer satisfaction and retention," a return on that investment is expected. By quantifying the desired outcome—such as "Increase renewal rate by 15%"—the anticipated gain can be calculated. Ideally, the expenditure associated with the goal should represent a fraction of its projected return.

Funding goals, not initiatives, should drive a redesigned annual budgeting process. While some may argue, "This is too difficult; altering our funding cycle isn't feasible," the question remains: if the Valorys model delivers significantly higher value, improved return on investment, and measurably better operational productivity, is the change not justified?

Shifting the evaluation cadence from annual to quarterly allows CFOs to observe capital deployment with greater immediacy—providing sharper economic insight and reinforcing the organization's financial governance processes.

Strategy Expression Best Practices

1: *Ensure clear, well-written goals shape the entity's trajectory.* Each level of the organization establishes its own GSOs, aligned with higher-level imperatives to create coherence from the executive suite to the front line. Valorys reframes strategy as a testable hypothesis—validated or refined before substantial capital is committed. Adopting GSOs as the common language of strategic expression promotes precision, shared understanding, and disciplined experimentation. This approach enables teams to learn rapidly, adjust intelligently, and treat failure as a source of insight rather than loss.

2: *Fund goals, not initiatives.* This principle anchors performance measurement in a consistent, monetized framework. While initiatives may signal intent, they lack the clarity and rigor of structured GSOs—the emerging standard for realized enterprise value. When goals fail to yield early returns, strategies can pivot based on empirical evidence, ensuring accountability and responsiveness. Quarterly financial reviews then evaluate GSO performance, directing capital toward efforts that generate the greatest sustained impact across the enterprise.

***

Organization Highlight: IBM

International Business Machines offers a long-standing institutional example of strategy expression operationalized through structured goal architecture. Since the 1920s, IBM has maintained a disciplined approach to objective-setting that has evolved alongside the company's repeated strategic reinventions—from hardware to services, from mainframes to cloud computing, from software licensing to AI-driven consulting. That continuity of method across fundamentally different business models makes IBM instructive for examining how goal structure functions as an organizational constant rather than a periodic exercise.

IBM's goal architecture cascades from enterprise level to individual contributors, establishing a structured hierarchy of intent. Annual corporate goals reflect long-term strategic priorities and translate into actionable targets across business units and teams. This top-down coherence is counterbalanced by bottom-up engagement that invites employees to co-author role-specific goals—creating a feedback loop that connects strategic foresight with operational reality. Goals are defined using the SMART framework, with embedded performance metrics that enable transparent evaluation and course correction. Real-time performance dashboards at multiple organizational levels allow managers to track progress and recalibrate as conditions change.

The results of this discipline are observable. As part of its internal enterprise transformation, IBM applied hybrid cloud, AI, and automation across its own operations, yielding $3.5 billion in productivity gains since early 2023.[6] A cognitive supply chain initiative achieved full order fulfillment while reducing supply chain costs by $160 million.[7] Within

IBM Consulting, alignment of business unit goals with client transformation metrics contributed to a 22% increase in consulting revenue in Q4 2023.[8]

What IBM's experience illustrates is not that goal-setting produces exceptional results in isolation, but that consistent structural discipline reduces organizational entropy over time. By synchronizing investment decisions, resource allocation, and innovation priorities around clearly defined goals, the company has repeatedly managed strategic transition without losing operational coherence—a challenge that defeats many enterprises facing comparable disruption.

1. Charles Spielberger, *Encyclopedia of Applied Psychology* (Academic Press, 2004).

2. Peter F. Drucker, *The Practice of Management* (Harper Business, 1954).

3. George Doran, "There's a SMART Way to Write Management's Goals and Objectives," *Journal of Management Review* 70, 35-36 (November 1981).

4. L. Pratt and N. Malcolm, *The Decision Intelligence Handbook* (O'Reilly Media, 2023).

5. George Miller, "The Magical Number Seven, Plus or Minus Two: Some Limits on Our Capacity for Processing Information," *Psychological Review* 63 (2): 81–97 (1956).

6. IBM, *Annual Report: Client Zero Transformation Overview* (Armonk, NY: IBM Corporation, 2023).

7. Joanna Martínez, "IBM Saves $160 Million, Achieves 100 % Order Fulfillment With Cognitive Supply Chain," *Cloud Wars* (October 25, 2023).

8. International Business Machines Corporation, "Q4 2023 Earnings Announcement," *IBM Investor Relations* (January 24, 2024).

Value Proposition

Uncovering Latent Desires

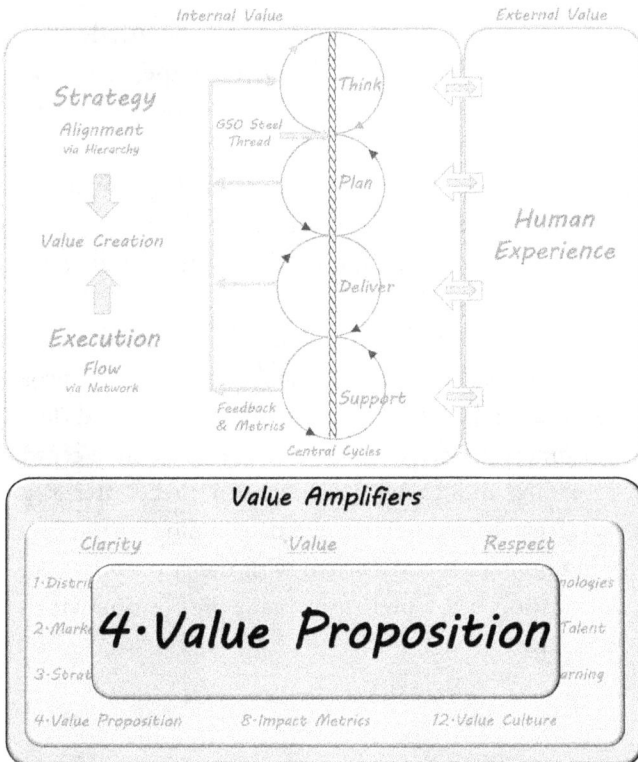

The Logic of Value Propositions

T oday's consumers exhibit remarkable acuity—they harbor distinct predilections yet frequently encounter difficulty articulating them with precision. Organizations that grasp the fundamental behavioral dynamics governing their clientele accumulate substantially greater shareholder returns than those operating without such comprehension.[1] This chapter presents a persuasive rationale for architecting and deploying products and services that encompass a customer's complete trajectory, purchasing psychology, and aspirational human experience.[2] Successful enterprises co-create value propositions collaboratively with their customers for each product family or service line.

Valorys concentrates on the manifestation of value, both within organizational boundaries and beyond. But, quantifying value presents formidable challenges owing to its fundamentally subjective character and individual variance. This intricacy renders it arduous for firms to establish unified definitions and metrics for value assessment.

Developing eloquently structured value propositions enables organizations to define their value architecture in terms comprehensible to all stakeholders. This facilitates enhanced discourse with consumers and personnel through a shared value-centric lexicon, providing an internal benchmark to direct enterprise conduct and an external standard for understanding customers' value interpretation. When constructed with the appropriate amount of sophistication, a comprehensive value proposition wields substantial influence.

Emotion as Value Driver

As previously noted, human nature remains perpetually evolving—what consumers desire today may diverge substantially from their priorities tomorrow. Countless narratives document companies that lost touch with their customers, erroneously presuming their purchasers would preserve identical proclivities for their offerings indefinitely, particularly when fortified by a formidable brand. Failing to sustain responsiveness to customer-perceived value precipitates organizational decline, especially within such a rapidly transforming commercial landscape. More often than not, *consumer purchasing decisions are predominantly governed by feelings*.[3] Successful entities attend assiduously to their purchasers' emotions and incorporate such insights into their value propositions. This value amplifier encourages leadership to maintain scrupulous market vigilance to comprehend what buyers regard as valuable and what they categorically reject.

Throughout the preceding five decades, numerous scholarly works have addressed the enhancement of customer acquisition, retention, fidelity, service excellence, and cross-selling opportunities. Nevertheless, authors have insufficiently emphasized the paramount element all purchasers pursue: *value commensurate with their investment*. Among the notable exceptions, Peter Fader, author of *Customer Centricity*, posits that when enterprises understand their consumers with profound intimacy, they harness customer lifetime value and additional buyer-centric analytics to render more astute decisions regarding the creation and delivery of meaningful offerings.[4]

Precision That Protects Value

It is well-established in aviation and maritime domains that even a single degree off course results in progressively greater departure from the intended destination as distance increases. This principle applies equally to product and service innovation, marketing endeavors, and sales initiatives requiring multiple phases and contributors. The more precisely a value proposition is articulated, the higher the probability an offering will achieve its prescribed objective. When product teams accurately discern specific customer needs and underlying motivations, development processes become considerably more efficient. Parties bearing responsibility for sales and marketing can engage their constituencies with enhanced precision when the subtleties of the premise are lucidly comprehended.[5]

Brand equity and share price resilience show direct correlation with clear comprehension of frequently shifting consumer and market preferences. For instance, by attending to potential vulnerabilities, such as sensitive data compromises and their psychological ramifications upon customers, shareholder valuations and product reputation can be safeguarded against the unintended consequences of external threats. Many consumers appreciate how an organization aligns with their social convictions, environmental consciousness, and ethical procurement practices. They remain cognizant of safety standards and personal health implications, alongside a company's participation in public service and community endeavors.

A robust brand can furnish insulation against short-term market turbulence while buttressing long-term shareholder value. By cultivating compelling value propositions to enhance brand equity and its potential influence upon share price, organizations express their dedication to brand cultivation and strategic decision-making excellence, thereby fortifying shareholder and investor confidence.

The Power of Fusion Teams

The term *fusion team* is relatively new, but the concept enjoys considerable heritage. It describes a group of self-organizing, self-managing individuals with cross-functional expertise who collaborate autonomously to achieve specific objectives.[6] Within the Valorys framework, fusion teams are among the most effective instruments for developing robust, accurate value propositions—precisely because they unite the knowledge, depth, and diversity of perspective that rigorous collaboration demands. Across four decades of advisory work, I have yet to encounter a more consistently effective mechanism for this purpose.

As depicted in the Valorys diagram, four sets of arrows illustrate the reciprocal intersections between external and internal value as they mutually inform one another throughout each central cycle. Given this framework, a fusion team characteristically encompasses a leader from product development and marketing/sales, a representative of the technological dimension of the offering (where applicable), a psychologist or individual possessing human-centered design proficiency, and one or more constituents representing the buyer ecosystem, including suppliers and distributors. The merit of this collaborative architecture lives in the heterogeneous frames of reference applied to both customer requisites and the entity's solution as value propositions undergo refinement.

Structuring Fusion Teams

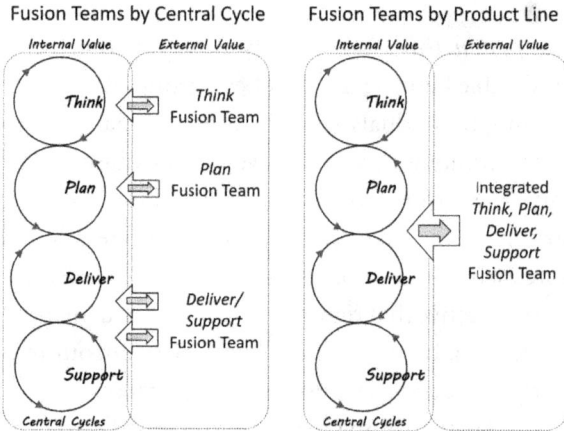

Fusion Teams by Central Cycle   Fusion Teams by Product Line

As illustrated above, organizations seeking to develop compelling value propositions through cross-functional collaboration may adopt one of several structural techniques for forming fusion teams. These include:

1. Assembling a singular team to address all related products within each central cycle—Think, Plan, Deliver, Support.

2. Creating a dedicated team for every product, product line, or service category that operates across all cycles.

3. Implementing a hybrid model that selectively blends both approaches.

The optimal configuration is contingent upon the organization's structural design, operating model, and degree of product diversification. Regardless of the pathway chosen, the process must originate from a strategic vantage point—beginning at the highest level of abstraction and proceeding through progressively finer levels of specificity.

For instance, fusion teams engaged in the Think and Plan cycles focus on broad consumer needs, competitive positioning, and macro-level market segmentation. By contrast, teams working within the Deliver and Support cycles address more granular concerns, such as individual product performance, customer satisfaction metrics, and service-level efficacy.

This cascading structure reinforces the notion that value propositions are inherently multidimensional, with distinct facets emerging at each phase of the enterprise cycle. By integrating both internal capabilities and external expectations, organizations are able to construct value definitions that are not only coherent across departments, but also reflective of stakeholder priorities. The resulting propositions embody a synthesis of institutional intent and customer aspiration—capturing the nuanced interplay between strategic vision and operational delivery.

***

The boardroom at Tuerin's headquarters in Parnell afforded a panoramic vista of Auckland harbor—silver light dancing across the water, sailboats capturing the afternoon breeze—yet no one at the elongated table was gazing outside. The space was subdued, utilitarian, designed for clarity and command. But clarity was precisely what had vanished.

Tuerin had long constituted a venerated name in the outdoor gear domain. Their signature product, the ApexShell, represented the kind of jacket that had constructed its reputation one tempest at a time. Dependable, field-validated, sustainably manufactured, it appeared on trampers in Fiordland, runners traversing Wellington ridgelines, and urban cyclists navigating morning drizzle in Christchurch. It wasn't ostentatious, but it performed.

Yet the metrics were beginning to narrate a different story. Online conversion rates were deteriorating. Customer growth had stagnated. The voice of the customer, once replete with unsolicited accolades, had diminished to a subdued, unenthusiastic murmur. On social platforms, Tuerin still received mentions—but the passion had dissipated. "Solid jacket," one comment articulated. "Still holding up." Faint praise in a competitive category where identity and aspiration frequently mattered as much as waterproof ratings.

Within the organization, execution remained precise. Fulfillment adhered to deadlines. Retail partners were adequately stocked. Warranty claims remained minimal. On paper, nothing appeared compromised. But momentum had waned. The team wasn't disregarding the transformation—they simply hadn't yet learned how to interpret it.

Dana, the CEO, had convened the meeting. Her leadership style was composed and inclusive, yet also unwavering when patterns failed to align. Around her sat the senior leadership: Marlon from operations, Doug from finance, Gina from marketing, several leads from digital and brand. They weren't scrambling. They were attempting to decode a shift they could perceive but hadn't yet mapped. The ApexShell hadn't changed. The world surrounding it had.

Over the preceding five years, outdoor performance gear had undergone a fundamental transformation. Technical features had become baseline expectations. Breathability and sustainability had evolved into prerequisites, not differentiators. Meanwhile, the customer base had diversified substantially. People were purchasing performance gear for reasons that bore little relation to summiting peaks. Urban dwellers sought gear that transitioned seamlessly between commute, café, and co-working space. Parents desired protection without bulk for children on scooters and bicycles. Dedicated trampers still prioritized pack weight and storm ratings—but they no longer represented the dominant voice in the marketplace.

Tuerin had not fallen behind in quality. It had fallen behind in relevance. The brand had continued to communicate with a singular voice. But the audience had fragmented. And that misalignment was quietly undermining them.

Three primary customer archetypes emerged as the team reviewed research, channel data, and anecdotal feedback:

- Urban commuters, who required versatile, weather-ready gear that didn't make them appear destined for Everest Base Camp. They sought a jacket that harmonized with their aesthetic, felt lightweight in motion, and appeared appropriate in both a staff meeting and a supermarket aisle.

- Backcountry trampers, who still comprised the brand's most devoted audience. They scrutinized materials, tested seams, prioritized packability and performance in extreme weather. For them, every feature required justification. They purchased gear like an engineer selects tools.

- Parents of teens, an emerging segment that frequently purchased the ApexShell because it promised simplicity and reliability. Their inquiries were pragmatic: Will it keep my child dry? Can it survive three seasons and ten wash cycles? Will I need to replace it mid-year?

These groups possessed unique needs, but until now, they had all been presented with the same proposition.

Gina, who had led brand strategy for years, acknowledged the drift. Hero banners were rotated based on seasonality, not segmentation. Messaging remained generic. "Waterproof. Breathable. Trusted." Accurate, but devoid of meaning when stretched too thin. Internally, they organized around climate. Externally, customers were choosing based on mindset and lifestyle.

That was the cultural moment this team encountered—not a crisis, but a crossroads. The realization was straightforward but sobering: the product didn't require modification. The narrative did.

What followed wasn't a brainstorming session, but a recalibration. They didn't need rebranding. They needed precision. Not new slogans, but refined value propositions tailored to each audience:

- For commuters: A jacket that adapts to city life—lightweight, breathable, tailored for movement. Rain-ready gear that fits your day, not just your hike.

- For trampers: Proven protection for unpredictable terrain. Built from field-tested materials with the durability and packability serious backcountry requires.

- For parents: Protection you don't have to think about. Waterproof, washable, built to last through school, sports, and storms.

The message wasn't about features. It was about alignment. Each segment needed to see themselves in the product—to feel that it was built for them, not just available to them.

Gina proposed forming cross-functional teams—incorporating product, marketing, customer support, retail partners, and end users—to test and iterate messaging that resonated emotionally, not just functionally. Dana concurred. The digital team could A/B test new landing pages. Retail leads could pilot in-store signage updates in high-traffic locations. Everything could be measured.

No one in the room questioned the value of the ApexShell. That wasn't the point. What had finally crystallized was the need to stop assuming value was self-evident. In today's marketplace, quality was a requirement—but relevance was the differentiator.

By the time the meeting concluded, there were no applause lines, no dramatic revelations. Just a quiet shift in posture. The same people who had arrived with questions departed with momentum. They hadn't changed the product, but they had changed how they would communicate it—and to whom. It was a brand stepping out of neutral and back into contention.

***

Defining Multilevel Value

In their influential 2016 Harvard Business Review article *The Elements of Value*, authors Eric Almquist, John Senior, and Nicolas Bloch drew upon Bain & Company's three decades of research to map the fundamental components of value as a hierarchical construct.[7] Much as Maslow's hierarchy of needs places physiological and safety requirements at the base—the prerequisites that must be satisfied before higher aspirations become relevant—the Elements of Value framework positions functional attributes such as features and performance at its foundation. These are the baseline expectations consumers bring to any purchasing decision.

At elevated levels, the framework surfaces the drivers that prove far more powerful in shaping loyalty and advocacy: emotional resonance, life-changing impact, and social meaning. Just as self-actualization represents the most profound level of human motivation in Maslow's model, these upper-tier value elements represent the most enduring sources of competitive differentiation—and the ones most organizations consistently underinvest in. So, what constitutes the hallmarks of a well-articulated, multi-layered value proposition?

Think Cycle

The Think cycle fusion team (typically at the enterprise level) emphasizes the altruistic impact of their product or service portfolio by asking themselves, "How are we enhancing the world?" Apple's enterprise-level value proposition has historically positioned the company around enriching customers' lives through premium, innovative, and intuitive technology—an expression broad enough to encompass its entire product ecosystem. This universality positions an organization in the broadest context for further exploration. Since the expression of the statement operates at such an elevated level, it encompasses the entire human experience to include customers' personal values and belief systems.

What of partners, distributors, and agents? Where do they integrate into value proposition development? Since external value is not wholly determined by consumers, these entities are regarded as a company's customers and should be appropriately represented among fusion teams.

Plan Cycle

Referencing the abstract Think cycle value propositions, the Plan-level fusion team (typically within a business unit) delves into greater specificity about the external value their buyers seek. Maintaining the Apple theme, each product line has historically emphasized simplicity and emotional resonance over feature enumeration—inviting customers to experience technology rather than merely operate it. At this tier, the collaborative team concentrates on the specific motivators or unique life-enriching benefits that would prompt individuals to purchase their products or services. As appropriate, customers' emotions and holistic experiences are considered.

Because Valorys considers internal as well as external value, fusion teams must determine how the organization will monetize its offerings. The Plan cycle's fusion teams deliberate how they would position products that would yield optimal returns by analyzing which extant core and peripheral business capabilities might be leveraged. Selling price, profit margins, ROI, organizational risk, regulatory compliance, and brand impact are scrutinized within this context, alongside less tangible factors such as a customer's requisite for trust, privacy, and security. This deliberation frequently precipitates nuanced refinements of the phraseology or inflection of the proposition statements themselves. The relative magnitude of the bi-directional vectors in the Valorys illustration shows that input from the customer receives marginally greater consideration than the entity's monetization imperatives.

Deliver and Support Cycles

Fusion teams responsible for articulating a value proposition for the Deliver and Support central cycles are predominantly concerned with fitness, form, function, total cost of ownership, and quality parameters. This tier's fusion teams ordinarily operate within a delivery arc (a business unit value creation mechanism detailed in Chapter 7: Value Streams) where they examine the details of the specific benefits a customer seeks. In the Apple exemplar, the emphasis would center on the aesthetics, technical attributes, and functionalities of distinct product models. At this juncture, there are likewise internal value specifications such as costs to create, distribute, configure, and support the products. Detailed calculations are executed here to confirm whether the organization's expected internal rate of return will be actualized.

While it may not appear immediately evident why this degree of granularity is necessary, the value propositional output of the Deliver and Support cycles establishes a critical input for strategic planning, market intelligence, value stream optimization, product design and testing, sales collateral, and brand messaging.

Elements of Strong Value Propositions

Several elements can influence the character and caliber of a value proposition, such as a company's core competencies, comprehending target markets and their segmentation, selecting the proper extent of personalization, and optimizing a customer's journey.

Designing Personalized Experiences

Most consumers appreciate individualized experiences when procuring products or services, even when those offerings are mass-produced and extensively distributed. Research has substantiated that customers are more inclined to repurchase and cultivate loyalty toward a brand that acknowledges their distinctive preferences, behaviors, and acquisition history.[8] Fortuitously, substantial volumes of available public and proprietary data may be examined, refined, analyzed, and organized to provide customized recommendations, content, and services predicated upon target audiences' cognitive biases and psychological motivators.

Mapping the Customer Journey

An efficacious approach to achieve some measure of personalization involves mapping each phase of a customer's procurement process and product utilization, identifying all touchpoints and interactions a purchaser experiences with the offering, from initial awareness to post-purchase support. Analysis of each stage within that trajectory provides supplementary insights into customer needs, expectations, frustrations, and opportunities for value creation.

Determining the emotional and experiential elements that align with an entity's brand and resonate with prospective customers enables fusion teams to creatively articulate what manner of interaction consumers desire at each stage of their journey and how they might perceive that experience.

Knowing Your Market

Continuously monitoring marketplace dynamics keeps organizations current on industry developments, emerging technologies, and evolving consumer segments—enabling ongoing assessment of the relevance and competitiveness of their value propositions. Methods such as A/B trials, focus groups, immersive design, surveys, AI prompting, and usability testing cultivate deeper comprehension of how customers perceive and respond to offerings.

Segmenting a target market through demographics, psychographics, and purchasing behaviors reveals how distinct groups harbor unique requirements that shape specific value propositions. Those propositions are subsequently refined to resonate with their intended audience, ensuring needs are addressed and desired benefits are delivered. Even competitors' value propositions yield useful intelligence—examining rivals' strengths and vulnerabilities identifies domains where the organization can advance a more distinctive and compelling position in the market.

Employees as Brand Ambassadors

Employees, associates, and support personnel prove instrumental for delivering exceptional consumer experiences. Companies cultivate more meaningful buyer interactions when they invest the appropriate time and effort to empower and train their workforce to serve as brand ambassadors. Fusion teams can derive substantial insights from regularly testing their value propositions upon customer-facing staff, as those positioned closest to the purchaser frequently possess the sharpest understanding of buying behavior.

Value Proposition Best Practices

1: *Use value propositions to illuminate customer-company relationships.* A strong value proposition commercializes experience and evokes emotion rather than simply describing a product. It must be specific, unambiguous, and aligned with both the company's product vision and the customer's deeper preferences. Leading organizations look beyond tangible features to integrate intangible qualities—crafting multi-layered propositions that reflect a holistic understanding of value.

2: *Extend value propositions throughout the enterprise.* Propositions gain precision at the levels where work is executed. Fusion teams integrate customer perspectives with business, human design, and technical insight, creating a synthesis of customer, company, and context. When these teams collaborate with purchasers to co-create thoughtful value propositions, they strengthen alignment, elevate performance, and increase the likelihood of sustained growth and profitability.

***

Organization Highlight: World Bank

The World Bank, a constituent agency within the United Nations system, stands as a vital enabler of global development through financial instruments, policy guidance, and technical support to low- and middle-income nations. Central to its mandate is designing value propositions that go beyond transactional aid and instead catalyze systemic transformation within diverse national contexts. These value propositions are not static declarations but living constructs—refined iteratively to reflect evolving geopolitical dynamics, developmental priorities, and ecological imperatives.

The World Bank's approach to value proposition development is highly diagnostic, integrative, and co-creative. Each engagement begins with systematic country diagnostics and partnership frameworks—analytical tools that identify critical constraints and opportunities for inclusive, sustainable growth. These designs are developed in close collaboration with national governments and stakeholders, ensuring interventions are both technically sound and locally relevant.

What differentiates the Bank's approach is its deliberate orientation toward longitudinal development logic. Rather than focusing solely on short-term deliverables or fiscal disbursements, each value proposition is architected to establish foundational capabilities—be it in regulatory reform, institutional accountability, or environmental sustainability—that outlast project timelines and political cycles. This positioning ensures that interventions are not only self-reinforcing but generative, enabling countries to evolve from aid recipients to development agents.

The Bank's strategic effectiveness lies in tailoring offerings to unique cultural, economic, and social architectures of member states. Diagnostic protocols examine fiscal sustainability, governance systems, infrastructure readiness, social equity, and climate vulnerability. This granular situational awareness empowers the Bank to craft interventions that address immediate development needs while building systemic resilience and capacity for autonomous progress.

An exemplary application occurred in India's Rajasthan, where the Bank supported the *24x7 Power for All* initiative. The value proposition involved financial support and deep policy engagement to restructure the state's power distribution companies through performance-based incentives, regulatory reforms, and digital monitoring tools. As a result, the combined financial loss of power distribution was reduced from $1.8 billion in 2014 to $560 million in 2017.[9] Importantly, the Bank's engagement extended beyond financial efficiency to include capacity-building for local utilities, enabling enduring institutional reform and improved service delivery for millions of citizens.

The Bank also integrates feedback and adaptive learning into its value proposition lifecycle. Post-implementation reviews, impact evaluations, and independent assessments are not merely compliance exercises—they serve as core design mechanisms for refining future engagements. This adaptive posture reinforces a culture of evidence-based iteration, enabling the Bank to evolve its service offerings in real time as local conditions shift.

Ultimately, the World Bank's enduring strength lies in its ability to unify technical rigor with diplomatic empathy. By embedding strategic adaptability, contextual intelligence, and durable partnerships into its development framework, the World Bank continually repositions itself as a global architect of inclusive growth—creating transformational levers for progress in an interdependent world. Its value propositions, grounded in co-creation and sustained engagement, ensure

that development is not a transaction, but a generative partnership built for continuity, relevance, and impact.

1. Sander F. M. Beckers, Jenny van Doorn, and Peter C. Verhoef, "Good,
   Better, Engaged? The Effect of Company-Initiated Customer Engagement Behavior on Shareholder Value," *Journal of the Academy of Marketing Science* Issue 46 (2018).

2. McKinsey Report, "Customer Experience: Creating Value Through
   Transforming Customer Journeys," *McKinsey & Company* (July 1,
   2016).

3. Gerald Zaltman, *How Customers Think: Essential Insights into the Mind
   of the Market* (Harvard Business School Press, 2003).

4. Peter Fader, *Customer Centricity: Focus on the Right Customers for
   Strategic Advantage* (Wharton School Press, 2020).

5. Lumen Strategies, "Value Proposition and a Whole Offer" (2020).

6. Ashutosh Gupta, "Why Fusion Teams Matter," *Gartner Research* (February 14, 2022).

7. Eric Almquist, John Senior, and Nicolas Bloch, "The Elements of Value:
   Measuring—and Delivering—What Consumers Really Want," *Harvard Business Review* (September 1, 2016).

8. Frederick Reichheld, *The Loyalty Effect: The Hidden Force Behind
   Growth, Profits, and Lasting Value* (Harvard Business Review Press,
   1996).

9. World Bank, "Supporting India's Transformation," *World Bank Results
   Report* (October 16, 2019).

Part Two: Value

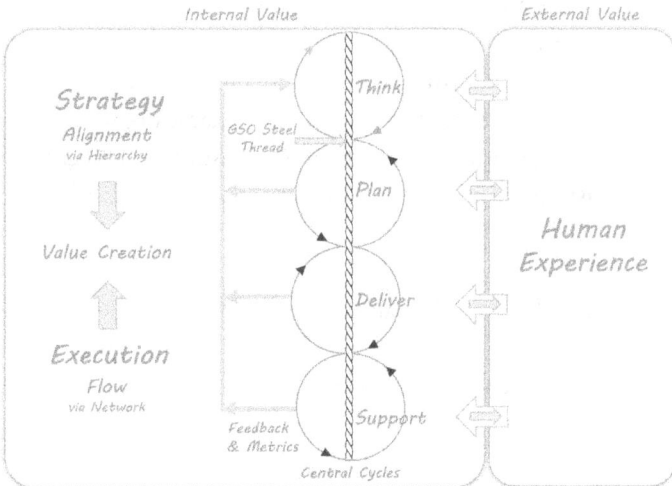

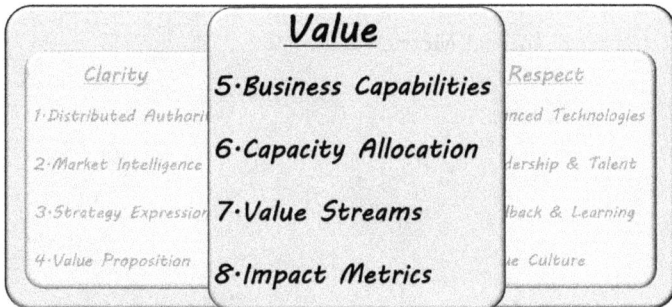

Strategy

Alignment
via Hierarchy

Value Creation

Execution

Flow
via Network

GSO Steel
Thread

Think

Plan

Deliver

Feedback
& Metrics

Support

Central Cycles

*Human
Experience*

Value

5·Business Capabilities

6·Capacity Allocation

7·Value Streams

8·Impact Metrics

Clarity

1·Distributed Authori...

2·Market Intelligence

3·Strategy Expression

4·Value Proposition

Respect

...nced Technologies

...dership & Talent

...back & Learning

...e Culture

V alue creation is the systematic conversion of organizational assets into stakeholder prosperity through the disciplined allocation of capital, talent, and strategic focus. It is what transforms strategy into enduring competitive advantage. In this section, I establish how the gains produced by distributed authority, market intelligence, strategic intent, and value propositions—introduced in Part One: Clarity—are maximized for operationalizing genuine value creation.

For many enterprises, the four value amplifiers explored here are frequently misclassified as operational functions rather than strategic imperatives—and consequently receive insufficient leadership attention. Yet, in practice, these competencies represent indispensable structural foundations that enable organizations to govern their operations with coherence, ensure process continuity, and sustain optimal value flow across the enterprise.

Chapter 5: Business Capabilities

Chapter 6: Capacity Allocation

Chapter 7: Value Streams

Chapter 8: Impact Metrics

Business Capabilities

Illuminating the Core

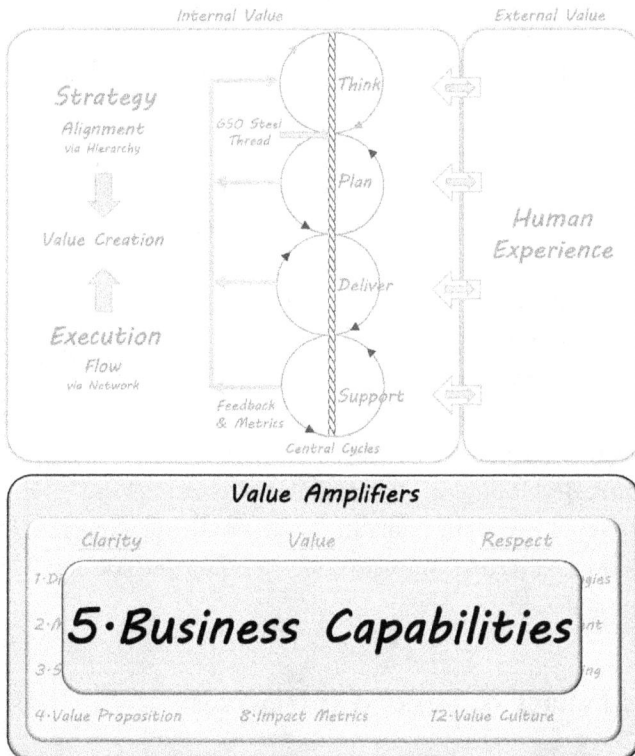

Building Composable Enterprises

B usiness frameworks that employ standardized design patterns to promote scalability, reusability, and adaptability across operational domains are often classified under the banner of composable architectures. Unlike traditional, monolithic constructs, flexible systems are inherently modular and thus more capable of accommodating shifts in market dynamics, regulatory mandates, and emergent customer expectations. They are also, in many cases, less costly to operate and maintain over time.[1]

A composable architecture necessitates the development and stewardship of a comprehensive catalog of business capabilities—the foundational building blocks upon which adaptable operations depend. Maintaining an up-to-date inventory is not merely an administrative exercise; it is essential to both quarterly growth and long-term resilience. In Chapter 7: Value Streams, I will explore in greater depth the strategic advantages afforded by a granular understanding of these competencies.

Given the increasing reliance on digital and electronics-based distribution models, technical capabilities have assumed an outsized role in enterprise success. However, it is erroneous to treat them as discrete entities. Technical capabilities are inextricably linked to a broader ecosystem of business capabilities—spanning product development, service delivery, customer support, and operational oversight. Isolating them from the comprehensive collection leads to incomplete understanding and suboptimal decision-making.

The Fallacy of Funded Initiatives

As discussed in Chapter 3: Strategy Expression, many organizations treat corporate initiatives as a proxy for strategy—a fundamentally flawed approach that wastes resources and undermines strategic progress. Without well-articulated goals, companies often develop annual priorities that amount to little more than a collection of appealing but disconnected ideas gathered from across the organization. This "suggestion box" mentality, where all ideas are welcomed regardless of strategic merit, creates portfolios of work that lack coherent direction.

The root cause of this fragmentation lies in structural misalignment between policy and execution, or worse, the complete absence of clearly stated goals. When enterprises follow cyclical funding processes—automatically disbursing capital each fiscal year without reassessing strategic alignment—they inevitably waste resources on endeavors that deliver little meaningful value. Work that operates independently of defined goals becomes functionally orphaned, making the wholesale funding of initiatives a structurally risky proposition.

This risk is compounded by the unstated assumptions underlying most initiatives. Given the significant investments at stake, these assumptions can be extraordinarily expensive when they prove wrong. Without defined goals, organizations lack the contextual framework needed to answer critical questions: How will this initiative materially advance our objectives? How does it relate to our broader strategy? Most importantly, how will we measure its success?

The absence of a value-based framework makes it almost impossible to assess the relevance, realized return, or ultimate success of any completed undertaking, prolonging a cycle of strategic drift masked by the illusion of perpetual activity.

Managing Capability Portfolios

Within Valorys, a portfolio—at its essence—is a curated collection of assets, comprising both existing and potential business capabilities that stem from capital investments. Its primary function is to ensure that the requisite competencies for business unit success are available, understood, and actively leveraged.

To illustrate: a prudent investor would not acquire additional equities without first evaluating the contents of their current holdings. Yet many corporations I have advised cannot produce even a rudimentary inventory of their internal capabilities, let alone demonstrate deep familiarity with the aptitudes and systems upon which their operations depend. Without this foundational awareness, how can one ascertain whether a new capability is genuinely needed?

In Valorys, annual business unit GSOs serve as the foundation for capability assessment. Upon issuance, the BU portfolio team conducts a detailed evaluation to determine what proficiencies must be built or enhanced to realize each stated outcome. The central question posed is: *What capabilities must exist—or be developed—to achieve this goal?*

If the required proficiencies are already in place, the portfolio team advises the responsible delivery unit to leverage them accordingly. If the capability is missing or insufficiently mature, the team creates a formal request for its development or augmentation. These requests populate the portfolio backlog—an ordered queue of work items required to generate the necessary capabilities for achieving goals and sustaining operations. Depending on scale and scope, backlog elements may be designated as projects, programs, initiatives, epics, or other unique terms familiar to the enterprise.

Importantly, items are added to the portfolio lineup only when there is verified need, as determined through a disciplined review of a business unit's GSOs. Any backlog component that does not support current or anticipated goals is subject to challenge and removal. This practice preserves alignment and safeguards against the accumulation of extraneous work.

Portfolio requests are funded through the annual goal-based allocation designated for each GSO. Once approved, the portfolio team determines sequencing, prioritization, and cost estimation. Complexity arises when goals or strategies evolve—often through the acquisition of experiential insight. In such cases, the backlog is revised in near-real time, enabling rapid reordering and reprioritization to reflect newly understood imperatives. This adaptive mechanism prevents the misallocation of resources to capabilities that may no longer serve the organization's direction. Just as equity portfolios require constant rebalancing to accommodate shifting markets, so too must business portfolios mature to remain strategically valid.

***

My business partner, Nishant, and I were contacted to provide guidance to a mid-sized insurance agency with an expanding roster of initiatives they believed necessary to maintain market relevance. We sat across from Jordan, the COO—a man whose expression made clear he had hired consultants before and been disappointed by all of them. I found myself wondering whether we should have taken this engagement. It was mid-morning, and the snow outside the Chicago Loop office had turned to slush, mirroring the atmosphere in the room.

"Here's my problem," Jordan started, his voice already strained. "We're hemorrhaging money on technology projects, and everyone's got their hand out. Client portal dashboard, new reporting tools, AI chatbots—you name it, someone's pitching it. But honestly? I don't think half these people know what they're asking for."

I maintained a neutral expression. "What are your actual business goals?"

"Goals?" He laughed bitterly. "My goal is to not get fired. The board wants policy renewals up 12% this year, and they want quote-to-bind time cut by 20% this quarter. Oh, and they want it done with the same budget we had three years ago."

Nishant interjected, "So, which of your current technology initiatives are driving those outcomes?"

Jordan's jaw tightened. "That's exactly what I'm paying you guys to figure out. Because right now, it feels like I'm throwing money into a black hole."

I leaned back. "We can't figure out what you won't admit. Your renewal process—is it working or not?"

"It's...adequate," he said, defensively. "Our CRM workflows are fine. The problem is quote-to-bind. Agents are still playing email tag with underwriters like it's 1995. No tracking, no accountability, no visibility into where things get stuck."

"Then why are you funding dashboard projects instead of fixing the actual bottleneck?" Nishant added.

His face flushed. "Because that's not how this place works, alright? The data team screams about outdated dashboards. The UX team wants their shiny new interface. I can't just tell department heads to go screw themselves."

I asked dryly, "Why not?"

Jordan stared at me. "Excuse me?"

"Why can't you tell them no? You're the COO."

He stood up abruptly, pacing to the window. "You know what? I don't need some know-it-all consultants coming in here and telling me how to manage my people. These are relationships I've built over years."

"And those relationships are costing you results," I said, not flinching. "Every dollar you spend on pet projects is a dollar you're not spending on fixing your actual problems."

"Pet projects?" He whirled around. "These are strategic initiatives proposed by department heads with twenty years of experience."

"Yes, initiatives that don't map to any measurable business outcomes," I shot back. "When's the last time someone pitched you something and showed you exactly how it would impact quote-to-bind time or renewal rates? Not 'this might help' or 'users would like this'—actual impact projections."

Jordan's voice rose. "What are you talking about? We won't know until the project's done. You can't determine that upfront."

"Not true!" I stood up to match his energy. "You absolutely can. High-performing organizations do it every day. They fund projects that are tied to results, not feelings."

"High-performing organizations," he repeated mockingly. "Right. Let me guess—you're going to tell me about some tech startup that moves fast and breaks things?"

"I'm going to tell you about other insurance companies that are making you obsolete because they can bind policies in hours while you're taking days."

That struck home. Jordan's shoulders sagged slightly, but his voice remained sharp. "So, what's your brilliant solution? Fire half my team and start over?"

Nishant intervened. "Our solution is that you start leading instead of managing. Every project proposal needs to show a direct impact on these two goals. No impact thesis, no funding. Period."

"And when my analytics director quits because I killed her dashboard project?"

"Then you hire someone who understands strategic priorities," he said. "Or you help her reframe the dashboard to show how it accelerates quotes. But stop funding work that doesn't move the needle."

Jordan laughed harshly. "Easy for you to say. You guys will be gone in three months. I have to work with these people every day."

Nishant countered, "Which is exactly why you need to set clear rules now. Otherwise, you'll keep having the same conversation with the board about missed targets and blown budgets."

He sat back down heavily. "You really think it's that simple?"

"I think it's that hard," I said. "Simple doesn't mean easy. It means you have to make uncomfortable decisions and stick to them."

Jordan rubbed his temples. "The leadership team is going to hate this."

"Some of them will. The ones who care about their pet projects more than company results. But the smart ones will appreciate the clarity."

His office fell silent except for the heating system cycling on. Jordan stared at his desk, weighing a decision he had been postponing for months.

Finally, he looked up. "Alright. But I'm not doing this alone. You guys are going to help me sell this to the leadership team. And when they push back—and they will—you're going to back me up."

"Fair enough," I said. "But once the rules are set, we expect you to enforce them. Even when it's uncomfortable."

"Especially when it's uncomfortable," he said, something more resolute creeping into his voice. "Because you're right about one thing—I'm tired of explaining to the board why we missed our numbers again."

We gathered our materials as Jordan retrieved his laptop to schedule his pitch at the next leadership meeting. Outside, the Chicago wind was merciless, but Nishant and I recognized that something had shifted in Jordan's thinking. In this instance, transformation emerged not through collaboration or consensus-building, but through the uncomfortable clarity that accompanies acknowledging what one has been avoiding all along.

***

Portfolio Governance and Fiscal Discipline

A high-functioning portfolio team demonstrates fiscal stewardship by ensuring that funded demands are explicitly tethered
to measurable impact metrics—namely, GSO outcomes—thus
affirming that its backlog of work is directly advancing enterprise-level objectives. In this context, CFOs play a critical oversight role: they ensure that portfolio managers are not administering requests whose relevance has expired, regardless of their
former utility. The objective is precision—capital should not be
extended to efforts that no longer contribute to organizational
advancement.

When strategic shifts or early-warning indicators trigger a
directional change, portfolio teams must often make difficult
calls—postponing, modifying, or discontinuing capability development work. These adjustments, while rational, might appear
arbitrary or disorienting to those at the product or delivery level. It
is therefore imperative that portfolio leadership clearly articulate
the rationale behind such decisions. In the absence of a transparent narrative, product development teams may interpret these
actions as reactive or indecisive, undermining trust and cohesion.

Value–Based Capital Distribution

GSOs serve as the anchor points for determining where investment should be increased, held steady, scaled back, or retired alto-
gether. These decisions shape the funding allocated to each business unit and inform its responsibility for maintaining a defined
catalog of business and technical capabilities. Chapter 7 will further demonstrate how value streams act as the primary conduits
for enterprise value creation. Consequently, business units allocate capital to their value streams based on their strategic book of

work—ensuring that funding reflects both demand and delivery capacity.

This method represents a marked departure from conventional budgeting paradigms, wherein funds are distributed directly to discrete functional domains such as sales, marketing, human resources, or compliance. In the Valorys model, these functions support value creation. As such, they receive budgetary allocations through the value streams they contribute to—via chargeback mechanisms calibrated to their role in developing, sustaining, or delivering products and services. This reconfiguration reduces the total number of cost centers in an organization, as value streams—and their collaborative enablers—are viewed not as administrative overhead but as interdependent profit centers. Notably, functional units are only engaged to the extent warranted by their contribution to GSO-aligned outcomes, reinforcing both accountability and fiscal discipline.

Value-centered enterprises structure funding based on defined goals and measurable outcomes rather than on long-lived programs or projects. Initiatives with multi-year timelines frequently drift from their original purpose. CFOs should, therefore, evaluate whether extended GSOs continue to deliver positive returns relative to the capital allocated. By anchoring financial plans to concise temporal horizons—annually or quarterly—organizations can more accurately assess the profitability of smaller increments of work and manage expenditures with higher promise and precision.

Business Capabilities Best Practices

1: *Build composable architectures for scalable adaptation.* Design composable frameworks that promote adaptability, modularity, and seamless scaling in response to change. Governed at the business-unit level and guided by GSOs, these architectures evolve through goal-driven requisitions in the portfolio backlog, ensuring flexibility without compromising alignment.

2: *Regulate work portfolios through forward-facing GSOs.* Keep each portfolio tightly synchronized with each GSO as defined by its business unit. Portfolio teams must continually assess and close the gap between existing capabilities and those required to achieve intended outcomes. Each backlog request should demonstrate clear relevance to designated targets within the active planning horizon.

3: *Replace assumptions with empirical discipline.* Ground every financial decision in experiential data rather than conjecture. Assumptions erode fiscal integrity and strategic focus; therefore, CFOs should withhold capital from initiatives lacking empirical validation or iterative testing. This disciplined approach ensures portfolio investments remain evidence-based, outcome-oriented, and fully aligned with enterprise objectives.

***

Organization Highlight: P&G

Procter & Gamble demonstrates how a capability-centric operating model yields superior strategic clarity, operational coherence, and enterprise-wide scalability—delivering repeatable excellence and measurable economic returns across international operations.

The cornerstone of P&G's competency-based approach is global business services (GBS), established in 1999, when company leaders recognized the need to revamp their business model for the 21st-century economy. The firm faced a critical challenge: eliminating duplication across operating units that were each supported by their own local service organizations, and leveraging economies of scale to reduce costs and improve efficiency.

Central to P&G's composable approach was the deliberate modularization of its business capabilities. Rather than embedding these competencies within individual business units—where they would remain siloed, duplicated, and difficult to scale—P&G consolidated them into reusable, standardized components administered through GBS. Finance and accounting, human resources, IT infrastructure, and facilities management were restructured not as departmental functions but as discrete capability modules, designed to be independently governed, consistently deployed, and shared across the enterprise. This architectural shift meant that any business unit could draw upon the same high-quality capability without maintaining its own local version—eliminating redundancy, enforcing standards, and enabling the kind of scalable, composable operation that defines a truly capability-centric enterprise. The result was an organization that could reconfigure its operational building blocks in response to strategic demands without disrupting the integrity of its core capabilities.

P&G's business capability consolidation strategy through GBS yielded substantial and well-documented performance gains. By 2008, GBS had generated cost savings exceeding $600 million, underscoring the efficiency of its shared services model. This centralized foundation also significantly enhanced the company's capacity for rapid post-merger integration, most notably demonstrated in the Gillette acquisition. The consolidation was completed in just 15 months—less than half the typical duration for a transaction of comparable scale. Given estimated synergy cost reductions of approximately $4 million per day, this accelerated timeline translated into nearly $2 billion in realized savings, exemplifying the transformative impact of GBS on operational mobility and strategic execution.[2]

P&G's capability improvements continued to evolve through enterprise outsourcing partnerships that enhanced rather than diminished their core capabilities. In 2003, P&G entered into $4.2 billion worth of third party agreements in IT infrastructure, finance and accounting, HR, and facilities management. By externalizing routine, commoditized tasks while retaining strategic functions internally, GBS was able to elevate the role of its shared-services organization—shifting focus toward innovation and the development of new business capabilities.[3]

This integrated approach enabled P&G to implement transformative programs, most notably its Connect and Develop platform that promotes innovation from outside the company. This open discovery framework now accounts for over 35% of the company's new products and has generated billions in revenue, demonstrating how strategic capability integration accelerates growth and drives commercial success.[4]

P&G's systematic approach to capability development, integration, and deployment reveals how treating business capabilities as strategic assets creates sustainable competitive advantage. Through its GBS model, strategic outsourcing partnerships, and continuous capability enhancement, P&G has built an organizational architecture that delivers both operational efficiency and innovation excellence—confirming that composability, when institutionalized with discipline, is not merely an architectural choice but a strategic one.

1. Duy Nguyen, "Quick Answer: How to Implement a Composable ERP Strategy?" *Gartner Research* (June 29, 2021).

2. Filippo Passerini, "From Internal Service Provider to Strategic Partner: An Interview with the Head of Global Business Services at P&G" *McKinsey Quarterly* (July 2008).

3. Ibid.

4. Larry Huston and Nabil Y. Sakkab, "Connect and Develop: Inside Procter & Gamble's New Model for Innovation" *Harvard Business Review* (March 2006).

Chapter 6

Capacity Allocation

Honoring Team Boundaries

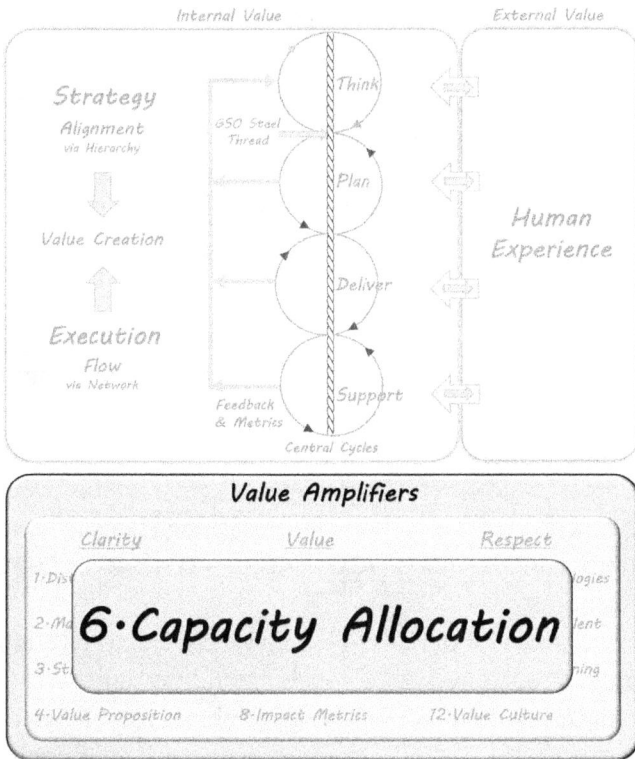

Internal Value   External Value

Strategy
Alignment
via Hierarchy

GSO Steel Thread

Think

Plan

Human Experience

Value Creation

Deliver

Execution
Flow
via Network

Feedback & Metrics

Support

Central Cycles

Value Amplifiers

Clarity   Value   Respect

6·Capacity Allocation

4·Value Proposition   8·Impact Metrics   12·Value Culture

The Ambition–Capacity Mismatch

Organizations across industries grapple with a fundamental discord: their aspirations consistently exceed their execution capacity. Leaders routinely assign more work than teams can realistically accommodate, creating a cascade of dysfunction that undermines the very outcomes they seek to achieve. This chronic overload manifests in predictable patterns—degraded profitability, eroded morale, diminished quality, and jeopardized customer loyalty. The root cause typically stems from inadequate capacity planning and haphazard work distribution.

But the ramifications extend far beyond immediate productivity losses. Organizations squander precious resources on activities that do not advance key objectives, forfeit market opportunities while competitors progress, and fail to deliver on crucial imperatives that could transform their competitive position. What appears to be a resource deficiency is a fundamental failure of strategic alignment and capacity management.

The Logic of Capacity

Capacity allocation is the deliberate practice of harmonizing finite talent and resources with the daily pressures of business execution in order to maximize enterprise value. It ensures that individuals are concentrated on efforts that advance critical objectives and yield superior returns. Conversely, burdening teams by treating all efforts as equally urgent reflects a pervasive—but costly—misjudgment.

In his influential work *The Goal*, Eliyahu Goldratt reveals how capacity overload impedes throughput and explains how it can be mitigated by transitioning from push-based to pull-based operational constructs. Push systems impose work indiscriminately, disregarding resource constraints; pull systems, by contrast, authorize only the volume of work that can be realistically absorbed by available capacity.[1] Pull-based systems demand that leaders prioritize tasks in accordance with well-defined goals, coherent strategies, and observable metrics—equipping teams with the clarity and focus necessary to concentrate on what truly drives value. One of the guiding precepts in value-centered organizations is elegantly concise: "Start less, finish more." By limiting work-in-process (WIP), enterprises accelerate delivery, capture value sooner, and unlock exponential gains over time.[2]

Flow-Based Allocation

In Chapter 7: Value Streams, I will explore how demand-driven resource allocation enables organizations to adapt swiftly to evolving conditions. When human and material assets within a value stream are governed by real-time market and customer pull rates, capacity becomes dynamically aligned with actual demand. This synchronization is realized through a flow-to-capacity construct that regulates WIP across each stream—optimizing output while honoring delivery constraints.

Implementing a high-functioning pull-based model necessitates the following foundational elements:

- Clearly defined value streams with formalized work entry protocols.

- Continuous visibility into capacity and demand, often enabled through digital dashboards or ERP system integration.

- Cultural coherence, wherein teams understand the strategic intent of controlled flow and are empowered to surface impediments early.

Effective capacity planning further requires rigorous assessment of critical enablers: staffing sufficiency, skill proficiency, tool accessibility, and historical throughput patterns. When demand surges, leaders allocate incremental funding to the most relevant value streams, scaling resources with precision.

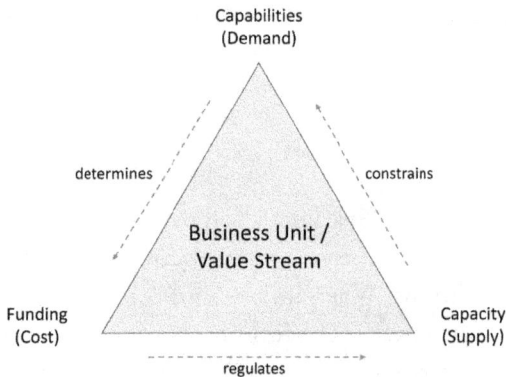

This model operates through three principal levers—demand, supply, and cost—each informing the others in a continuous cycle of adjustment and alignment. Organizations that master this discipline respond deftly to shifting priorities and extract maximum value from every hour expended, dollar invested, and decision made.

***

I still remember the weight in my stomach as I walked down Toorak Road toward that café in Melbourne's South Yarra. It was one of those crisp July mornings where the wind cuts through your jacket, but the real chill I felt had nothing to do with the weather. After three months of working with Clarissa, her fintech startup was still hemorrhaging cash and burning out talent—despite following my advice to the letter.

I'd screwed up. Badly.

When Clarissa first came to me, the problem seemed obvious. Her team was scattered, working on everything and nothing, with no clear direction. Classic startup chaos. I'd seen it many times before. So I did what any experienced consultant would do: I helped her sharpen her strategic focus. We spent weeks refining her annual goals, crafting clear outcomes, and rolling them out to the entire organization with military precision.

The goals were beautiful. Specific, measurable, aligned with market opportunities. Her leadership team embraced them. The board loved them. I felt quite good about myself.

Three months later, very little had changed.

Actually, that's not true. Things had gotten worse. The team was working even harder, now with the added pressure of clearly defined targets they couldn't seem to hit. Investor patience was wearing thin. And Clarissa? She was angry—not just at the situation, but particularly at me.

"Your strategic clarity isn't working," she'd told me bluntly during our last video call, her voice tight with exhaustion. "We're still spinning our wheels, people are still working nights and weekends, and we're burning through cash like it's kindling. I need solutions, not more talk about vision statements."

That stung. Because she was right.

I'd been so confident in my diagnosis that I never bothered to look deeper. Strategic clarity was my hammer, and every startup problem looked like a nail. But as I sat in my home office in San Diego, I finally admitted what I should have seen months ago: I'd treated the symptom, not the disease.

The real problem wasn't that they didn't know what to do. It was that they were trying to do everything at once, with no regard for their actual capacity to deliver. All my beautiful goal-setting had simply given them a clearer view of their own chaos. I'd been

so focused on Clarissa's strategic challenges that I'd completely missed the operational breakdown happening right under my
nose.

So there I was, walking into that Melbourne café, about to have
the most uncomfortable conversation of my consulting career. I
was going to admit I'd been wrong, explain what I should have
seen from the beginning, and hope Clarissa would not fire me, but
give me a chance to make it right.

"This is our life right now," she said flatly. "Four product
launches in parallel. Twelve 'must-have' initiatives. A team working seventy-hour weeks. It's an absolute mess. And I still can't tell
you which of these things is actually moving the dial."

I took a deep breath. Time for the confession.

"Clarissa, I need to apologize. I got this wrong from the beginning."

She looked up, eyebrows raised.

"Three months ago, when you came to me, I was so focused on
strategic clarity that I missed the real problem. Your goals aren't
the issue—they're actually quite good. The issue is that your staff
is trying to execute everything simultaneously, with no regard for
your team's actual capacity to deliver."

I explained what I should have seen from day one: her startup
was suffering from a classic case of work overload, not strategic
confusion. No amount of goal refinement would fix a system that
allowed unlimited work to flow to a finite team.

"You need a gatekeeper," I told her. "Someone whose sole job is
to control the flow of work into your organization. Someone who
can say no when your team is at capacity, who can kill projects
that don't directly support your goals, and who can protect your
people from the chaos of constant context-switching."

Clarissa stared at me for a long moment. "You're telling me the
last three months were for nothing?"

"Not nothing," I said carefully. "Having clearer goals is valuable—it gives us criteria for what work should be prioritized.

But goals without capacity discipline are just wishful thinking. I should have seen that sooner."

I outlined my proposal: find someone with deep operational experience, preferably from outside the startup world. Someone senior enough to push back on leadership, disciplined enough to enforce hard trade-offs, and detached enough from the startup's emotional drama to make tough decisions objectively.

"This person reports directly to you, but their job is to say no to everyone—including you—when new work threatens to overwhelm the system. They'll plan work to fill only about eighty-five percent of your team's capacity, leaving room for the inevitable surprises and urgent requests."

Clarissa rubbed her temples. "And you think this will actually work?"

"I know it will," I said. "Because I've seen it work before. I should have recommended this approach from the beginning."

To her credit, Clarissa didn't fire me on the spot. Maybe she was too exhausted to fight, or maybe she recognized that my mistake came from overconfidence rather than incompetence. Either way, she agreed to let me help her find the right person.

Three weeks later, we hired Marcus Webb.

Marcus was perfect for the role—a fifty-something former operations manager from a regional bank who knew nothing about startup culture and cared even less about being popular. He had the gravitas to stare down pushy product managers, the experience to spot when projects were poorly scoped, and the backbone to tell everyone—including Clarissa—when they were asking for too much.

More importantly, he understood that his job wasn't to be liked; it was to protect the team's capacity and ensure that only the most critical work made it through the gates.

I spent the next month coaching Marcus through the transition. We mapped every current initiative against the team's actual bandwidth. We killed six projects that couldn't be directly tied to annual goals. We established a visual prioritization board that made trade-offs explicit and transparent. And we instituted a simple rule: no new work gets approved unless something else comes off the plate first.

The resistance was immediate and predictable. Other members of the C-suite were furious. Product managers complained about bureaucracy. Engineers grumbled about process overhead. Even some investors questioned whether the company was losing its edge.

But Marcus held the line. Every request had to justify itself against the goals we'd defined months earlier. Every new project had to identify what existing work would be delayed or cancelled. Every "urgent" request had to explain why it was more important than what the team was already doing.

Within six weeks, something remarkable happened. The seventy-hour weeks became fifty-hour weeks. Projects that had been stalled for months suddenly started moving forward. The team stopped looking like they were drowning and started looking like they were performing with purpose.

Five months after that uncomfortable conversation in South Yarra, Clarissa called me with news: they'd closed their Series B round, two months ahead of schedule. The investors had been impressed not just with the company's progress, but with the discipline and focus they'd demonstrated in execution.

"You know," she said during our debrief call, "I wasn't angry with you for getting it wrong the first time. Your work on strategic clarity did add value—we needed those goals to give Marcus criteria for what work to approve. But you're right that goals without capacity discipline are just wishful thinking dressed up as strategy."

That comment hit me harder than her initial frustration had. She was being generous, finding value in my mistake rather than dwelling on the chaotic months. But I knew better. I'd let my confidence in a familiar solution blind me to what was actually happening in her organization.

The experience taught me something crucial about consulting, and about leadership more broadly: real problems often hide behind obvious symptoms. When a client comes to you with what seems like a straightforward challenge, the temptation is to apply your best-known solution and move on to the next project. But the most valuable thing you can do—for them and for yourself—is to dig deeper, question your assumptions, and remain open to the possibility that your first diagnosis might be wrong.

Marcus stayed with Clarissa's company for eighteen months, long enough to embed the capacity management discipline into their culture. By the time he transitioned to a part-time advisory role, the organization had learned to protect its own bandwidth instinctively. They'd discovered that saying no to good opportunities was often the key to saying yes to great ones.

As for me? I now spend at least twice as long on problem diagnosis as I used to. I've learned to embrace the uncomfortable questions that challenge my initial assessment. And I've gotten much better at recognizing when a client's presenting problem might be masking something deeper.

It was a defining moment in my career that helped me think differently in subsequent engagements. Sometimes the most important thing a consultant can do is admit they got it wrong the first time—and then commit to getting it right the second time. Clarissa's startup didn't succeed despite my initial mistake; it succeeded because we were both humble enough to acknowledge when our first approach wasn't working and disciplined enough to try something different.

***

The Run, Grow, Transform Framework

Every enduring enterprise must not only sustain core operations but also pursue expansion and periodically reinvent itself to maintain relevance in a shifting landscape. The *Run-Grow-Transform* framework offers a strategic construct for classifying and harmonizing these three essential domains of activity. It enables executives to allocate resources judiciously, evaluate portfolio risk, and guide systemic decision-making across the organization.[3]

- *Run the Business* encompasses the essential activities required to maintain operational infrastructure, ensure continuity of service, and preserve institutional stability. Often referred to as keep-the-lights-on (KTLO) work, these undertakings ensure compliance, mitigate disruption, and uphold the baseline functions upon which all other endeavors rely. As these efforts maintain existing capabilities rather than create novel assets, they are typically financed through operating expenditures (OpEx).

- *Grow the Business* focuses on extending the reach of current offerings, penetrating adjacent markets, and amplifying organizational capabilities. These activities leverage core competencies to boost performance, stimulate innovation, and drive top-line growth. Growth-oriented work often requires a blend of OpEx and capital expenditures (CapEx), depending on the maturity and scope of the effort.

- *Transform the Business* represents the most ambitious and future-defining category—typically CapEx-intensive ventures that redefine business models, disrupt markets, or establish entirely new revenue streams. These transformational efforts demand visionary leadership, directed investment, and strategic alignment.[4]

Funding and Integration

Funding allocation across Run, Grow, and Transform varies significantly by context. High-volatility sectors may emphasize Transform investments, while stable or mature industries often prioritize Run optimization and incremental Grow pursuits.

Conventional portfolio management often overlooks OpEx-funded initiatives, focusing predominantly on capital requisitions. The GSO framework of Valorys challenges this limitation by ensuring that all work—regardless of funding source—is traceable to clearly defined strategic imperatives. This end-to-end visibility reduces allocation ambiguity, reveals hidden KTLO burdens, and eliminates ad hoc efforts not aligned with enterprise goals. When Run activities demonstrably support GSOs, they merit goal-based funding structures, inclusive of compensation and operating costs—a shift that may require significant revision of traditional budgeting models.

The contemporary workplace further complicates these distinctions. Whereas legacy organizations historically separated operations from innovation, today's technology-infused enterprises demand integrated expertise. It is increasingly common for the same individuals to support day-to-day operations, lead growth projects, and contribute to transformative innovation—often without managerial recognition of this triadic workload. Engineers who architect systems also maintain them. Operations staff who ensure continuity frequently serve as the source of next-generation improvements.

This reality reflects a broader shift within the experience economy: the most impactful innovations often arise from those closest to products and customers. Integrating Run, Grow, and Transform efforts within a unified portfolio structure acknowledges this reality and provides the analytical depth necessary for refined resource allocation. It enables a more systematic accounting of how talent, time, and capital are deployed across all strategic categories.

Preserving Adaptive Capacity

Traditional management orthodoxy has long pursued maximum resource utilization, often pushing teams to full capacity in the pursuit of efficiency. Yet contemporary leadership models—grounded in both research and real-world outcomes—recognize this posture as both counterproductive and unsustainable.[5]

High-functioning organizations understand the imperative to preserve adaptive capacity—the ability to absorb unforeseen demands without disrupting ongoing workflows. This is achieved not through heroic overextension, but through the deliberate establishment of operational buffers. Unfortunately, many enterprises neglect this principle, breeding systemic dysfunction and operational fragility.

Empirical evidence suggests that optimal resource utilization hovers around 80%, reserving the remaining 20% to accommodate volatility, emergent requests, and unexpected pivots. This margin is not wasted capacity—it is strategic foresight. It allows organizations to respond to the inherent unpredictability of business life without compromising delivery performance or workforce well-being.

Capacity Allocation Best Practices

1: *Capacity allocation reveals an organization's true operating bandwidth.* Disciplined capacity allocation is the foundation of value realization. When GSOs are clearly defined and cascaded across the enterprise, they create a natural, pull-based system—anchored in genuine priorities and tempered by real constraints. Precision requires confronting organizational limits, not wishful assumptions. Scarcity, when managed intelligently, becomes a powerful engine for focus and meaningful progress.

2: *Design work portfolios that reflect true value.* Structure business unit portfolios as strategic instruments that integrate funding, operations, and outcomes. By encompassing Run, Grow, and Transform work, they provide a complete picture of resource distribution. Unlike capital-focused models, value-aligned portfolios balance OpEx and CapEx according to strategic direction—ensuring that investment follows intent and delivers measurable impact.

3: *Manage capacity as a strategic constraint.* Miscalculating capacity exacts heavy costs—overextended teams, eroded quality, and lost talent. To preserve resilience, plan no more than 80% of total bandwidth for committed work, reserving the remainder as adaptive capacity. This disciplined buffer safeguards execution quality, responsiveness, and the long-term sustainability of performance.

***

Organization Highlight: Zara

Zara, the flagship brand of Inditex, exemplifies a retail enterprise that has institutionalized capacity management as a central driver of strategic execution. Renowned for its vertically integrated and demand-responsive operating model,

Zara has built a supply chain that continuously senses, interprets, and acts upon consumer demand signals in near real time. This responsiveness is not incidental—it is the result of deliberate capacity design and a disciplined operational philosophy that prioritizes market relevance over volume optimization.

Zara's approach is rooted in the principles of a pull-based system, where work and resources are mobilized only when downstream signals indicate verified demand. Unlike push systems—where production is forecasted in advance and work is preloaded into the system—pull systems limit work-in-process, reduce waste, and preserve operational flexibility.

Zara's mastery of capacity allocation stems from its refusal to chase economies of scale at the expense of strategic flexibility. Rather than preemptively committing production resources to long forecasting cycles, Zara engages in deliberate small-batch manufacturing, often refreshing collections biweekly. Its factories are intentionally underutilized—running at approximately 85% utilization, compared to the industry norm of 95%—to preserve the ability to respond rapidly when consumer preferences shift.[6]

This margin of reserved capacity functions as a strategic hedge, offering decision-making optionality and mitigating the operational risks associated with forecast errors, demand spikes, and regional volatility. It also enables Zara to compress the design-to-store cycle to as little as 15 days, a feat nearly unmatched in the global apparel sector.

The impact of Zara's pull-based model is empirically evident: inventory turnover is among the highest in retail, with an estimated 12 inventory turns per year, compared to a global industry average of 3–4, indicating rapid stock movement and minimal obsolescence. Stockout rates are higher by design (approximately 10%)—a tradeoff that discourages deep discounting and reinforces brand desirability through scarcity.[7]

Zara sells 85% of inventory at full price versus the industry average of 60%. Annual unsold inventory remains at 10% compared to industry averages of 17-20%, demonstrating superior demand matching.[8] Inditex reports gross margins exceeding 55%, outperforming most peers in the fast fashion space, due in part to reduced markdown dependency and minimized inventory waste.[9]

A key enabler of this model is Zara's versatile workforce—employees capable of performing multiple roles across logistics, merchandising, and retail operations. During seasonal peaks or new store openings, labor is reallocated dynamically, allowing Zara to meet surges in demand without excessive overtime or reliance on temporary workers. This flexibility converts human capital from a fixed cost into a responsive, value-driven resource, while also fostering employee engagement and skill development.

For organizations facing volatile demand environments, tight labor markets, or geopolitical uncertainty, Zara offers a blueprint for operational resilience. Its model illustrates how intentional underutilization, when paired with real-time market sensing and modular resource deployment, can create structural advantages in speed, cost control, and customer satisfaction.

Moreover, Zara aligns its operational model to its value streams with precision. It minimizes latency between consumer signal and organizational response, treats capacity as a finite resource governed by strategic objectives, and ensures that cross-functional teams are deployed in alignment with enterprise-level goals. It resists the temptation to view busy systems as productive systems—recognizing instead that true value lies in relevant execution, not constant activity.

Zara's enduring success is not simply a product of fashion acumen, but from deliberate operational architecture. By institutionalizing pull logic, dynamic capacity allocation, and modular workforce deployment, Zara transforms complexity into advantage. It confirms that, in a world of accelerating uncertainty, operational demand-based discipline is not a constraint, but a foundation for profitable adaptability.

1. Eliyahu Goldratt and Jeff Cox, *The Goal: A Process of Ongoing Improvement* (North River Press, 1984).

2. Donald Reinertsen, *The Principles of Product Development Flow: Second Generation Lean Product Development* (Celeritas Publishing, 2009).

3. Suzanne Adnams, et al., "CIOs Can Use the Run-Grow-Transform Model to Align IT Functions and Roles to Strategic Business Priorities," *Gartner Research* (August 10, 2017).

4. Steven Bell, et al., *Run Grow Transform* (Routledge, 2012).

5. David Paulson, *The Importance of Resource Loading Explained* (Playbook, June 2020).

6. Statista, "Apparel Market Worldwide – Statistics & Facts," *Statista*, accessed June 28, 2025.

7. Martin Roll, "The Secret of Zara's Success: A Culture of Customer Co-creation," *Martin Roll* (blog) (November 6, 2021).

8. Ibid.

9. Fashion United, "Zara-owner Inditex Posts Sales and Profit Growth," *Fashion United* (September 10, 2024).

Chapter 7

Value Streams

The Nexus of Power

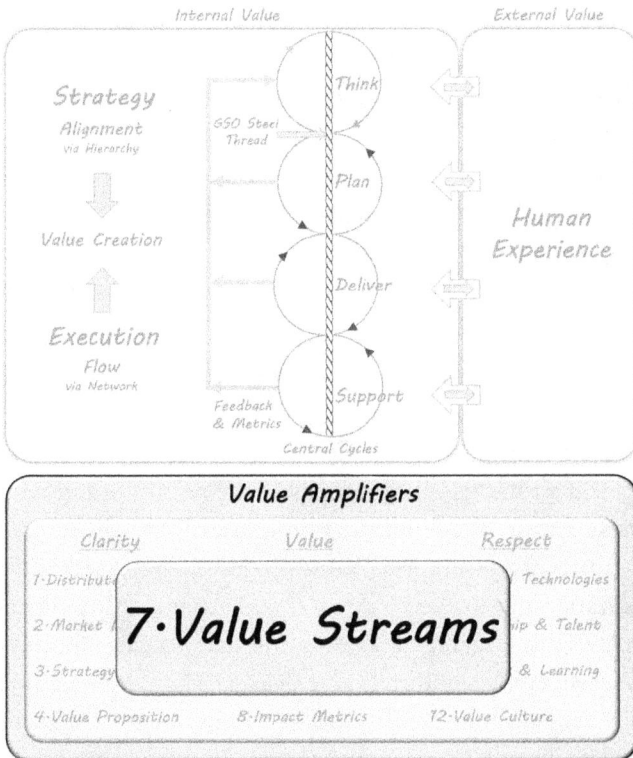

Exposing Operational Waste

I am consistently struck by the extraordinary volume of squandered effort prevalent in most organizations. Inefficiencies often emanate from the ambiguity or invisibility of how value is conceived and delivered, rendering this phenomenon comprehensible. Frequently, companies suffer from inadequate insight into the temporal and asset requirements for each phase in their value development cycle, the latencies between phases, the quantity and nature of handoffs, and the complex dependencies between functional units that further complicate the process. Enterprises that remain oblivious to the specific mechanisms for creating and delivering value tend to mismanage substantial financial and material resources.[1]

My consulting experience corroborates this assertion. Only through lucid appreciation of how value accumulates from one stage to another have my clients been able to identify and resolve previously enigmatic deficiencies concealed behind opaque internal boundaries. Most often, it is optimal to create a visual representation of value flow, which I will address subsequently.

Flow-Driven Institutional Design

A value stream is an intangible construct that transcends organizational structure—it encompasses the resources and competencies requisite for value creation and distribution across disparate parts of an enterprise. Value progression represents how an organization generates the internal and external value critical to its operations. Organizing work in this manner can substantially enhance an entity's culture, value delivery, and corporate performance. The magnitude of value, and the velocity at which it is created, is directly proportional to how disciplined a company is regarding its flow-based behavior.

In a 1994 Harvard Business Review article, James Womack and Daniel Jones argued that the concept of the value stream should define an institution around the complete flow of activities required to supply a good or service—from development and production through sales and maintenance—in a manner that delivers maximum value to the customer.[2]

At their core, value streams translate strategic intent into operational reality—bridging the distance between what an entity aspires to achieve and the hierarchical structures through which it must act. This is foundational to Valorys: an organization must define itself through its value streams, understand them with rigor, and embed their logic into how it actually functions.

I distinguish two categories of value streams: *delivery arcs* and *asset warehouses*. Delivery arcs represent the outward flow of value creation—customer-facing pathways through which revenue is directly generated. They encompass the continuum of activities that transform enterprise capabilities into the offerings clients ultimately demand. Asset warehouses, in contrast, function as internal engines of scalability. They develop and distribute reusable components and shared capabilities that equip delivery arcs to deliver revenue-generating value with consistency and precision.

To ensure efficacy, delivery arcs are managed comprehensively from inception to completion, employing a comprehensive set of value stream management practices that are not extensively covered in this work, but include supply chain optimization, product development flow, organizational velocity and output, distribution methodologies, and compliance factors, to name a few.

Eliyahu Goldratt's groundbreaking *theory of constraints* influences the behavior of both delivery arcs and asset warehouses to achieve optimal throughput by channeling the appropriate volume of work to each one's finite capacity.[3] When adhering to these foundational pull-based principles, businesses realize superior-quality offerings, enhanced efficiency, and increased productivity. This approach also generates high consumer satisfaction and minimizes non-value-added activities.

The Value Accountability Gap

As previously noted, organizations are characteristically structured along hierarchical lines. This arrangement presupposes a pyramidal framework anchored in conventional functional domains, such as operations, finance and accounting, marketing and sales, human resources, facilities, and others. However, these discrete functions in isolation fail to generate and deliver substantive value. Genuine worth emerges *across* the functional constituents of an enterprise, not *through* its vertical top-down command systems.

Business units represent the actual architects of valuable products and services, yet their established methodologies exhibit considerable variation and are frequently burdened with inefficient expenditures of resources. The foundational step in cultivating a value-centric enterprise requires senior leadership to recognize that the absence of coherence and efficacy in product and service delivery represents a formidable obstacle to enterprise success. The pivotal inquiry leaders must advance is: *"Who assumes accountability for delivering comprehensive value for each market offering?"*

Many organizations cannot articulate the processes through which value is created, nor identify the specific components that contribute to that worth. Without a clearly mapped arc of value creation, refinement becomes impossible. I have yet to encounter a prospective client who has institutionalized a role explicitly dedicated to value stewardship—such as a value manager or value stream custodian—underscoring that value considerations often remain peripheral. In truly value-driven enterprises, executive leadership designs and orchestrates value delivery mechanisms intentionally and comprehensively, rather than permitting them to emerge arbitrarily from local initiatives.

Structuring Value Creation

Valorys incorporates both classifications of value streams—delivery arcs and asset warehouses—to forge a direct correlation between strategic imperatives and operational execution, culminating in a demand-driven system optimized through capacity allocation and work-in-process limitations. This orientation inherently cultivates a concentration on outcomes rather than mere outputs. Because value streams function as conceptual architectures, they do not require the restructuring of existing business units. Instead, orchestrating virtual value streams necessitates cross-functional collaboration and requires stakeholders to possess an intimate understanding of how value is generated and how it traverses through and across the organization's components.

Value streams are not parochial pursuits; they serve as the enterprise's central engines of influence, guided by business unit GSOs and value propositions that resonate both within the organization and across the broader market. The objective elements of GSOs function as the parameters for value creation, as the allocation of capital toward achieving those aims provides the financial foundation for value stream operations. The efficacy of a value stream is evaluated by its capability to fulfill the targeted GSO outcomes.

It is equally important to clarify what value streams are not. Value streams are not small operational segments delivering incremental results—a misconception that frequently leads to organizational confusion. Delivery arc value streams do not function on a restricted scale; instead, they represent comprehensive, multi-team and multi-functional architectures that deliver products to clientele in their entirety.

Each business unit maintains a thoughtfully curated portfolio of value streams, encompassing both delivery arcs and asset warehouses, determined by the breadth of product lines, service offerings, and business capabilities under its stewardship. This portfolio-based structure ensures that value creation remains coherent, strategically aligned, and operationally scalable.

Defining Value Flow

The purpose of a delivery arc is to facilitate an offering's progression from one condition to another, thereby effectuating transformation and enhancing its inherent value. I characterize it as an arc because it transcends functional demarcations and organizational architectures, embodying the convergence of hierarchical and networked structures. It manifests as the nucleus of an entity's influence, where substantive worth materializes, substantiating Womack and Jones' contention that the concept of a value stream fundamentally defines an enterprise.[4] Like the solar plexus of human anatomy, a company's dynamic and innovative energy radiates from this central point.

Organizations should possess comprehensive cognizance and mastery of all activities integral to crafting their offerings in order to optimize that flow. However, they must first apprehend the essence of their delivery arcs. Do these consistently manifest with clarity, or does their identification call for profound business acumen? The response is decidedly the latter; virtually all of my clientele initially presumed they comprehended the nature of their value streams, yet upon rigorous examination, discovered they did not.

Why does this present such a formidable challenge? As discussed, most institutions are functionally configured and lack familiarity with conceptualizing value progression. Traditional departmental boundaries are commonplace in businesses that encounter collaborative difficulties because of sectional preoccupations. It is entirely normal to lack comprehensive visibility into key value creation flows, so organizations should not be discouraged if their value streams remain unidentified. I recommend engaging a qualified specialist to help discover an entity's distinctive value streams, thereby preventing the misallocation of critical time and resources on non-strategic efforts.

Delivery arcs are not contained within functional units; rather, they traverse conventional operations. To surmount this institutional inertia, I employ a tripartite technique to discern the authentic delivery arcs of an organization:

1. Engage the finance and accounting departments to confirm the company's customer constituency. Inquire: "Who receives invoices? Who remits payment? What revenue classifications appear in our financial statements?" These responses provisionally identify the entity's customer demographics and product and service taxonomies.

2. Subsequently interrogate the sales and marketing divisions: "Through what mechanisms do we commercialize products and services to our customers (distribution channels, product portfolios, geographical territories, market segments, etc.)? How is the sales organization structured? To whom do we direct our marketing efforts?" Their insights serve to validate and refine offering classifications for each customer demographic.

3. Finally (and this represents the most intellectually demanding component), query the operations personnel: "For each product classification and customer demographic, how is value conceived and delivered? Who participates in and contributes to generating that value (in-

ternal units, vendors, suppliers, strategic partners, etc.)?"
The responses to these inquiries culminate in the identification and foundational architecture of a company's
delivery arcs.

Once an organization's delivery arcs are comprehended and
consensus is achieved, they are graphically rendered in industry-standard notation. Delivery arc mapping and analysis are formidable instruments for revealing bottlenecks, redundancies, superfluous transitions, ineffectual processes, and non-value-adding
activities. Upon completion, the delivery arc map presents a comprehensive visualization of how work progresses through the entity for that particular product or service family. Mapping transforms intricate pathways into lucid, elevated abstractions that all
stakeholders can grasp, from executive leadership throughout the
organizational hierarchy. Almost invariably, leaders and personnel
experience pleasant surprise and satisfaction when they finally
comprehend their value flow through clear, illuminating representation.

Enterprise Delivery Dynamics

As previously articulated, external value is generated and transmitted through delivery arcs—sustained activities executed in a
continuous, sequential, and cross-functional progression across
an enterprise. The sophistication of a delivery arc dwells in its capacity to engage centralized business functions as necessary while
value is being conceived and conveyed through successive phases
of the arc. It constitutes a matrix-based mechanism that precludes
the need for maintaining proprietary specialized competencies;
instead, the arc draws expertise from multiple domains of the
organization to cultivate and deliver a product or service. The

diagram below illustrates several of these centrally administered corporate functions and illustrates how they might interface with a delivery arc at each stage of value creation.

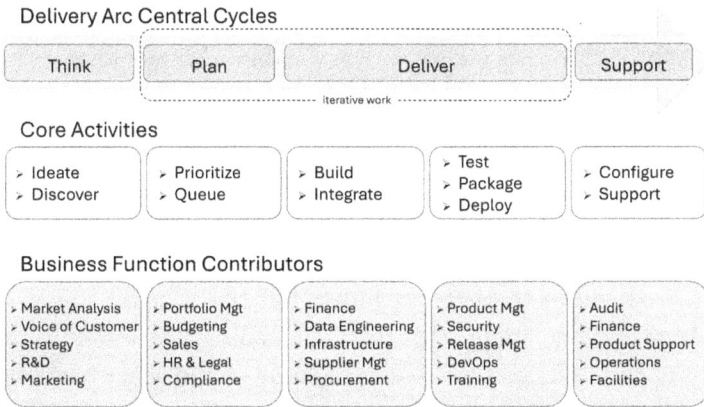

Delivery Arc Central Cycles

Think	Plan	Deliver	Support

Iterative work

Core Activities

‣ Ideate ‣ Discover	‣ Prioritize ‣ Queue	‣ Build ‣ Integrate	‣ Test ‣ Package ‣ Deploy	‣ Configure ‣ Support

Business Function Contributors

‣ Market Analysis ‣ Voice of Customer ‣ Strategy ‣ R&D ‣ Marketing	‣ Portfolio Mgt ‣ Budgeting ‣ Sales ‣ HR & Legal ‣ Compliance	‣ Finance ‣ Data Engineering ‣ Infrastructure ‣ Supplier Mgt ‣ Procurement	‣ Product Mgt ‣ Security ‣ Release Mgt ‣ DevOps ‣ Training	‣ Audit ‣ Finance ‣ Product Support ‣ Operations ‣ Facilities

Delivery arcs epitomize how enterprises leverage and distribute resources to generate optimal customer value with speed and precision. This configuration demands collaboration and cooperation among constituent functions and their readiness to contribute value to delivery arcs for the organization's collective benefit.

Because delivery arcs necessitate input from most, if not all, corporate business functions, enterprise-wide alignment and comprehensive optimization yield substantially greater returns than concentrating on isolated efficiency enclaves. Functionally oriented firms traditionally show sectional predispositions because funding, compensation, and departmental performance metrics are frequently contingent upon one division operating more efficiently than another. This common anti-pattern establishes counterproductive competition among organizational components that cannot generate value independently. Only when each function collaborates within the framework of an enterprise's overarching goals to create worth through delivery arcs is their genuine contribution actualized.

Each business unit employs a predictable, rhythm-based flow to serve as the pulse of its value streams. Consequently, multiple delivery arcs and asset warehouses within a business unit operate synchronously, a principle underscored in Goldratt's theory of constraints.

Inside Asset Warehouses

Business capabilities demonstrating inherent synergy are centralized within an asset warehouse. Through the distribution of reusable operational elements, a cross-disciplinary asset warehouse facilitates customer-facing delivery arcs in achieving optimal value creation and distribution efficacy. An example follows:

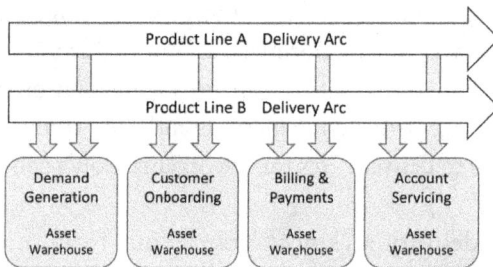

Structuring business capabilities into modular constituents that can be independently developed, deployed, and refined enables an entity to seamlessly integrate disparate building blocks as required by various delivery arcs. Asset warehouses function as a repository of production-ready capabilities designed to enable comprehensive offerings rapidly. Characteristically, asset warehouses do not deliver products or services directly to an enterprise's clientele, though occasionally, an array of capabilities is monetized and independently commercialized in the market-place.

Asset Warehouse Design

Asset warehouses are ecosystems wherein analogous capabilities are frequently clustered by customer journey, product portfolios and markets, or technological platforms. Configuring an entity's asset warehouses depends upon several determinants, including the enterprise's fundamental nature, its market and customer engagement modalities, and the organization's core competencies, among other considerations.

Customer Journey

A customer's trajectory represents a prevalent, efficacious method for architecting asset warehouses. Constructing reusable components for discrete segments of the consumer experience enables the distribution of comparable capabilities across multiple delivery arcs.

Product Lines and Markets

When an entity's product offerings and market domains exhibit substantial differentiation, maintaining an asset warehouse concentrated on a particular segment may become the optimal approach. In this configuration, an asset warehouse generates essential components for a circumscribed collection of product lines or markets, which are subsequently leveraged across multiple delivery arcs.

Platforms / Capabilities / Business Logic

Aggregating fundamental technical capabilities that make up elements of a specific platform or possess computational logic similarities represents an alternative approach for organizing asset warehouses.

Asset Warehouse Structure

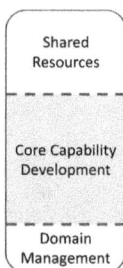

An asset warehouse encompasses three strata: shared resources, core capability development, and domain management. The shared resources level provides specialized competencies that aid delivery arcs through multiple mechanisms, including embedded subject matter expertise, dedicated support teams, knowledge dissemination, and fulfillment of specific work requests from delivery arcs. These shared resources enable delivery arcs to effectively integrate the core capabilities developed and managed by an asset warehouse.

Core capability development specializes in crafting composable, reusable business capabilities. Through the synthesis of diverse business architecture components, this unit establishes a standardized method for various systems, solutions, and services to interact and exchange data, ensuring compatibility and interoperability.

Business capability domains are administered by a proficient team supervising the overarching trajectory of an asset warehouse. Domain managers govern architectural patterns, sophisticated tooling, standards compliance, and the intellectual repository of its capability portfolio while maintaining currency with emerging technologies, industry developments, and customer imperatives.

They continuously refine and adapt their architectures to provide seamless transformation and expansion while preserving
alignment with delivery arc desires and corporate goals.

Asset Warehouse Evolution

Asset warehouses manifest a dynamic character, evolving as
they solidify and reach maturation. They do not adhere to
standardized architectural paradigms; the fundamental nature
of each enterprise may require distinctive configurational attributes. Asset warehouses characteristically progress through
three sequential phases, with each stage emphasizing a unique
strategic dimension.

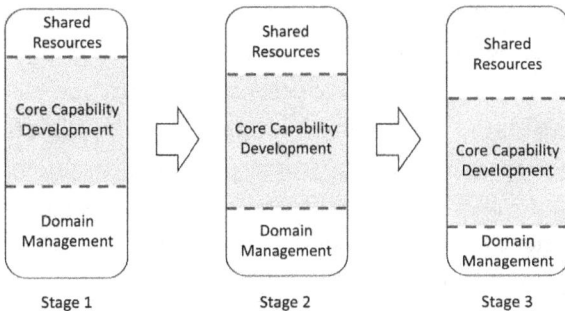

Shared Resources	Shared Resources	Shared Resources
Core Capability Development	Core Capability Development	Core Capability Development
Domain Management	Domain Management	Domain Management
Stage 1	Stage 2	Stage 3

Stage 1: Nascent and Growing

During early collaborative planning sessions, representatives from
key capabilities engage directly with delivery arcs to surface and
consolidate future requirements. Foremost among the priorities
is the formal establishment of the domain management function—an essential step in defining the domain's structure, scope,
and governance. This process integrates foundational capabilities
into a cohesive operational construct, enabling clarity of pur-

pose, strategic alignment, and sustained execution within the asset warehouse.

Stage 2: Developing and Maturing

Multiple teams are deployed to delivery arcs for product development cycles and subsequently repatriated to the asset warehouse as circumstances warrant. While primary competencies are enhanced for diverse distribution mechanisms, platforms undergo consolidation, microservices are abstracted into reusable elements, and emergent capabilities are nurtured to reinforce innovative and transformative product propositions.

Stage 3: Stable and Optimized

Myriad teams furnish direct support to delivery arcs for ambitious product launches while preserving operational excellence. Core capabilities are preserved and refined while pioneering innovations are explored and prototyped through systematic experimentation. Domain managers cultivate and shepherd core development teams alongside the shared personnel allocated to delivery arcs, ensuring sustained organizational capability advancement.

***

The sun had scarcely ascended over Dubai's skyline when my business partner, Nishant, arrived at the headquarters of one of the UAE's most formidable logistics and supply chain enterprises. The edifice, architecturally sophisticated and contemporary, commanded a panoramic view of the Port of Jebel Ali—a perpetual testament to the company's pivotal role in regional commerce.

Within the organization, however, conditions were considerably less harmonious. Despite the firm's distinguished reputation, their operations had become convoluted. Projects languished indefinitely, teams duplicated efforts systematically, and tensions percolated beneath ostensibly collegial meetings.

The firm's Deputy CEO, Mr. Kareem, had finally summoned external expertise—not as an admission of organizational failure, but out of profound respect for the complexity of the challenge.

"Brother Nishant," Kareem said, rising from his seat as my partner entered the executive lounge. His kandura was immaculate, and his demeanor was cordial yet measured. "Shukran for responding so quickly. I know your time is valuable."

Nishant offered a slight bow of his head. "It is a privilege, Kareem. When a respected partner calls, I must respond."

An attendant unobtrusively poured coffee into delicate cups as Kareem gestured toward an elegant low table, where fresh dates were arranged with meticulous care.

"We are not failing because of laziness," Kareem said, taking a seat. "Our teams are loyal and committed. But things feel...fragmented. Disconnected."

Nishant nodded respectfully, and replied, "In my experience, it is rarely the people. It's the structure that often holds them back."

Kareem leaned forward slightly. "The foundation was built more than a decade ago. Many who laid it are no longer here. Documentation is sparse, and each department seems to be moving on its own timeline. It's no longer one system. It's many."

"Then we begin by reconnecting the flow," Nishant said. "Let's map how value moves across your organization—from the moment a customer request comes in, all the way to fulfillment and feedback. But we'll do it with your people. They hold the real insight."

Kareem pondered this proposition in contemplative silence, then nodded deliberately. "Very well. We'll give you access starting next week. Meet with whoever you need. Start where you believe the blind spots are."

"Understood, Kareem. And I'll make sure your people feel heard—not just consulted."

A subtle smile illuminated Kareem's countenance. "That is the kind of work that earns trust here. And trust, Brother Nishant, is our real currency."

A month later, with the analysis finalized and the foundational architecture secured, Nishant led a three-day value stream discovery session.

Day 1: Mapping the Unknown

An expansive conference hall was carefully prepared. Operations, IT, customer service, and finance representatives—dozens of professionals congregated. Men in traditional dishdashas stood alongside women in impeccably tailored business attire. There was courteous curiosity, but also palpable skepticism.

Nishant positioned himself at the front of the assembly.

"We are not here to judge. We are here to learn. From each other."

With whiteboards, adhesive notes, and sophisticated process mapping instruments, they commenced their investigation. One team meticulously traced how orders penetrated the system. Another pursued the digital trajectory. Participants posed questions to one another they had never contemplated previously. They even contacted former colleagues to illuminate informational voids.

By late afternoon, the walls were completely covered. The value stream began to materialize—a cartographic representation not merely of process, but of organizational anguish.

A logistics coordinator shook his head in bewilderment. "I've worked here eight years and never realized how many times we re-enter the same data."

Another colleague confided quietly to Nishant, "There's a part of the process no one seems to own. We just...hope it happens."

Nishant nodded. "The map does not lie. It simply reveals."

Day 2: Bottlenecks and Stewardship

The teams reconvened with renewed vigor. They began to identify the vulnerable points—bottlenecks where antiquated databases precipitated delays, and where manual circumventions added hours to elementary tasks.

What struck everyone most profoundly was the pervasive ambiguity. Until now, no individual could articulate, with unwavering confidence, who owned what.

"We are pulled left and right," said one project manager. "Every executive has a different priority."

By midday, a comprehensive visual display was prepared—illuminating fractured handoffs, infrastructure deficiencies, and leadership conflicts. When they presented it to the senior leadership cohort, profound silence descended over the room.

Kareem examined the convoluted stream displayed on the wall and whispered reverently, "Now I see it."

Day 3: Strategic Realignment

The final day was dedicated to executive leadership. Nishant facilitated the discourse with patience and intellectual clarity.

"This map is not a critique," he said. "It is a gift. It shows us where to invest, where to assign true ownership, and where to say 'no' to competing demands."

One executive rose deliberately. "We have been asking our teams to be efficient—without giving them the clarity to do so."

Another contributed, "It is time to rebuild the foundation. This time with transparency."

By the session's end, roles had been definitively clarified. Infrastructure priorities were systematically established. Ownership was unambiguously assigned.

When Nishant and Kareem departed the meeting room that evening, there was no celebration—merely quiet, profound confidence.

"We've never had a plan this grounded," Kareem said. "And more importantly, I believe the teams now feel seen."

"They do," Nishant replied. "You honored their knowledge. That's why they responded."

Kareem smiled with genuine satisfaction. "You were respectful as to how you challenged us. That made all the difference."

Within the organization, lucidity had supplanted confusion, and previously scattered efforts were now aligned beneath one comprehensive map—drawn not by an external consultant, but by the hands of those who labored each day.

***

Value-Driven Business Units

A value-centric enterprise encompasses business units that function as semi-autonomous profit centers, each cultivating emerging endeavors while maintaining governance of core capabilities. These units comprise value streams—both delivery arcs and asset warehouses—with delivery arcs emerging from established operational domains as integrated product cohorts. Through comprehensive understanding of how centralized shared services integrate with each delivery arc, organizations optimize value by determining which functions contribute to value-creation processes, along with their optimal timing, to enhance alignment and advance strategic imperatives.

Given that value streams bear the predominant operational burden within a business unit, divisional overhead remains materially low. Business units principally depend upon corporate auxiliary business functions, though they may occasionally develop specialized expertise directly. Through coordinated vendor management and supply chain oversight on behalf of constituent value streams, business units achieve economies of scale while optimizing value generation.

When systematically mapped, delivery arcs effectively illuminate extraneous expenditures by revealing activities that do not enhance the fundamental merit of an offering. This represents another compelling rationale for the growing organizational embrace of value-centered paradigms.

Value-Aligned Economics

Financial stewardship centers on translating value stream performance into measurable returns, ensuring that investments drive both near-term profitability and enduring shareholder value. Each product evolves through an intentionally choreographed delivery arc—progressing from GSOs through supply-chain genesis, development and market emergence, and ultimately to order fulfillment, distribution, and customer-service distinction.

Organizations pursuing value-centric transformation often establish enterprise directives requiring functional departments to embed specialized acumen across designated value streams during both strategic formulation and operational execution. I have witnessed the corrosive effects when pivotal functional domains cannot or will not provide adequate support, invariably triggering delays, organizational discord, and the erosion of precious resources.

Both delivery arc and asset warehouse value streams operate through demand-responsive pull mechanisms. As operational bandwidth becomes accessible, business unit portfolio backlog items are introduced into value streams where they undergo validation, prioritization, sequencing, and preparation for active deployment. During quarterly strategic planning assemblies, value stream teams—supported by representatives from indispensable functional domains—determine the optimal workload capacity within specific implementation cycles, governed by resource availability. Teams arrive at these strategic gatherings prepared to define feasible production parameters and calculate the requisite investment to design, produce, and deliver value units, whether for internal consolidation or direct release to distribution networks and end consumers.

Optimizing Enterprise Flow

The pinnacle of value delivery lies in attaining the "sustainably shortest lead time," which directly expedites revenue realization.[5] Optimizing value creation demands the comprehensive employment of value-driven principles, methodologies, and techniques. Systems thinking furnishes the analytical framework for evaluating opportunities to enhance enterprise-wide flows. Nevertheless, streamlining these flows presents formidable challenges, as institutional behaviors are profoundly entrenched and resistant to modification. Realigning—rather than restructuring—organizational constructs can initially disrupt established paradigms and challenge individuals' sense of autonomy and professional equilibrium, despite value streams embodying virtual architectures. True value stream optimization requires unwavering determination and sustained dedication. When leaders, managers, and practitioners comprehend their pivotal role in enhancing flow dynamics and eliminating non-value-added activities, organizational transformation becomes considerably more attainable.

Value streams achieve optimal efficacy when equipped with appropriate equipment and properly configured operating environments. Adaptive leaders judiciously allocate requisite financial and technological resources to sustain delivery arcs while nurturing essential business capabilities within their asset warehouses. They ensure that necessary talent, competencies, and experiential knowledge align with both enterprise intent and business unit goals. Peak performance emerges from purposeful design that enables seamless collaboration with suppliers and third-party partners across organizational boundaries.

Extending Value Ecosystems

Under specific conditions, the span of delivery arcs and asset warehouses extends well beyond the confines of the enterprise itself, encompassing entire supply ecosystems, distribution configurations, and affiliated intermediaries. Forging strategic partnerships or formal alliances with external entities that possess reciprocal competencies becomes indispensable for achieving excellence in the end-to-end provisioning of products and services. This integration may take the form of technology consortia, trusted partners, targeted acquisitions, or the engagement of domain specialists and seasoned industry advisors. Such collaborative structures may be orchestrated either at the enterprise level or within discrete business units, depending on strategic design and operational scale.

By refining supply chain orchestration and embracing a just-in-time ethos, organizations maintain more rigorous oversight of the peripheral components across their extended value compositions. As vendors and ancillary network contributors are woven into the broader economic architecture, their seamless alignment with the organization's culture and operational cadence becomes a prerequisite for sustained performance.

At the demand interface—where producer meets consumer—organizations embed demand-side wisdom with cross-functional value proposition fusion teams to uncover stakeholder expectations, latent frustrations, and emerging needs within the market.

But the benefits extend beyond demand stimulation. By aggregating representative voices, fusion teams ensure consistent experiences across distribution channels and customer touchpoints, creating a coherent framework for value delivery while optimizing logistics. This approach builds lasting customer loyalty and satisfaction. Ultimately, cultivating deep demand intelligence—and actively shaping market direction—remains fundamental to value-driven enterprise success.

Value Streams Best Practices

1: *Center the enterprise around value streams.* Make value streams the organizing nucleus of how goods and services are conceived, developed, delivered, and sustained. Their institutionalization marks a decisive step toward full value alignment—requiring executive sponsorship, reflective leadership, and sustained commitment. Even in early stages of cultural readiness, consistent progress fosters eventual coherence and organizational maturity.

2: *Practice value stream management with rigor.* Anchor value stream management in disciplined principles, coherent frameworks, and enabling technologies. Employ virtual value streams to structure product and service lifecycles, ensuring timely, high-quality delivery that adapts to shifting customer needs. The results are accelerated time-to-market, deeper employee engagement, and elevated customer satisfaction.

3: *Base the principal organizing logic of the firm on value-centered constructs.* Traditional functional silos become secondary, while business units—encompassing distinct delivery arcs and asset warehouses—act as the primary engines of value creation. Enterprise specialists embed directly within BUs, infusing expertise that sharpens execution and strengthens outcomes. Asset warehouses cultivate modular, reusable components consumed by delivery arcs to strengthen efficiency, coherence, and strategic scalability.

***

Organization Highlight: Caterpillar

Caterpillar, a global leader in heavy equipment manufacturing, demonstrates how an enterprise-wide commitment to value stream identification and optimization can serve as a strategic lever for operational efficiency, product quality, and financial performance. Unlike traditional process-improvement initiatives that isolate operational functions, Caterpillar treats value streams as end-to-end ecosystems—defining the complete sequence of activities required to deliver value to the customer, from concept to aftermarket service.

Caterpillar's approach to value stream design begins with a rigorous delivery arc mapping exercise where cross-functional teams are mobilized to analyze the flow of materials, information, and effort across the full product lifecycle. Rather than defining value streams solely by functional lines such as manufacturing or logistics, Caterpillar organizes them around customer-facing outcomes, including large engine production, hydraulic excavator systems, and aftermarket parts distribution. These streams are architected not for internal convenience but to reflect the actual pathways through which value is created, delivered, and sustained.

Each stream is evaluated against key criteria, such as lead time, first-pass yield, inventory turnover, and cost-per-unit of value delivered. This analytical precision ensures that their value streams reflect real operational logic rather than arbitrary organizational structures. For example, in its excavator division, Caterpillar restructured its delivery arc by co-locating engineering, manufacturing, procurement, and quality assurance teams under a single stream-aligned leadership structure. This shift improved coordination, reduced handoffs, and created faster resolution cycles for production constraints. In 2022, its revenue reached $60 billion, ranking first in the market, with a year-over-year growth of 17%.[6]

Caterpillar's value stream logic encompasses supply chain, dealer network, and service infrastructure as integrated components extending beyond internal operations. The company orchestrates collaborative supplier planning through digital demand signals, reducing upstream lead times while optimizing material availability and market responsiveness. Concurrently, the company refines its global distribution architecture—parts depots and regional logistics centers—to embed dealer and customer support within the value stream rather than treating it as a secondary consideration.

These capabilities are supported by advanced digital systems—including IoT-based telematics, machine health diagnostics, and predictive service algorithms—that feed data directly into value stream operations. Caterpillar's product platforms collect equipment performance data across thousands of field-deployed assets, enabling remote diagnostics and preemptive service scheduling. These insights not only enhance customer experience but reduce unplanned down-time, reinforcing lifetime value and increasing aftermarket margins.

Caterpillar's value stream transformation is not merely a matter of operational theory—it has translated into concrete, enterprise-wide performance gains. The company achieved $250 million in cost reductions, attributed largely to operational efficiency and supply chain optimization.[7] Equally important is the cultural shift: employees now understand their roles not just in departmental terms but in relation to the full flow of customer value. Caterpillar has embedded value streams as a permanent operating logic—one that ensures capital, talent, and technology are orchestrated to produce the greatest possible return on value delivered. This systemic awareness creates alignment across functions, streamlines decision-making, and fosters innovation where it matters most.

Caterpillar's exemplar confirms that the path to resilience and profitability lies not in working harder, but in working smarter—and by aligning every facet of the enterprise around strategic flow. It offers a compelling case for leaders seeking to transcend legacy silos and build organizations where value is not merely measured but methodically engineered.

1. James Womack and Daniel Jones, *Lean Thinking: Banish Waste and Create Wealth in Your Corporation* (Simon & Schuster, 1996).

2. James Womack and Daniel Jones, "From Lean Production to the Lean Enterprise," *Harvard Business Review* (March-April 1994.)

3. Eliyahu Goldratt, *Theory of Constraints* (North River Press, 1999).

4. Womack and Jones, *Harvard Business Review*.

5. Dean Leffingwell, et al., *SAFe® 4.0 Reference Guide: Scaled Agile Framework® for Lean Software and Systems Engineering* (Addison-Wesley, 2016).

6. Yan Huang, "King of Construction Machinery: How Does Caterpillar Achieve Long-lasting Prosperity?" *Equal Ocean* (August 7, 2023).

7. GR, "Caterpillar: Building the Supply Chain of the Future," *Harvard Business School Digital Initiative (RC-TOM)* (November 15, 2017).

Chapter 8

Impact Metrics

Mining for Gold

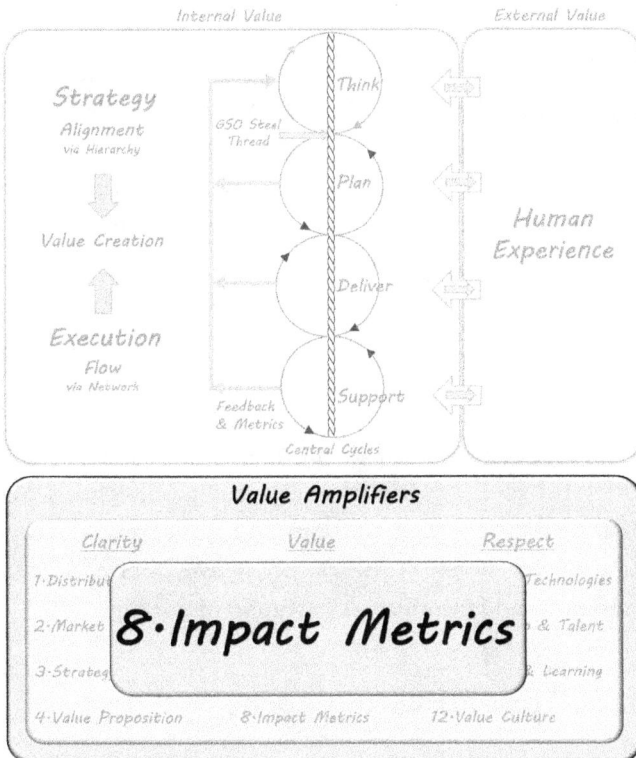

Analytics-Driven Adaptation

As previously discussed, transitioning from functional hierarchies to value streams is indispensable in optimizing operational dynamics and embedding value-centric organizational behavior. This structural reorientation minimizes systemic friction and resource dissipation while enabling strategic decision-making grounded in empirical evidence rather than intuition or assumption.

The architecture of a value-centered enterprise is built upon small, autonomous, cross-functional teams, aggregated into cohesive teams-of-teams—scalable structures that remain aligned through shared objectives. Organizations that institutionalize multidisciplinary integration across all levels exhibit greater responsiveness to shifting market conditions and evolving customer needs. Yet, this adaptability is best supported by rigorous measurement frameworks that elevate reactive adjustments into intentional, forward-looking strategy.

Value streams become an enterprise's principal mechanisms of value generation, serving as the core repositories for performance data that illuminate not only what transpired, but why—and what future outcomes are likely. In this case, measurement extends beyond conventional accounting, incorporating predictive analytics, behavioral indicators, and dynamic value flows. When orchestrated effectively, this infrastructure functions as an organizational nervous system—a distributed network of feedback loops that monitors and informs value creation in real time.

Data as Transformation Agent

When GSOs are paired with well-defined metrics, organizations are better positioned to track actual value as it emerges. The principle widely attributed to Peter Drucker holds, "What gets measured gets managed."[1] This foundational observation underscores measurement not merely as oversight, but as an agent of behavioral transformation—reinforcing accountability, surfacing hidden dynamics, and aligning efforts with enterprise goals.

GSO outcomes serve as definitive indicators of value creation within the Valorys system—truth-tellers that cut through organizational bias and reveal the genuine impact of strategic initiatives. However, GSOs can lose efficacy in the absence of relevant data. Data scarcity obscures the causal links between action and outcome, undermining comprehension and diminishing strategic clarity. Addressing this gap demands more than technology.

Rather than treating data as a passive byproduct of operations, forward-looking enterprises elevate it to the status of a core organizational capability—on par with financial stewardship or brand equity. This shift repositions data not as an operational detail, but as a vital lever of enterprise performance, demanding deliberate cultivation, protected investment, and cross-functional ownership.

Predictive Leading Indicators

Consider the example introduced in Chapter 3: Strategy Expression. If the goal is to "Improve customer satisfaction and retention," with an outcome to "Increase renewal rate by 15%," success depends on tracking leading indicators such as engagement frequency, support resolution time, feature adoption, and sentiment trends. These precursors to lagging results create a predictive canvas for early intervention, enabling hypothesis testing and iterative refinement that allow organizations to anticipate rather than simply respond to market developments.

With this type of visibility, CFOs evolve from fiscal reporters into strategic partners. They monitor profitability pro-

jections through metrics that eclipse traditional financial statements—operational efficiency ratios, customer acquisition costs,
and market penetration indices—enabling timely reallocations
and informed recalibration. Poor performance in early quarters
may still prompt the need for adjustment, but rich, real-time data
ensures those decisions are deliberate rather than reactive.

In its 2023 strategic plan, the American Psychological Association declared a deliberate shift from measuring outputs to measuring outcomes—committing to an approach where the goal,
not the tactic, drives the work, and where impact is rigorously
assessed rather than assumed.[2]

Integrated Measurement Discipline

While most organizations acknowledge that data collection demands significant investment, they often undervalue the exponential returns derived from well-architected measurement systems. In *Measure What Matters*, John Doerr champions the
use of objectives and key results (OKRs) to focus exclusively
on meaningful metrics—an approach validated across industries
ranging from technology, manufacturing, and service sectors.[3]

Valorys GSOs share foundational intent with OKRs but advance the model by incorporating hypothesis statements—strategic assumptions to be tested through structured experimentation. This transforms measurement into an active learning system
that uncovers causality, correlation, and optimal leverage points.
Complementing this, GSOs apply the steel thread method to
ensure consistency, clarity, and traceability among decision layers,
supporting both tactical execution and long-range pattern recognition.

Steel threads are especially critical. Unlike conventional reporting structures that fracture data within silos, this technique preserves the continuity of value-generating narratives across units,

maintaining strategic relevance wherever data resides. As a result, measurements remain contextually anchored, enabling coherent interpretation throughout the enterprise.

Foresight Through Discovery

The fidelity that outcome-focused enterprises require doesn't emerge naturally, and results-oriented data collection remains uncommon. Precision matters—but so does timing. Because the data needed to determine value realization is often absent from traditional reporting, organizations must acquire it swiftly and purposefully, typically within timeframes of a month to one quarter. This often demands rapid deployment of purpose-built data-collection mechanisms—temporary structures built for specific analytical purposes, then retired. Their transient nature reflects the aggressive reality of value creation in evolving markets.

The economic rationale is compelling: in dynamic markets, the cost of inadequate or delayed information often dwarfs the expense of robust measurement systems. Timely perception can prevent resource misallocations and enable swift responses to emergent opportunities—capabilities that compound in value over time. Real-time intelligent systems enable leaders to course-correct proactively, transforming leadership from hindsight to foresight through live interpretation rather than retrospective analysis.

In my advisory work, I encourage organizations to consider the strategic utility of consolidating fragmented information assets into centralized data warehouses or searchable repositories. Such platforms support both structured queries and exploratory analysis, enabling entities to extract decision-critical observations through advanced analytics, machine learning, and AI. These tools amplify human capability, thus allowing deeper pattern recognition while preserving executive judgment for crucial choices.

Where a centralized data architecture does not yet exist, building the instrumentation needed to evaluate GSOs generally initiates its creation. This incremental approach—laying the groundwork in tandem with urgent strategic needs—may appear less elegant than comprehensive design, but can prove more sustainable. Aligning infrastructure development with immediate organizational priorities rather than speculative future projections ensures relevance, adaptability, and long-term utility.

Dynamic Measurement and Strategic Evolution

In contrast to more enduring key performance indicators (KPIs) used for continuous operational oversight, the measures required to assess GSO outcomes are intentionally ephemeral—crafted to address central questions within defined timeframes. Their significance is tethered to the lifespan of an active goal, forming a dynamic measurement ecosystem that evolves alongside shifting strategic priorities. Once a goal is achieved or retired, its associated metrics are replaced by new indicators aligned with emerging objectives.

This temporal specificity marks a deliberate departure from traditional measurement approaches that emphasize consistency and long-term trending. While uniformity is essential for operational stability, strategic evaluation demands time-bounded metrics that prioritize relevance and actionable awareness over historical continuity. The key challenge is to preserve organizational learning without burdening measurement systems with obsolete metrics which obscure focus and consume resources.

As each GSO is conceived, its own measurement blueprint may be formed, specifying required data, collection methodologies, and analytical frameworks in advance of implementation. This forethought avoids a common pitfall: discovering key data gaps only after work is underway. As execution unfolds, incremental outcomes are evaluated for alignment and value contribution, establishing a continuous feedback loop that facilitates early course corrections and minimizes sunk cost risk.

Beyond Legacy Frameworks

Over the past three decades, the balanced scorecard has been widely adopted as a strategic performance framework designed to align organizational activities with overarching objectives.[4] While once valuable, it now shows its limitations. Legacy models like the balanced scorecard tend to reduce the complexity of modern enterprises into overly simplistic visuals, making them poorly suited to today's fast-moving and unpredictable conditions. These outdated frameworks emphasize retrospective reporting and rigid categorizations, constraining innovation instead of enabling the imaginative energy adaptive organizations require.

One cannot refine what one cannot measure. Effective organizations build measurement systems not merely to monitor performance, but to sharpen strategic focus and accelerate learning. These systems provide early signals that clarify what is working, reveal where realignment is needed, and expose leverage points for accelerating progress. When structured properly, measurement becomes a real-time operating model—bridging strategic intent with tactical precision.

Because GSO outcomes are expressed as forward-looking metrics, performance can be assessed within specific segments of a value stream at defined intervals—monthly, quarterly, or semi-annually. This temporal granularity permits micro-adjustments that maintain strategic direction while adapting execution to evolving conditions. The result is a governance rhythm that blends long-term persistence with short-term adaptability.

Strategic Review Discipline

Strategic review begins with each planning interval, forming a continuous cycle of learning, adjustment, and investment validation. Senior leaders assess whether subordinate GSOs continue to merit capital allocation based on projected returns, opportunity cost, and strategic flexibility. At the end of each iteration, structured evaluations examine alignment between actual results and intended impacts, triggering cascading retrospectives that promote understanding across organization levels.

Value-centered assessments consistently return to three essential inquiries:

- What quantifiable value is being created to support the annual goal? This involves impact attribution, ROI analysis, and consideration of both direct and indirect effects.

- Is the underlying hypothesis still valid, or must the approach evolve? This entails rigorous testing using statistical and causal inference methods to assess validity amid changing conditions.

- Can confidence be maintained that current investments will yield their projected returns by the end of the increment? Forward-looking appraisals rely on performance trend analysis, scenario modeling, and competitive benchmarking to forecast likely outcomes.

Analytical Rigor and Leadership

For those responsible for implementing GSOs, this undertaking is far from simple. Constructing temporal systems that reliably monitor intended outcomes demands both resolve and sustained discipline. It also requires equipping team members with a firm grasp of the strategic imperative behind them—so the rigor feels justified, the effort becomes meaningful, and the temptation to circumvent the process or dilute the measures is replaced with a commitment to uphold their integrity.

Moreover, strategic measurement requires emotional intelligence and leadership maturity to maintain objectivity, challenge assumptions, and encourage a culture where revising course is not seen as failure but as discipline. Teams often become attached to their initiatives, introducing confirmation bias and inertia that must be actively countered. Creating a safe space for acknowledging missteps is essential to preserving analytical integrity.

The inclusion of the CFO—or an equivalent financial steward—is critical throughout this process. Financial modeling provides crucial insight into the expected economic return of key pathways but must be sophisticated enough to capture complex, time-distributed value relationships. These models, while quantitative, are still built on assumptions and require sensitivity testing and scenario planning to remain credible. Ultimately, financial intelligence deepens strategic dialogue, ensuring investments are not only intentional but also proportionate to expected value, aligned with the organization's risk profile, and adaptive to changing market conditions.

Quantitative benchmarks undergo continual assessment—not merely for variance—but through trend analysis, predictive modeling, and scenario planning. This level of analytical rigor clarifies whether the expected value is materializing and reveals the performance dynamics behind deviations. Strategies can then be recalibrated in rhythm with quarterly outcomes, replacing annual retrospection with timely, data-driven adaptation that mirrors market cadence.

***

The Shenzhen boardroom held a gravity beyond its skyline view. Through the floor-to-ceiling windows, the Pearl River shimmered with restless energy—its waters coursing past ports that carried the company's ambitions to the world. Inside, however, ambition had become entangled with complexity.

Chen Hao, the business unit president, leaned forward at the table. "We're not on track," he said flatly. "Not just behind on quarterly targets. We're jeopardizing our annual goal."

That goal had been set months earlier by the board: "Reduce customer-impacting service failures by 40% across regions." It was a directive with reputational weight and financial teeth—delays, emergency shipments, and failed fulfillment were eroding trust and margins alike.

The digital wall projected a network map that, at a glance, looked impressive. But behind the dense lines and icons lurked missed delivery windows, surging air freight costs, and mounting client complaints. The markers were not achievements, they were warning signals.

Liu Wei, VP of Logistics, presented her findings with quiet precision. "We're running reactive. Freight spikes in Europe. Inventory stagnation in Southeast Asia. LATAM orders arriving a week late. If we stay on this trajectory, we'll fall short of our objective by at least 18%."

Zhang Ming, the data architect, offered little reassurance. "Each region defines 'on-time' differently. Our systems show green while customers report red. We're not disagreeing on facts—we're simply not aligned on definitions."

I turned to Chen. "What's your current method for tracking progress toward the annual goal?"

He hesitated. "We do retrospective reviews. Postmortems at quarter close."

That answer clarified everything. They weren't failing due to bad intentions or insufficient technology—they were trying to steer the vehicle by looking through the rear-view mirror.

I suggested a shift: deploy a targeted outcome-tracking model with real-time visibility on failures most correlated with customer loss. Not an elaborate dashboard built for appearances, but a lightweight, adaptable measurement tool designed to highlight where misalignments were generating the most operational drag.

Liu Wei leaned in. "You're saying we stop measuring everything and start measuring what matters?"

"Yes. Start where failure hurts you most—emergency shipments," I replied. "Every expedited order is a story of something that broke."

Zhang Ming, initially skeptical, opened his laptop and began pulling historical data. The correlation between emergency freight and customer churn was almost embarrassingly clear. "We can map this against forecast accuracy and cycle time," he said. "It'll show us which sites are causing the most downstream risk."

Chen Hao stood. He turned toward the window, scanning the luminous sprawl of Shenzhen. "We've got three quarters left," he said. "Missing this goal isn't an option."

"What do you need to hit it?" I asked.

"Continuity," he replied. "Not a temporary task force. A standing capability."

He proposed forming a Strategic Outcomes Cell—a permanent, three-person cross-functional team embedded within the business unit. Their mandate: translate annual goals into measurable micro-metrics, activate near-term feedback loops, and codify learnings into operational playbooks. They wouldn't build empires; they'd build clarity.

Liu Wei offered a senior logistics analyst. Zhang would contribute a data systems integrator. Chen himself committed a strategy liaison. No hierarchy. No fluff. Just focus.

Right then, in the boardroom, work began in earnest. As the team assembled around Zhang's prototype interface, something shifted. What was perceived as a reporting gap was now a strategic inflection point. Liu identified categories of shipment failures to track. Zhang began building a live correlation engine. Chen drafted an internal memo reframing the annual goal—not as a metric to hit, but as a system to evolve.

"This cell won't just monitor," Chen said. "They'll operationalize the goal."

Before leaving, I offered one caution: "Keep it lean. And when the goal changes, change the measurement."

Chen nodded, absorbing it all. "If we can reduce emergency shipments by even 20%, we're halfway to goal. But the real shift is cultural. We're not reacting anymore. We're designing."

At the elevator, he turned to me one last time.

"Funny," he said, watching the lights of the city reflect off the river below. "We thought the goal was 40% fewer service failures. But it's really about 100% better alignment."

The doors closed, and I was convinced they'd make it.

***

Evidence-Driven Adjustments

When leading indicators trend positively, confidence is reinforced, justifying further investment and accelerated execution. If metrics reveal underperformance, responsible leadership should be prepared to reconsider methods—or even goals—recognizing that strategic dexterity is not indecisiveness but a vital competency. Well-designed GSOs are constructed to generate measurable financial value while retaining the flexibility needed for continuous optimization.

This data-centric orientation clarifies both the timing and location of value creation, offering a defensible foundation for capital allocation decisions that transcend intuition and internal politics. It enables organizations to refine work intake, prioritize intelligently, and allocate capacity based on verified performance—results that withstand scrutiny from stakeholders, investors, and regulators alike.

Often, early analytics reveal hidden constraints, vague assumptions, or emerging issues before significant resources are committed. This foresight facilitates timely interventions that reduce costs and improve outcomes, preserving momentum without the disruption of major course corrections. Impact metrics assume a dynamic function, continuously reshaping inner workings and outward offerings with near real-time precision. This fluidity marks a departure from static planning models, empowering entities to operate at the speed and complexity required by today's volatile environment.

Impact Metrics Best Practices

1: *Pursue clarity through meaning, not volume.* Strategic clarity arises not from amassing data but from distilling insight with precision. True intelligence demands diagnostic inquiry, disciplined reasoning, and pattern recognition. When applied thoughtfully, predictive analytics evolve from trend jargon into instruments of foresight—linking emerging realities to timely, informed action.

2: *Measure what truly matters.* Make impact metrics the empirical foundation of value creation. Value-centered enterprises quantify outcomes that reflect genuine progress, focusing on leading indicators that reveal performance in motion and enable proactive, evidence-based management.

3: *Build a system of strategic measurement.* Adopt modern measurement systems that transform data into learning and adaptation. Invest in analytical capability, sound infrastructure, and a culture of disciplined reasoning. The power lies not in complexity but in precision—using relevant metrics to guide judgment, allocate resources intelligently, and sustain innovation, responsiveness, and long-term advantage.

4: *Review financial alignment with intentional cadence.* Conduct quarterly financial reviews that balance analytical rigor with executive judgment. If results reflect value proportional to investment, sustain the course; if not, recalibrate to refine strategy, rebalance spend, or redefine goals to preserve both fiscal discipline and strategic integrity.

***

Organization Highlight: Costco

Costco's ascent to becoming the world's third-largest retailer hinges not only on scale and pricing but on a rigorously disciplined, metrics-driven operating framework. From its origins as Price Club in 1976 through today's global presence, Costco has embedded data-centric precision into all aspects of its culture—transforming strategic ambitions into operational experiments and validated initiatives.

At the core of this discipline lies a hypothesis–experiment–evaluation loop: every new service or pilot—whether an in-store beauty salon, optical center, or pizza counter—is launched with well-defined hypotheses, performance thresholds, and decision triggers. This ensures each initiative is rigorously evaluated, and either optimized or discontinued based on tangible outcomes.

One striking example was the conclusion to shutter underperforming in-store photo centers. By 2021, Costco was using transactional data and cost-to-serve analysis to determine that on-line photo services delivered stronger margins and better member convenience than in-store counters, leading to an internal estimate of 18% annualized return on the reallocated space and labor.

Perhaps the most compelling evidence lies in Costco's e-commerce transformation, which was never conceived as a replacement for physical retail. The company initially viewed its online channels as performance amplifiers—tools to enhance in-store traffic, inventory velocity, and customer experience. Yet, as real-time data from A/B testing, customer behavior analysis, and app engagement patterns accumulated, the digital business began producing outsized returns. In fiscal Q3 2024, e-commerce surged 20.7% year-over-year, while app downloads grew 32% to 35 million users.[5] For the full year, online revenue expanded 16.1%, far outpacing overall comparable sales of 5.3%. [6] These gains, though unanticipated in scale, now inform physical retail strategy—tightening promotional cycles, improving shelf turnover, and expanding cross-category spend.

But throughout its e-commerce rollout, Costco did not abandon its core belief in physical retail dominance. Instead, it evolved its strategic posture as the data showed unexpected upside in digital, signaling a sign of mature, adaptive strategy—letting evidence reshape emphasis without undermining the original goal. Digital is no longer merely a channel—it has become a core driver of enterprise-wide performance.

Costco's success shows that a comprehensive data measurement structure—rooted in goals, strategies, and outcomes—is not simply a governance mechanism, but a key enabler of profitability, adaptability, and institutional alignment. By ensuring every initiative, from high-level expansion to localized pilots, is tested against transparent metrics, Costco maintains the lucidity and discipline necessary to scale without losing cohesion. The company exemplifies how specific measurements can anchor strategic clarity, operational flow, and cultural congruity—empowering the enterprise to respond to complexity not with reactive improvisation, but with evidence-based precision.

---

1. "What gets measured gets managed" is one of the most widely cited aphorisms in management literature—and one of the most thoroughly misattributed. Despite near-universal attribution to Peter Drucker, the Drucker Institute confirmed in a 2013 article that he never said it. What Drucker actually wrote, in *The Effective Executive* (1967), was nearly the opposite in spirit, noting that knowledge work resists the kind of measurement applied to manual tasks. The phrase's most credible origin is V.F. Ridgway's 1956 paper "Dysfunctional Consequences of Performance Measurements"—though Ridgway's argument was a warning against overreliance on quantitative measures, not an endorsement of them. The axiom is used here in its conventional, constructive sense, while acknowledging that some of the most important things in organizational life resist quantification entirely.

2. American Psychological Association, "Impact in Action: Reflecting on APA's Strategic Plan and Progress To-Date," *American Psychological Association* (February 2023).

3. John Doerr, *Measure What Matters: How Google, Bono, and the Gates Foundation Rock the World with OKRs* (Portfolio-Penguin Books, 2018).

4. Robert Kaplan and David Norton, *The Balanced Scorecard: Translating Strategy into Action* (Harvard Business School Press, 1996).

5. Business Insider, "Costco Third Quarter Wagyu Beef, Fake Trees Boost Sales," *Business Insider* (May 31, 2024).

6. Digital Commerce 360, "Costco e-commerce sales rise 18.9% in fiscal Q4," *Digital Commerce 360* (September 27, 2024).

Part Three: Respect

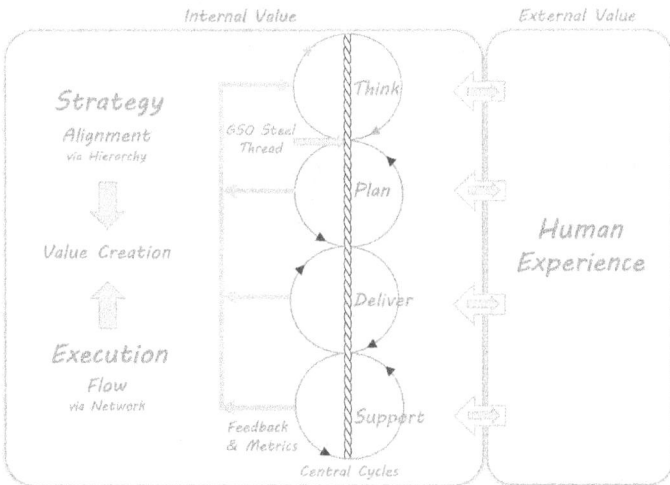

V alue creation converts resources into outcomes that advance purpose, benefit stakeholders, and are central to enterprise success. In Part Two: Value, I explored how organizations convert the strategic coherence established in Part One: Clarity into meaningful value delivery through measurable outcomes. Part Three now turns to the foundational principle that underlies every dimension of a value-centered enterprise: *Respect*.

The four value amplifiers introduced in this section form the basis upon which clarity and value depend. Without these core elements, the pursuit of sustained excellence lacks both authentic foundation and strategic viability.

Chapter 9: Advanced Technologies

Chapter 10: Leadership & Talent

Chapter 11: Feedback & Learning

Chapter 12: Value Culture

Advanced Technologies

Breaking All the Rules

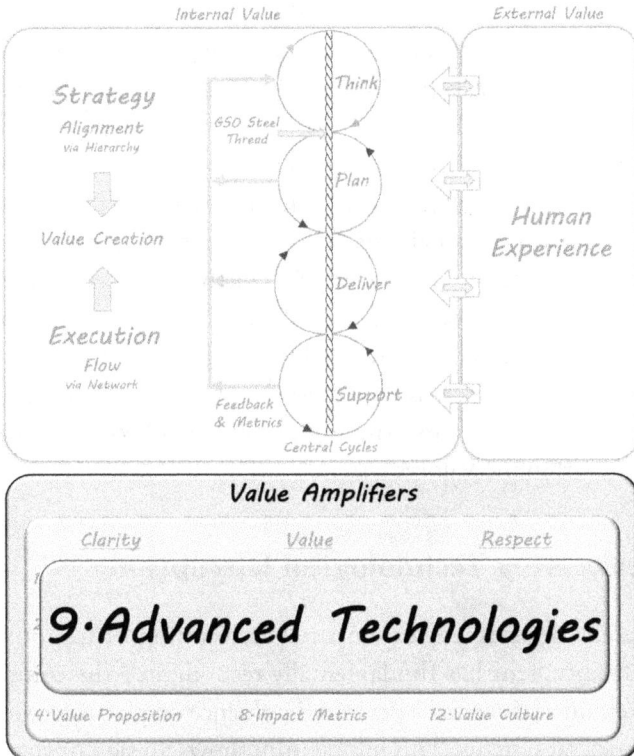

Modernization for Survival

The modern landscape is being reshaped by advanced technologies at such an unforgiving pace that many organizations, burdened by legacy thinking and sluggish adaptation, are not just falling behind—they are witnessing their own demise. As discussed in Chapter 3: Strategy Expression, the GSO construct—reinforced by its integrated steel thread and iterative feedback loop—enables entities to respond with exceptional speed to shifting conditions. The structural flexibility inherent in GSOs empowers enterprises to incorporate innovative advancements fluidly, enhancing both customer experience and operational effectiveness without necessitating disruptive organizational overhauls. This capability becomes particularly potent when technological integration is purposefully embedded within the enterprise's strategic goals.

This value amplifier underscores the pivotal role that contemporary technology plays in driving institutional growth, resilience, and long-term sustainability. Indeed, an entity's continued viability may depend on its ability to swiftly and strategically assimilate modern advancements in alignment with its overarching imperatives. This chapter delves into the multifaceted effects of such innovations across the enterprise domain, with particular emphasis on how transformative technologies become strategic drivers within the Valorys system.

Accelerating Technological Disruption

In recent decades, the exponential acceleration of technological advancement has fundamentally reconfigured the commercial terrain and exerted a profound influence on global economic and societal systems. This momentum shows no sign of abating; on the contrary, emerging technologies continue to disrupt and redefine entire industries, recalibrate monetary frameworks, and reform social constructs. While these developments present extraordinary opportunities for innovation, efficiency, and strategic growth, they also usher in a degree of volatility and complexity that can challenge even the most well-resourced enterprises.

One of the most pressing imperatives facing modern-day organizations is the capacity to remain synchronized with the rapid cadence of technological metamorphosis. The compression of digital lifecycles has become a defining feature of the modern era, with yesterday's innovations rendered obsolete by the accelerating emergence of newer models. This continuous state of transformation compels institutions to cultivate structural responsiveness and adopt forward-leaning approaches to technology integration.

For various enterprises—particularly those constrained by limited capital, talent, or infrastructure—this velocity of change may engender what might be termed *technological fatigue*.[1] The unremitting pressure to invest in incipient systems, retrain and upskill personnel, and re-engineer operational models can stretch internal capacities to the breaking point. Yet, the alternative—failing to maintain innovative relevance—poses existential risks: erosion of competitive position, declining market significance, and deteriorating customer experience. Each organization, therefore, must discern and calibrate its optimal level of equilibrium—balancing the imperatives of innovation and stability, investment and return, transformation and continuity.

Integrating Emerging Technologies

Assimilating nascent technologies into existing operational ecosystems presents a formidable challenge for contemporary enterprises. Many entities remain tethered to legacy systems that are inherently resistant to seamless alignment with modern innovations. Resolving these integration complexities is both capital intensive and time-consuming. The proliferation of heterogeneous technological solutions—each governed by its own standards, protocols, and architectural assumptions—further magnifies the difficulty. Achieving interoperability and functional cohesion across disparate platforms requires not only technical precision but also deliberate strategic orchestration. These realities compel a fundamental shift away from static, long-range forecasting models toward more adaptive, responsive decision-making frameworks—ones capable of absorbing and responding to critical developments with dexterity and coherence.

Valorys explicitly confronts these challenges by embedding technological adaptability directly into strategic planning. When a particular innovation attains sufficient competitive salience, it is elevated to the status of a formal organizational goal, appropriately tiered within the enterprise hierarchy and allocated resources commensurate with its anticipated impact. Under this model, system enhancements and integrations are no longer treated as ancillary or discretionary "side-of-desk" efforts. Instead, they are institutionalized as central imperatives—receiving the executive focus, company commitment, and operational rigor necessary for successful execution.

Shifting Competitive Dynamics

The accelerating evolution of technology profoundly influences organizational behavior, reshaping business functions, customer engagement models, and competitive positioning. Emerging innovations empower enterprises to iterate pricing strategies, redefine product-market fit, and recalibrate industry trajectories with unprecedented speed and precision. Digital ecosystems have dismantled many of the structural barriers that once insulated incumbent players, allowing nimble, tech-native entrants to disrupt mature markets with greater ease. Legacy firms currently find themselves contending with lean startups that wield technology as a strategic multiplier—delivering novel products and services at velocity and scale.

This redistribution of competitive advantage demands a fundamental reorientation among leadership. Adaptive leaders must now harness sophisticated tools to generate actionable insights, optimize organizational throughput, and craft differentiated value propositions capable of commanding sustained relevance.

Concurrently, advanced technologies are driving a transformation in the nature of work itself. Automation and intelligent systems increasingly enable employees to focus on higher-order tasks, enhancing overall productivity and engagement. Collaborative platforms have augmented organizational communication, particularly in distributed environments, fostering real-time coordination and strengthening cross-functional connectivity.

Cloud computing and mobile infrastructures have unlocked unprecedented workforce flexibility, enabling remote operations and fluid scheduling. Decision-making is increasingly supported by a new generation of artificial intelligence—spanning generative, analytical, and agentic modalities—delivering insights that inform the formulation and refinement of strategically aligned GSOs. In addition to AI, education and development practices are similarly undergoing transformation as augmented reality and virtual reality converge to deliver immersive, hybrid learning experiences that seamlessly integrate the physical and digital realms—amplifying both knowledge retention and collaborative engagement across the enterprise.

Navigating Workforce Transformation

Yet, not all employees are equally positioned to embrace emerging technologies, introducing layers of complexity into workforce dynamics. The adoption of advanced tools often necessitates the acquisition of new competencies—requiring targeted investment in training and capability-building initiatives. These transitions can be particularly challenging, as they risk creating fissures within the organizational fabric. Employees who feel unprepared or unsupported may exhibit resistance or apprehension, undermining morale and impeding productivity if not addressed with foresight and care.

Technological innovation often precipitates deeper cultural transformation, displacing rigid hierarchical models in favor of more integrated, horizontally oriented structures. These reconfigurations require not only procedural adjustments but also a fundamental shift in mindset and behavior. In this context, effective change management becomes indispensable.

Leaders play a critical role in orchestrating these transitions. Through the articulation of well-designed GSOs, they communicate a clear and compelling vision for technological adoption—anchored in strategic value and shared benefit. By ensuring that sufficient resources are allocated to support employee development and change enablement, organizations encourage smoother adaptations and mitigate friction. Concurrently, leadership should promote cultures rooted in innovation, continuous learning, and adaptive resilience—creating environments in which the workforce has the potential to thrive amid constant transformation.

Embracing Technological Challenges

While the challenges posed by rapidly advancing technologies are formidable, they are by no means insurmountable. Through the Valorys system, organizations not only mitigate these complexities but also unlock the transformative potential of innovation to drive sustained growth and strategic advancement.

In many cases, I have observed the transformative force of technology reshape organizational outcomes. In one instance, a nonprofit with which I collaborated realized a 36% increase in revenue by implementing state-of-the-art e-commerce and data analytics platforms—expanding donor engagement while optimizing contribution workflows. In another case, within a large financial institution, I witnessed executive leadership revitalize a chronically underperforming unit by setting annual goals with clearly defined targets while granting teams the autonomy to determine the most effective methods for achieving them. In this particular instance, one group, exhibiting exceptional resolve and prescience, proactively researched and piloted a newly released innovation. Their initiative enabled the department to deliver successful outcomes in just two months—dramatically ahead of the original one-year projection. It was, by all measures, a remarkable demonstration of the power of aligned strategy, empowered execution, and technological fluency.

Enabling Future Readiness

Conceived during the Plan cycle, a comprehensive implementation roadmap is indispensable for organizations seeking to navigate the inherent complexities of technological transformation with precision and foresight. Anchored in annual or multi-year goals, this dynamic blueprint articulates a clear and compelling technology vision, delineating priority areas for capability development and establishing defined milestones and timelines to guide execution. To remain responsive to emerging innovations and shifting conditions, the plan is subjected to regular review and iterative refinement.

Equally critical is the elevation of an organizational culture that embraces innovation as a core operating principle. With the Valorys system, this cultural shift is advanced by promoting experimentation, incentivizing creative problem-solving, and facilitating an environment in which failure is recontextualized as a catalyst for learning rather than a marker of deficiency. Adaptive leaders play a pivotal role in shaping this ethos by providing strategic clarity, modeling creativity-affirming behaviors, and sustaining a psychologically safe climate conducive to exploration and bold thinking.

At its core, Valorys equips organizations to develop resilient, future-ready solutions. The modular business and technology capabilities described in Chapter 5: Business Capabilities support the design of scalable architectures, enabling the smooth replacement and refinement of discrete components as strategic requirements evolve. This componentized approach not only enhances operational prowess, but also ensures long-term adaptability in a continuously shifting technological landscape.

***

The whiteboard in the fourth-floor conference room looked like a battlefield. Nina's hand hovered above the maze of lines and boxes she'd drawn—each a relic of some past solution that had temporarily held the company together.

"Twenty years of workarounds," she said under her breath, recapping the marker with a snap. "A legacy built on patches, not progress."

As Chief Technology Officer of a regional health insurer serving over a million members across California, Oregon, and Washington, Nina carried the weight of systems designed for another era. What had once been the company's digital backbone now creaked under the strain of growth, regulation, and rising consumer expectations. From Medicare Advantage to employer-sponsored plans to the company's fast-growing Medicaid contracts, Nina's technology estate was a latticework of disconnected platforms—each designed to solve one problem but never built to work in concert.

She'd done what she could over the last eight years—cloud migrations, fraud detection practices, automation upgrades—but every improvement was a battle. Budget approvals dragged. Innovation felt like a disruption. And year after year, the Board sent her modernization proposals back with polite deferrals: it's not the right time, we're in the middle of open enrollment, the market's uncertain.

What no one wanted to admit was this: the company's own systems were now impeding its future.

Her latest plan sat thick and professionally bound in front of me—seventy pages of architecture diagrams, integration plans, rollout phases. I flipped through it, noting the thoroughness. But then I looked up.

"This is a solid blueprint," I said. "But how do you want the Board to feel when they read it?"

She paused, uncertain. "Confident, I suppose. That we have a plan."

I nodded. "They don't need a plan. They need a reason."

Nina looked down. "They don't see the urgency. Every year, I make the case—technical debt, outdated infrastructure—and every year, they nod and stall."

"Because you're asking them to modernize systems," I said. "You need to ask them something else entirely: How long can we afford for our business strategy to be constrained by legacy architecture?"

She was quiet. And then she looked defeated. "I'm not even sure what to say to them anymore."

So I offered her a way forward.

"Start with their language," I said. "Don't explain what a containerized architecture does. Ask which business goals they believe are achievable. Then show them why the answer depends on the technology they've been postponing."

A week later, she walked into a cross-functional meeting with leaders from operations, strategy, and compliance. Together, they reviewed the company's declared priorities: reduce administrative costs, boost member retention, expand Medicaid coverage, increase provider network transparency, and improve CMS ratings.

I asked one question: "How many of these can we actually deliver on with the systems we have today?"

The room was still. Then Nina broke the silence.

"We've added three new teams just to manage handoffs between platforms. Our retention strategy is dead in the water because our app can't even push notifications. And the idea of expanding Medicaid in Oregon?" She exhaled. "We can't even get the eligibility engine to sync across counties."

Suddenly, what had seemed like IT bottlenecks were revealed as business risks—undermining strategy, delaying growth, driving up cost.

In that moment, Nina stopped fighting for tech upgrades. She started fighting for the future of the company.

Over the next month, she rewrote her proposal from the ground up. This time, every technical recommendation was paired with a business outcome. She linked automation to cost containment, integration platforms to market expansion, system unification to ratings improvement. And critically, she added a section titled "Organizational Alignment and Workforce Redeployment." It addressed the anxiety she knew was growing across teams—fear of layoffs, fear of irrelevance. She laid out training programs, mobility pathways, and new roles that reflected a human-centered transition strategy.

Presentation day arrived. This time, Nina didn't open with infrastructure. She opened with a question.

"We say our strategy is to reduce costs, retain members, and grow in Medicaid. Can we honestly do that with the technology we have today?"

Silence. It was clear no one on the Board knew.

Then she walked through the strategic goals—one by one—mapping each to the systems required, the gaps that existed, and the cost of doing nothing. She never used jargon. She talked about strategic enablement, risk mitigation, and organizational readiness. She said nothing about modernizing for its own sake. She spoke of performance ceilings that technology alone could lift.

Halfway through, the CFO leaned forward. "Why wasn't I told about this risk profile before now?" he asked, his tone sharp.

"You were," she said evenly. "But it was framed as an IT issue. This time, it's framed as a business one."

The CEO, who had been quiet until now, spoke up.

"What's the real blocker here?" he asked.

Nina didn't hesitate. "It's not budget. It's belief. We've siloed technology from strategy. Until we treat them as inseparable, we're operating with a built-in disadvantage."

The vote to fund the first phase passed—with vocal support from the CEO and grudging acceptance from the CFO. The Board had not only approved the plan—they had absorbed the message.

Technology ceased to be a back-office function. It had become a strategic lever.

After the meeting, Nina paused at the whiteboard. The diagram still bore the scars of compromise, but it no longer felt like a defeat. It was, at last, acknowledged for what it truly was: a working draft of what lies ahead. This patchwork wasn't something to erase, but something to build upon—a foundation of hard-earned lessons that, with clarity and resolve, could become the architecture of the company's future.

***

Empowerment Drives Technological Lift

The strategic deployment of advanced technologies to generate measurable financial impact and catalyze organizational growth is most effectively realized within frameworks of distributed authority. Paradoxically, the act of empowering others—giving up control to take control—emerges as a decisive enabler of transformative success, allowing organizations to unlock the full potential of materializing technological innovations.

In a Harvard Business Review analysis, Adobe CEO Shantanu Narayen observed that the strategic dimension of technological transformation, while demanding, is far less challenging than the operational execution and the human elements that accompany it—and that inspiring employees to apply their own ingenuity to the change is the critical differentiator.[2]

Numerous exemplars reveal how enterprises have harnessed cutting-edge technologies through differentiated, high-impact applications. Starbucks, for instance, integrated sophisticated data analytics with wireless technology platforms to deliver personalized marketing experiences and frictionless mobile ordering, thereby enhancing customer loyalty and driving revenue expansion. UPS implemented advanced routing algorithms and logistics optimization systems to refine delivery networks, reduce fuel consumption, and accelerate service performance. Levi Strauss revolutionized its production model by adopting laser-enabled finishing for denim processing, significantly compressing output cycles while advancing its sustainability commitments—reinforcing its relevance in a fiercely competitive industry.

These cases underscore a broader trend: the transformative potential of technology to reshape core organizational capabilities when adopted through deliberate, strategically aligned mechanisms. Ford Motor Company invested heavily in robotics and automation across its manufacturing processes, yielding substantial reductions in operational costs and improving throughput—critical factors in maintaining its position within the global automotive sector. Similarly, Domino's Pizza undertook a sweeping digital transformation, integrating advanced online ordering systems and mobile applications. This investment not only enhanced the customer experience but also streamlined internal operations, resulting in significant gains in both revenue and market penetration.

Collectively, these examples illustrate that technological innovation, when embedded within a framework of distributed authority and aligned with strategic intent, can serve as a powerful engine of growth, differentiation, and sustained competitive advantage.

Technologies Reshaping Tomorrow

A range of pioneering technologies holds significant promise for reshaping the organizational landscape and redefining the parameters of performance, innovation, and societal progress. Quantum computing, with its potential to exponentially enhance data processing and resolve previously intractable computational challenges, stands poised to disrupt industries ranging from finance to pharmaceuticals. Likewise, advancements in nanomedicine offer the prospect of revolutionizing healthcare through precision-targeted therapeutics and next-generation diagnostic modalities.

Neuromorphic structures—designed to emulate the neural architecture of the human brain—promise to deliver unparalleled gains in computing efficiency and adaptive learning. Meanwhile, blockchain applications are transforming global supply chain operations by encouraging transparency, traceability, and transactional trust across increasingly complex commercial ecosystems.

These technological frontiers are already driving transformative shifts in operational models, enabling more intelligent and responsive work environments. Yet, what lies on the horizon suggests even more profound implications for the future of human enterprise.

Fusion power, long a scientific aspiration, holds the potential to deliver virtually limitless, clean electricity—substantially altering energy economics and geopolitical dynamics. Molecular assemblers may herald a new era in manufacturing, enabling atomic-scale material synthesis with unprecedented precision. Programmable matter introduces the concept of materials that dynamically alter their properties in response to environmental stimuli, unlocking entirely new design and engineering possibilities.

Universal translation systems promise to overcome linguistic boundaries in real time, facilitating seamless global collaboration and cultural exchange. Artificial general intelligence (AGI) aspires to replicate human-level reasoning, judgment, and problem-solving, raising profound questions about the future of work, creativity, and cognition. Perhaps most revolutionary, brain-computer interfaces offer the potential to integrate thoughts directly with computational systems, amplifying cognitive capabilities and redefining the limits of human-machine interaction.

Together, these technological breakthroughs represent not merely incremental advancements, but foundational shifts with the ability to reshape civilization's trajectory, redefine organizational purpose, and elevate the human condition across the decades to come. For leaders operating within the Valorys framework, these possibilities are not abstractions to be monitored from a distance—they are emerging variables to be evaluated against declared goals, assessed for strategic fit, and incorporated deliberately when the evidence warrants, ensuring that the organization's response to transformative change remains purposeful rather than reactive.

Mitigating Digital Friction

While advanced technologies offer substantial operational benefits, they also introduce complex workplace challenges that demand thoughtful and deliberate management. Automation-induced job displacement could heighten employee anxiety, resulting in occupational uncertainty. Excessive reliance on technological solutions may inadvertently erode critical thinking and diminish the capacity for nuanced, analytical problem-solving. The ubiquity of electronic connectivity increasingly dissolves the boundaries between professional and personal life, contributing to worker burnout and heightened stress levels. Moreover, the persistent digital divide—particularly among employees with lesser degrees of technical fluency—may exacerbate disparities in productivity and career progression, threatening internal equity and cohesion.

Despite their operational promise, emerging technologies require vigilant leadership to ensure they are implemented objectively and responsibly. Senior executives play a critical role in facilitating this balance. By nurturing organizational cultures grounded in innovation, adaptability, and psychological safety, leaders accelerate the adoption of advanced tools while mitigating objections. Comprehensive training and enablement programs are essential to bolster employee confidence and competence with unfamiliar systems. Moreover, involving personnel in the co-creation of GSOs strengthens engagement, reinforces shared ownership, and reduces resistance to change.

Adaptive leaders employ iterative, low-risk experimentation—piloting technologies at a contained scale to assess operational and cultural impact before pursuing broader deployment. Such methodical approaches allow organizations to learn, adjust,

and improve implementation strategies without unnecessary per-
il.

Crucially, technological integration must be tightly aligned
with strategic imperatives. Digital innovations are evaluated not
for their novelty, but for their capacity to fulfill specific corporate
needs and advance published GSOs. Technologically enthusiastic
employees, while valuable, may advocate for tools based on excite-
ment rather than organizational fit; it is incumbent upon management to ensure that adoption decisions reflect enterprise-level
priorities.

Advanced Technologies Best Practices

1: *Confront technological acceleration as a strategic imperative.* Technological advancement is no longer a singular challenge
but a multidimensional force reshaping every domain of enterprise. Executives must steer dynamic markets, integrate emerging
tools, and cultivate a culture grounded in learning, innovation,
and adaptive judgment—ensuring that progress becomes a disciplined, repeatable capability.

2: *Harness Valorys to transform complexity into advantage.* Apply the Valorys system to master technological complexity and
convert modernization into enduring growth. By aligning structure, behavior, and technology, leaders create organizations that
do more than adapt—they flourish amid change.

3: *Embed distributed authority to sustain technological resilience.*
Institutionalize distributed authority to build enduring capacity for decisive, coordinated action. A resilient foundation—anchored in empowered judgment, strategic communication, and
coherent culture—enables organizations to thrive amid the continual disruption of breakthrough technologies.

***

Organization Highlight: Shopify

Shopify's emergence as a transformative force in global commerce underscores how the strategic application of emerging technologies can propel an organization from niche origin to market disruptor. Initially conceived in 2004 as a technical solution to a practical problem—namely, the absence of robust, user-friendly e-commerce infrastructure—Shopify was born out of necessity. Co-founder Tobias Lütke, leveraging his software engineering acumen, constructed a proprietary platform tailored to Snowdevil, the founders' budding online snowboard shop. What began as a purpose-built tool soon revealed broader potential, as other merchants sought access to the system's seamless transactional capabilities.

Recognizing the market's structural deficiency and latent demand for accessible digital storefronts, Lütke and his team launched Shopify in 2006, transforming a functional workaround into a scalable platform. By embracing modular architecture, cloud infrastructure, and accessible development tools, Shopify established itself as a fluid, customizable e-commerce solution—one that did not require retailers to possess deep technical expertise. This commitment to technological enablement became central to the company's strategic identity.

Shopify's timing proved advantageous. Between 2011 and 2021, global e-commerce sales more than quadrupled, growing from approximately $1.3 trillion to over $5.2 trillion,[3] a trend that provided fertile ground for the firm's expansion. By

2023, Shopify powered over 4.4 million live websites across 175 countries,[4] serving businesses ranging from micro-entrepreneurs to multinational brands such as Kraft Heinz and Hyatt.

But Shopify's success is not simply a matter of market timing—it lies in the platform's sustained capacity to integrate and monetize advanced technologies in ways that create compounding value for both the company and its users. At its core, Shopify functions as a full-stack digital commerce infrastructure, offering tools that transcend the transactional layer to optimize the entire commercial lifecycle. For instance, its machine learning-based fraud detection system dynamically monitors purchasing behavior to reduce chargebacks and protect merchants at scale, preserving profit margins while enhancing consumer trust.

Equally transformative is Shopify's use of AI-driven personalization engines, which empowers even small sellers to deliver Amazon-level customer experiences. These tools analyze behavioral signals to recommend products, optimize page layouts, and automate promotional timing—all of which increase conversion rates and average order values. The platform also integrates augmented reality features that allow customers to visualize merchandise in their physical spaces, significantly reducing return levels for high-consideration purchases, such as furniture or home décor.

The monetization logic behind these tools is elegantly self-reinforcing: each technological improvement increases merchant success, which in turn grows Shopify's gross merchandise volume and revenue. In 2023 alone, Shopify merchants generated more than $235 billion in global economic activity, a testament to the platform's capacity to enable entrepreneurial value creation at scale.[5]

More than a transactional platform, Shopify has reshaped the landscape of modern retail by enabling creators and companies to move with greater speed and independence. Its technology infrastructure democratizes access to sophisticated technical capabilities, significantly reducing the marginal cost of innovation. This allows businesses of all sizes to test, scale, and improve their offerings in real time.

Today, Shopify's influence transcends commerce. It represents a fundamental shift in how digital systems can remove barriers to entry, flatten competitive hierarchies, and accelerate innovation—showcasing the transformative potential of technology when deployed with vision, precision, and user-centric purpose.

1. Craig Brod, *Technostress: The Human Cost Of The Computer Revolution* (Basic Books, 1984). While Brod did not specifically use the term "technological fatigue," he is credited with creating the foundational concept and academic framework that underlies all modern discussions of technology-related stress and burnout.

2. Shantanu Narayen, "Adobe's CEO on Making Big Bets on Innovation," *Harvard Business Review* (November–December 2023).

3. Statista, "Retail e-commerce sales worldwide from 2014 to 2026," *Statista*, accessed June 28, 2025.

4. BuiltWith, "Shopify Usage Statistics," *BuiltWith*, accessed June 28, 2025.

5. Shopify, *2023 Shopify Economic Impact Report* (Ottawa: Shopify, 2024), accessed via Wayback Machine archive, June 28, 2025.

Chapter 10

Leadership & Talent

Elevating Human Potential

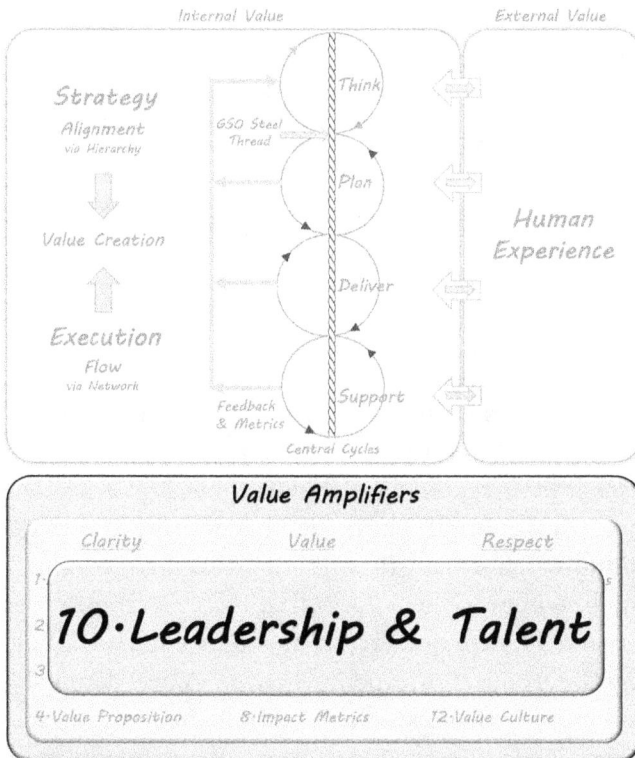

Long-Horizon Stewardship

I n *Good to Great,* Jim Collins identifies a defining trait
of exceptional leaders: they combine unwavering resolve
with personal humility, remaining more concerned with the
success of the enterprise than with their own individual ac-
complishments.[1] This blend of determination and modesty
enables them to build a strategic value-creation framework
focused on sustained prosperity rather than short-term gains.
What makes these leaders enduringly effective is their ability to
embed adaptive mechanisms that respond fluidly to evolving
customer needs and market conditions.

Research published by McKinsey in 2021 confirms that
executives who consistently make decisions with long-term
objectives in mind generate more shareholder value, create
more jobs, and contribute more to economic growth than
peers focused on short-term returns—and that attending to
the interests of employees, customers, and other stakeholders
produces better long-term outcomes.[2]

The Discipline Imperative

As introduced in Chapter 7: Value Streams, one of the defining attributes of a value-centered enterprise is its commitment
to disciplined execution. Yet, this discipline is not merely procedural—it is cultural. The pursuit of enduring value requires
continuous refinement through rigorous introspection and
methodical improvement. Organizations must come to recognize that errors are not aberrations to be concealed, but the
natural byproducts of experimentation. What distinguishes
mature firms is their capacity to surface, interrogate, and re-
mediate such failures with intention and clarity of purpose.

Such an orientation reflects a fundamental evolution in how organizations lead, manage, and develop talent. Rather than constructing mechanisms to prevent failure at all costs, value-focused enterprises normalize it as a crucible for learning—cultivating a workforce that is not only resilient and resourceful, but continuously aligned with long-term strategic aims.

A disciplined culture, however, must not be conflated with a controlled one. Indeed, discipline—properly understood—stands in stark contrast to micromanagement. As Jocko Willink and Leif Babin assert in *Extreme Ownership*, the disciplined ethos cultivated within U.S. Navy SEAL teams empowers individuals to operate with extraordinary autonomy, even amid the most volatile and consequential conditions. This sovereignty is not accidental; it is the byproduct of rigorous preparation, unambiguous intent, and a deep-seated ethic rooted in trust and moral courage.[3]

Because discipline is internalized, elite military units such as the SEALs require neither incessant oversight nor rigid supervision. Instead, they are entrusted with precise objectives and clearly defined parameters—within which they are free to determine the most effective course of action. This reality reveals a profound organizational truth: when self-regulation is coupled with clarity and trust, it becomes a force multiplier for initiative, accountability, innovation, and sustained performance.

Leadership Shapes Value

Organizations that most effectively prioritize value creation are invariably guided by senior executives who embody a lived commitment to shaping culture, articulating strategic direction, and refining operational models. Transformation at scale must be anchored at the top, where leadership behaviors consistently align with declared values. When there is dissonance between rhetoric and action, middle management and frontline contributors perceive the inconsistency almost immediately—undermining trust and corroding credibility.

Empirical evidence confirms that some of the most significant innovations originate not in the boardroom, but at the operational edge—particularly among individuals with sustained, unmediated contact with customers. These actors are uniquely positioned to discern emerging needs, refine existing offerings, and contribute substantively to the co-creation of unique value.[4]

By granting bounded freedom—discretion within a well-defined frame—organizations can activate a form of distributed intelligence that counters the inertia and complacency that so often afflict mature enterprises. Teams should be entrusted with the latitude to prototype new offerings, enhance service experiences, or pursue improvements they believe will resonate with those they serve. It is the responsibility of senior leaders not only to permit such exploration, but to actively encourage and support it—materially and structurally.

Adaptive leadership forms the foundation of synchronic organizations: those capable of remaining directionally aligned while responsive to emergent complexity. Today's workforce is no longer content with transactional labor; it seeks purposeful engagement and values affirmation through meaningful contribution. Within this context, value creators constitute the organization's most indispensable asset. Accordingly, they must be treated not as interchangeable units of work, but as individuals worthy of dignity, respect, and care.

Workforce as Value Engine

To attract, inspire, and retain this caliber of talent, organizations should reconsider how they engage their people. This entails fostering an environment of trust, transparency, inclusion, and deliberate patience—a culture in which everyone feels seen, heard, and empowered to fulfill both personal ambitions and collective goals.

Authors Bob Chapman and Raj Sisodia offer a persuasive argument for the equitable and compassionate treatment of employees. In their publication *Everybody Matters*, they attest that when organizations authentically prioritize the well-being of their people, individuals reciprocate with deeper engagement, sustained loyalty, and elevated performance.[5] While this philosophy may not be universally embraced, its efficacy across diverse organizational settings asserts its pragmatic viability.

Enhanced workers, after all, are drawn from the broader population and carry with them the same cognitive intricacies, social conditioning, and behavioral variability observed in society at large. Yet, within many corporate environments, these fundamental realities are frequently marginalized or insufficiently acknowledged. The discipline of industrial-organizational psychology exists precisely to address this disconnect—applying empirical insight to improve workplace productivity, satisfaction, and psychological well-being. The field reveals a simple truth: when the human dimension is integrated into managerial systems, performance reliably follows.

The Valorys system aligns closely with principles advanced by behavioral scientists and organizational psychologists, integrating best practices in job architecture, motivation theory, and applied social economics. Its value amplifiers are designed to cultivate environments where individuals flourish, purpose becomes operationalized, and long-term talent retention is achieved. By addressing both operational efficiency and human sustainability, Valorys equips organizations to build cultures that are not only strategically potent but also psychologically viable.[6]

The Empathy Advantage

Central to this uplifting transformation is the role of emotionally intelligent leadership. First conceptualized by Peter Salovey and John D. Mayer in 1990[7] and later expanded by Daniel Goleman in his classic 1995 work *Emotional Intelligence*, the framework outlines five core competencies essential for effective leadership: self-awareness, self-regulation, motivation, empathy, and social skill.[8] These capacities are not abstract ideals—they are practical imperatives in organizations seeking to humanize performance without sacrificing rigor.

In my experience with multinational enterprises, it has become increasingly evident that senior leaders serve as the architects of cultural development. Their ability to model emotional intelligence directly influences organizational character, reinforces strategic clarity, and boosts coherence across complex systems. Leaders attuned to their own values and emotions—and to those of others—are uniquely equipped to cultivate trust, model integrity, and enable environments where principled action and collective purpose can thrive.

When organizations undertake a deliberate inquiry into their cultural architecture, a recurring realization emerges: empathetic engagement is not peripheral to performance—it is foundational. Workers who are recognized and supported as multidimensional individuals become indispensable contributors to enterprise value. Conversely, neglecting their affective needs and intrinsic motivations weakens commitment and invites attrition.

Even the integration of foundational emotional intelligence competencies—such as empathy, self-regulation, and reflective listening—into leadership development efforts can yield outsized returns. These skills not only elevate interpersonal dynamics but also enhance organizational stability, strengthen talent continuity, and underpin sustainable long-term performance.

Leading the Modern Workforce

The expectations of today's workforce differ markedly from those of prior generations. Enhanced workers—characterized by elevated skills, reflective awareness, and vocational autonomy—demonstrate a declining tolerance for traditional command-and-control models. Instead, they seek environments defined by meaning, inspiration, and the opportunity to contribute purposefully. For organizations to harness their full potential, leaders must establish a nuanced understanding of these motivational drivers and construct pathways that support professional development and intrinsic engagement.

It is unrealistic to expect consistent value contribution from any cohort without first equipping them with the requisite knowledge, context, and tools. In this capacity, middle managers assume a pivotal role—ensuring that employees, regardless of functional assignment or compensation level, receive substantive exposure to value-centric thinking. These leaders must also internalize the rationale that underpins the organization's value framework and act as interpreters of its relevance.

Recurring, well-structured training programs are essential to embed this orientation, providing the cognitive bedrock necessary for performance in a value-based firm. This mindset should also extend beyond internal stakeholders. Strategic suppliers, vendors, and ecosystem partners operating within extended value streams should likewise display fluency in value-driven principles to sustain alignment across the broader enterprise context.

The primary mechanisms through which work is executed are small, self-organizing, cross-functional teams—autonomous, interdependent groups empowered to act decisively. This versatile team structure represents a universal organizational building block, equally effective whether deployed within value streams or across other areas of an enterprise. Middle managers are instrumental in enabling their success: they apply rigor, facilitate alignment, and maintain a cadence of contextual engagement through ongoing, often daily, interaction. This requires a fundamental shift—from supervisor to coach, from controller to enabler.

To fulfill this mandate effectively, managers strive to assume an adaptive approach to leadership and eschew the trappings of micromanagement. They are charged with cultivating environments in which individuals exercise discretion, contribute insight, and maintain accountability for value delivery. A substantial body of literature affirms the behavioral traits and governance conditions necessary to support high-functioning, value-oriented teams. Accordingly, managers require targeted development and continuous reinforcement to become the connective tissue of a truly value-aligned enterprise.

Equally important is the provision of time and space for reflection. Insight and creativity—those essential drivers for innovation—rarely emerge amid unbroken execution. Rather, they arise during moments of cognitive disengagement, often while commuting, engaging in routine tasks, or pausing intentionally to reflect. These intervals of mental quietude allow individuals to reconceptualize challenges and envision alternative approaches with greater clarity and imagination.

Leaders in high-performing organizations recognize that sustainable value creation is not the byproduct of constant motion, but of deliberate reflection—of creating the conditions in which insight is permitted to emerge.

Promoting Workforce Excellence

Investment in human capital remains a defining attribute of value-centered enterprises and a strategic differentiator in increasingly competitive markets. Central to this investment lies the systematic development of leaders and managers capable of operating effectively within value-based frameworks. Robust and adaptive training programs are essential not only for implementation but for cultural integration. These efforts must go beyond mere procedural instruction, instead instilling a deep understanding of value principles that are often absent from traditional curricula.

Technologies such as AI-enabled learning platforms hold considerable promise. These tools generate personalized, role-specific content responsive to the unique responsibilities of each participant, thereby enhancing engagement, comprehension, and applied relevance across the organizational spectrum.

Senior leaders should act as visible champions of workforce training, allocating both fiscal resources and institutional bandwidth to ensure its success. Given the scale and complexity of enterprise-wide transformation, phased rollouts often provide the most viable path forward. Ideally, these phases coincide with periods of strategic inflection—such as the launch of a new value stream—when corporate receptivity and impact potential are highest.

Middle managers serve as critical enablers in this process. They identify skill gaps, assess team readiness, and implement targeted interventions to ensure talent is properly aligned with the organization's evolving strategic architecture. This includes upskilling, reskilling, and cross-training initiatives that respond to real-time performance needs.

A well-structured curriculum should include themes such as consumer empathy, communication precision, applied prob-

lem-solving, and service excellence. Executive and managerial associates may benefit from targeted workshops designed to deep-
en understanding of consumer expectations and sharpen the organization's value delivery mechanisms. These sessions should
emphasize cascading GSOs, establishing effective feedback pro-
cedures, and reinforcing an ethos of customer commitment
throughout the hierarchy.

Value-focused middle managers also operate as internal com-
municators—leveraging formal and informal channels to dissem-
inate compelling narratives that illustrate the tangible outcomes
of value-based practices. These stories serve a dual function: they
provide insight into operational alignment and inspire broader
commitment through the articulation of purpose. When leaders
consistently display congruence between intention and action,
they not only model expectations, but elevate the organization's
collective capacity for value creation.

***

I encountered Erich in a break room situated mere steps from
the manufacturing floor. He presented as a youthful, physically
fit engineer who had dedicated four years to a mid-sized industrial
automation firm in Munich. I sought to gain deeper insights regarding my client Karl, the Chief Operating Officer.

"How do you like working for Karl?" I asked.

Erich furrowed his brow. "He's a nice enough guy, friendly
and smart. But I don't think he really has a handle on what's
happening down here—he started as an engineer, you know."

He continued, looking a bit more receptive to sharing his
thoughts with an outside consultant. "All the managers are talking about innovation, but no one in the shop knows what that
means. We have some very concrete ideas on how to improve the
processes, but there's no way to implement them with the tools we

already have. There's a ton of new technology we could leverage, but no clear path to make that happen."

The subsequent morning found me positioned in Karl's executive office. Floor-to-ceiling windows provided an elegant frame for the Isar River, where early commuters navigated purposefully through the morning fog that enveloped the cityscape.

"You know," he began, his voice formal but clear, "we've spent over fifty million euros in the last eighteen months on modernization. The PLCs talk to the production monitors. Predictive maintenance has cut downtime by 37%. Quality control systems are capturing more data than we've ever had."

He adjusted his wire-rimmed glasses with deliberate precision. "And yet... something's missing. The way our people operate hasn't really changed. Not where it counts."

I tilted my head with curiosity. "What do you mean?"

He pressed his lips together, then spoke slowly. "Culture. Ownership. Mindset. We have exceptional engineers, committed technicians. But the spark for true innovation is not there. We're automating everything—except how we solve problems."

I acknowledged his observation with understanding. "You're not alone. The companies that truly create value—the ones moving markets—are the ones who give their teams the space and support to think and act differently."

Karl leaned forward with evident interest. "The best ideas we have come from the floor. Engineers who customize servo drives for pharmaceutical clients. Field techs who solve packaging issues in automotive plants. But our board keeps prioritizing standardization, predictability, efficiency."

"That's the classic tension," I said. "Engineering excellence versus business pragmatism. But the people who interact with real customer problems—those are your value creators. Mechanical engineers debugging specification dissonance. Software teams optimizing runtimes. They live the challenges."

He traced the polished oak table's surface thoughtfully. "So how do we make space for them to contribute strategically? Germans love systems."

"Bounded freedom," I said. "Give them room to innovate—within clear parameters. Think like an engineer: define the boundaries. Encourage experiments with PID logic, custom human-machine interfaces, or entirely new product variations. But support it visibly."

Karl's eyes narrowed slightly with analytical focus. "We've talked about innovation labs. Cross-functional teams testing Industry 4.0 use cases. Machine learning models for injection molding. But the board thinks it's a distraction from core business."

"That's the old mindset," I said. "The companies that thrive now? They know exploration isn't a luxury—it's a requirement. And they don't treat engineers like interchangeable parts. They treat them like partners."

He appeared genuinely amused by this observation. "We are ...not known for our organizational flatness."

"Few legacy firms are. But the shift starts with how you engage your people. Today's engineers want to know how their work fits into the bigger picture. That their decisions matter beyond tolerances and timelines."

Karl leaned back in his chair, adopting a contemplative posture. "And you think that kind of thinking can be taught?"

"I think it can be cultivated. Through trust. Through communication. Through leadership that respects expertise—not just titles."

He offered a quiet laugh of recognition. "Patience with ideas that haven't yet proven themselves? That's not our strong suit. We prefer data. Documentation."

"Emotional intelligence is becoming just as important as technical expertise," I said. "It's what allows teams to navigate ambiguity, to explore without fear. EQ isn't fluff—it's capability."

Karl redirected his attention toward the river, observing a sleek commuter train traversing the bridge. "So you're saying the real value isn't just in hardware or software. It's in human potential."

"Exactly. When engineers feel their ideas matter, when they're entrusted with real problems and supported to solve them—they do more than build systems. They drive innovation."

He nodded slowly, processing the implications. "We've spent years getting the tech stack right. Maybe now it's time to focus on the people who make it work."

"What if," I asked, "we looked at your leadership development programs? Not just for soft skills, but for strategic alignment. What if you trained your mid-level managers to coach innovation, not just manage throughput?"

Karl straightened in his chair with renewed attention. "You mean real training. Not workshops. Not pointless seminars."

"Exactly. Real EQ development. Peer coaching. Cross-functional immersion. Reflection practices. It's not about teaching engineers to be extroverts. It's about helping them create despite complexity."

He considered this proposition thoughtfully. "We've wanted our engineers to think bigger. Maybe we just haven't given them the tools."

I responded with encouragement. "Or the permission."

Karl extended his hand across the conference table. "Let's explore this further. I want to see what leadership looks like when we stop optimizing people and start empowering them."

He paused with evident anticipation. "And if we get it right?"

"Then innovation won't just live in your systems. It'll live in your people."

***

Capability-Centric Management

As previously established, value-driven organizations are structured not around traditional hierarchies, but centered on value streams. In this model, cohorts of enhanced workers—once embedded within static resource pools or departmental silos—are reconstituted as asset warehouses, aligned according to specialized capabilities rather than rigid functional divisions. Resource managers drawn from the legacy model frequently transition into domain managers, assuming responsibility over talent consistent with their specific technical or professional disciplines.

Domain managers occupy a critical role in preserving and advancing institutional capability. They are entrusted with defining standards of excellence, curating individualized pathways for career progression, and ensuring that each member of their discipline receives ongoing education informed by value-based principles. This dual alignment model allows enhanced workers to operate under the day-to-day guidance of delivery arc managers while maintaining a parallel, developmental relationship with domain leads responsible for the long-term cultivation of professional acumen.

Such a structure preserves deep technical expertise while aligning workforce development with strategic intent. Executives are encouraged to adopt this shift from conventional functional oversight to domain-centric leadership, as it enables the organization to maintain specialization without compromising the coherence and responsiveness of value stream operations.

Sustaining Transformational Focus

To pursue value orientation in earnest is to principally reimagine how an enterprise operates, leads, and evolves. The hard truth is this: meaningful transformation requires substantive change.

Without it, organizations remain encumbered by legacy structures that constrain their capacity to respond to evolving strategic demands.

Transformation must be championed from the top. In the absence of committed executive sponsorship, efforts to reorient around value risk devolving into ephemeral exercises in rhetoric. To effect enduring change, leaders should internalize value principles not only intellectually, but emotionally—embodying them consistently in conduct, communication, and decision-making. Authentic metamorphosis begins with conviction, not compliance.

Adaptive leaders recognize the importance of pacing organizational progression with care. Cultural integration cannot be forced. Individuals absorb structural and behavioral shifts incrementally, and attempts to accelerate transformation without adequate support often yield counterproductive resistance. In an environment of accelerating global demand, various enterprises extend themselves into new markets and expedite feature delivery in pursuit of growth. Yet, in the absence of rigorous prioritization and careful validation, such expansion may produce dissonance rather than progress.

This strain is notably acute when initiatives proliferate without clear linkage to strategic direction. Employees, overwhelmed by simultaneous imperatives, lose visibility of the mission and the value outcomes their efforts are meant to support. Amid such ambiguity, day-to-day decisions become fragmented, priorities blur, and adherence to executive guidance wanes—particularly when market movements or customer demands appear misaligned with the organization's core trajectory.

To navigate this complexity, leaders must create disciplined governance systems that maintain strategic clarity and guide thoughtful decision-making. This focused approach ensures the organization stays aligned while preserving employee engagement and achieving the full benefits of transformation.

Leading Through Obstacles

As outlined in Chapter 6: Capacity Allocation, the inadvertent overextension of personnel is effectively mitigated through the use of pull-based systems. These structures ensure that only high-priority tasks are introduced into the workflow, calibrated to the available capacity within each value stream. By limiting work-in-process and anchoring effort to strategic relevance, organizations optimize resource utilization while safeguarding the long-term sustainability of their workforce. This operational discipline is best enacted through orderly business unit portfolio management—emphasizing small teams, incremental delivery scaled to the appropriate level of inter-team interaction, and the continuous progression of validated, prioritized activity.

The path to organizational transformation is seldom linear. Value-driven reforms often encounter resistance—from passive disengagement to active obstruction. Some dismiss the value focus as a passing trend, while others default to the comfort of familiar routines. Left unaddressed, these behaviors can impair cultural alignment, erode morale, and stall momentum.

Effective leaders act with clarity and resolve. Addressing resistance early, constructively, and unequivocally prevents it from calcifying into permanent dysfunction. Even when initial messaging fails to resonate, consistent reinforcement of strategic intent—through action and communication—signals the durability of the transformation. Over time, this principled follow-through yields more streamlined operations, stronger alignment, and enhanced value realization across an enterprise.

Leadership & Talent Best Practices

1: *Architect value-centered governance from the top down.* Senior executives must act as the designers of value-based ecosystems—cultivating disciplined thinking and embedding emotional intelligence, ethical judgment, and adaptive leadership into the organization's core. Their custodianship establishes the principles that shape both culture and competence, ensuring that every layer of the enterprise operates in harmony with its purpose and strategic intent.

2. *Empower the middle as the engine of transformation.* Middle managers serve as pivotal integrators—translating executive intent into practical approaches. By mentoring empowered contributors through structured learning and performance coaching, they foster the conditions for creativity, accountability, and sustained contribution. Their leadership bridges vision and execution, transforming aspiration into consistent practice.

3. *Develop people as a system's greatest asset.* Modern enterprises thrive when human growth and business performance evolve together. Domain managers must look beyond functional oversight to nurture both the well-being and capability development of their teams. Synchronic organizations invest deliberately in cross-training and upskilling, attracting those motivated by purpose beyond profit and cultivating a workforce that is resilient, intellectually engaged, and aligned with long-term value creation.

***

Organization Highlight: IRC

The International Rescue Committee, renowned for its frontline engagement in global humanitarian crises, exemplifies how adaptive leadership and strategic talent development can simultaneously elevate organizational performance and drive cost efficiency. Operating in volatile and resource-constrained environments, the IRC recognizes that the strength of its executive pipeline directly correlates with its capacity to deliver mission-critical outcomes while minimizing the operational drag associated with high turnover and underperformance.

Central to the IRC's approach is a deliberate investment in cultivating adaptive leadership—leaders who exhibit resilience, contextual intelligence, and the acumen to make high-stakes decisions amidst uncertainty. Through structured mentorship, immersive training programs, and situation-based learning, the IRC equips individuals across all organizational tiers with the tools necessary to lead with fortitude and efficacy. The impact is measurable: a 2021 evaluation of IRC's leadership development program showed that 90% of participants felt significantly more equipped to guide their teams through crises.[9]

What distinguishes the IRC's governance model is its emphasis on distributed decision-making under conditions of complexity. Rather than defaulting to centralized control, the organization trains leaders to operate autonomously within a coherent framework of values, ethics, and outcome-oriented accountability. This approach enhances operational responsiveness while reinforcing trust across hierarchical layers. IRC management programs incorporate experiential learning and scenario planning specifically designed to simulate the ambiguity and pressure of humanitarian contexts—an environment where textbook management models often fall short. This commitment not only strengthens day-to-day operations but also promotes a culture of responsibility, continuous improvement, and respectful workplace dynamics—reducing attrition and mitigating the costly cycle of recruiting and onboarding replacements.

Retention gains reflect this investment. In a sector where turnover often exceeds 30% annually, the IRC achieved staff retention rates of 84% across high-stress field positions in 2023.[10] These improvements not only preserve continuity, but reduce the estimated $4,000–$10,000 per employee in replacement costs typically borne by nonprofits managing frequent personnel transitions.[11] More importantly, high retention supports deeper contextual knowledge, stronger local relationships, and a more capable organizational memory—all of which are invaluable in fluid and unpredictable operating environments.

In parallel, IRC's emphasis on talent diversification—drawing from disciplines such as logistics, finance, technology, and advocacy—broadens its institutional ability to respond to multifaceted challenges. The organization's cross-disciplinary approach enables integrated solutions that reflect the true complexity of human needs. For example, technologists embedded in field teams support real-time data collection and predictive modeling, enabling resource allocation decisions that are both cost-effective and mission-aligned.

The IRC champions the integration of local authority within its operational framework, advancing community-based potential as a lever for sustainable impact. As of 2023, over 60% of IRC country programs are led by national staff, reflecting its intentional shift toward nationally led humanitarian operations.[12]

Succession planning is the culmination of this strategy. By proactively identifying high-potential individuals and systematically preparing them for future management roles, the IRC ensures continuity, preserves institutional knowledge, and avoids the disruption and inefficiency commonly triggered by leadership vacuums. These pipelines are not just reactive—they are deliberately aligned with organizational foresight, allowing the IRC to anticipate gaps, shift personnel dynamically, and maintain operational integrity in regions undergoing rapid change.

Ultimately, the IRC's focus on adaptive leadership and talent development is not a peripheral initiative—it is a core operational strategy that drives performance, curbs avoidable costs, and sustains mission fidelity in the world's most demanding contexts. It affirms a broader truth for leaders across sectors: that the cultivation of human capital—when grounded in contextual insight, inclusive design, and systemic investment—forms the backbone of institutional resilience and strategic excellence.

1. Jim Collins, *Good to Great: Why Some Companies Make the Leap...And Others Don't* (Harper Business, 2011).

2. Ariel Babcock, Sarah Keohane Williamson, and Tim Koller, "How Executives Can Help Sustain Value Creation for the Long Term, *McKinsey on Finance* (July 22, 2021).

3. Jocko Willink and Leif Babin, *Extreme Ownership: How U.S. Navy SEALs Lead and Win* (St. Martin's Press, 2015).

4. Sang M. Lee and Silvana Trimi, "Innovation for Creating a Smart Future," *Journal of Innovation & Knowledge* (2018).

5. Bob Chapman and Raj Sisodia, *Everybody Matters: The Extraordinary Power of Caring for Your People Like Family* (Gildan Media, 2015).

6. Dr. Alise Cortez, *The Great Revitalization: How Activating Meaning and Purpose Can Radically Enliven Your Business* (Practical Inspiration Publishing, 2023).

7. Peter Salovey and John D. Mayer, "Emotional Intelligence," *Imagination, Cognition and Personality* (1990).

8. Daniel Goleman, *Emotional Intelligence: Why It Can Matter More Than IQ* (Bantam Books, 1995).

9. IRC, *Leadership Development Program Impact Evaluation: Internal Impact Report Summary*, internal report (IRC, New York, 2022).

10. ALNAP, *The State of the Humanitarian System, 2022 Edition* (London: ALNAP/ODI, 2022).

11. Heather Boushey and Sarah Jane Glynn, "There Are Significant Business Costs to Replacing Employees," *Center for American Progress* (November 16, 2012).

12. IRC, *Strategy100: Year Three Progress Report* (New York: International Rescue Committee, 2023).

Chapter 11

Feedback & Learning

Harvesting Insights

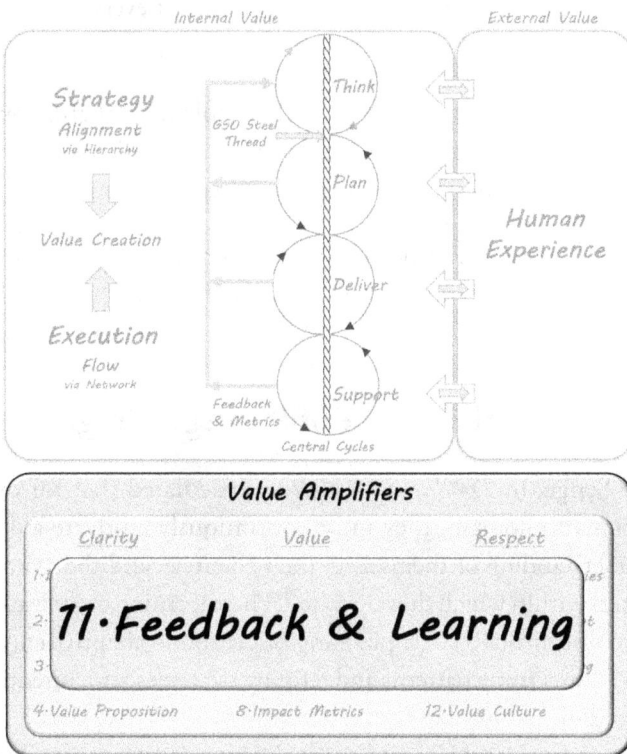

Markers of Value Excellence

E nterprises genuinely grounded in value exhibit four defining characteristics that distinguish their performance and culture. They:

- Continuously refine the flow and composition of their value streams, accelerating the delivery of outcomes that matter most to their stakeholders.

- Embed value-centric thinking throughout the organization, investing in comprehensive workforce education and modeling principled leadership at every managerial level.

- Promote environments that enable meaningful contribution—nurturing collaboration, open dialogue, and a culture of mutual respect and shared accountability.

- Maintain a dedication to discovery, refinement, and the deliberate pursuit of purposeful progress.

Learning as the Engine of Strategic Progress

Peter Senge, in *The Fifth Discipline*, articulated that for organizations to flourish, they must continuously cultivate a deeper understanding of themselves, their clientele, and the dynamic markets within which they operate.[1] These learning organizations evolve not through static planning but through adaptive engagement—discerning patterns and refining strategies with intentional precision.

Henry Ford is widely credited with observing that the only real mistake is the one from which we learn nothing[2]—a sentiment echoed by Jack Welch, who argued that an organization's ability to learn and translate that learning into action rapidly represents its utmost competitive advantage.[3] If the wisdom of these widely cited voices is heeded, it becomes evident that institutional progress hinges on the capacity to harness knowledge as a strategic asset. Pragmatic methods for structured experimentation—rooted in hypothesis generation, outcome measurement, and repeated refinement—have been thoroughly chronicled by contemporary thinkers, most notably Eric Ries in *The Lean Start-up*.[4] Such approaches render speculation unnecessary; the foundation for iterative, knowledge-driven transformation already exists.

However, to leverage these methods effectively, leaders must reframe their understanding of failure—not as a deficiency, but as a necessary antecedent to insight. When experimental efforts are anchored in thoughtfully articulated GSOs, a disproven hypothesis ceases to be a setback. Rather, it becomes a valuable input in the iterative progression toward more robust, goal-aligned strategies.

Foundations of Value Thinking

Enduring value transformation demands a profound reorientation of thought—a departure from conventional mindsets to more sophisticated interpretive models. Within today's complex economic landscape, a range of intellectual frameworks—including critical reasoning, fiscal logic, lean thinking, and systems analysis—offer essential lenses through which value-centric behaviors can be cultivated. While this text does not examine these practices exhaustively, the following abstract provides a conceptual baseline. Executives and organizational stewards are encouraged to cultivate proficiency in at least one of these frameworks, tailored to the specific exigencies of their environment.

Principles of Critical Inquiry

Critical thinking functions as an intellectual discipline grounded in rigorous inquiry and lucid judgment. It enables individuals to engage with problems through structured analysis, thereby enhancing the integrity of decision-making. Core attributes consistently include disciplined cognition, clarity of argument, and sound evaluative capacity—capabilities indispensable for dissecting causal feedback loops and refining organizational learning mechanisms. Within a value-centered enterprise, critical inquiry extends beyond problem-solving—it challenges the assumptions embedded in strategy, scrutinizes the validity of performance data, and surfaces the cognitive biases that distort organizational judgment. Cultivating this discipline across managerial cohorts produces a workforce that interrogates rather than accepts, distinguishes evidence from assertion, and resists the institutional inertia that so frequently masquerades as conventional wisdom. When applied consistently, critical thinking transforms reactive organizations into reflective ones—capable of learning not only from outcomes but from the reasoning that produced them.

Embedded Fiscal Logic

Economic acumen lies at the heart of effective value realization. Within any decision framework, strategic alternatives invariably produce fiscal consequences—beneficial, detrimental, or neutral. The cornerstone of economically responsible behavior lives in the capacity of individuals throughout the enterprise to make financially prudent choices, cultivated through deliberate education and adherence to clearly articulated economic standards embedded within the organization's value architecture. Fiscal logic, as applied within Valorys, extends well beyond accounting literacy—it encompasses an understanding of how capital flows through value streams, how investment decisions compound over time, and how the cost of inaction rivals the cost of misallocated spend. Practitioners fluent in this discipline evaluate proposals not merely for their operational appeal but for their demonstrable return relative to declared GSO outcomes. Embedding this orientation broadly across the enterprise transforms fiscal stewardship from a CFO function into a distributed organizational competency.

Lean Principles and Practices

Popularized by James Womack and Daniel Jones in *Lean Thinking*, this approach draws directly from the foundational tenets of the Toyota Production System. At its core are five principles: value, value streams, flow, pull, and perfection.[5] Subsequent adaptations have expanded the model's emphasis to include not only operational efficiency but also the empowerment of frontline contributors and the advancement of organizational cultures that sustain long-term excellence. Within Valorys, lean principles are not applied as a discrete improvement methodology but as an embedded operating orientation—one that continuously investigates whether each activity genuinely advances stakeholder value or merely sustains organizational habit. By eliminating non-value-added work, compressing cycle times, and anchoring flow to actual demand, lean-informed enterprises reduce waste not as an end in itself but as a direct consequence of pursuing purposeful, outcome-aligned execution. This discipline proves especially potent within delivery arcs, where the clarity of lean logic accelerates throughput and sharpens the organization's capacity to deliver on its strategic commitments.

Holistic Systems Insight

Emerging from the discipline of system dynamics in the mid-20th century, systems thinking presents a holistic framework for comprehending the intricate web of interdependencies that define organizational ecosystems. As the Institute for Systemic Leadership describes it, the approach centers on understanding a system by examining the linkages and interactions between its component parts as a unified whole.[6] Mastery of this discipline enables leaders to uncover both overt and latent interdependencies, positioning their enterprises to pursue comprehensive value creation while enhancing the coherence and resilience of internal processes. Within Valorys, systems thinking provides the conceptual architecture through which GSOs, value streams, and feedback cycles are understood not as discrete mechanisms but as interdependent elements of a living organizational system. Leaders who internalize this perspective resist the impulse to treat symptoms in isolation—recognizing instead that interventions in one part of the enterprise invariably produce effects elsewhere. This awareness is foundational to sustainable transformation, enabling organizations to design for coherence rather than optimize for local efficiency at the expense of enterprise-wide performance.

Cycles That Drive Value

A central insight of systems thinking is that closed-loop structures—those in which outputs are continuously fed back into the system as inputs—constitute the bedrock of adaptive, high-performing organizations. Such mechanisms thrive only when information circulates through clearly defined channels of meaning. In this context, the GSO steel thread acts as a conduit across the four interlocking central cycles, enabling transparent communication of value-centric objectives and achievements.

Feedback originating from any stratum of the enterprise can be directly mapped to higher-order GSOs, expressed in a common evaluative vernacular. This uniformity eliminates the need for interpretive guesswork when gauging efficacy. When a course of action fails to produce intended value, the information it generates holds intrinsic worth—guiding the recalibration of methods, refinement of outcomes, or, where necessary, the redefinition of overarching goals.

High-functioning feedback systems are predicated on short-cycle rhythms and the regular reassessment of business impacts. Value streams, by design, support rapid iteration and work completion within compressed timeframes, thereby accelerating organizational learning and value generation. In contrast, elongated operational cycles delay insight, often leading to squandered capital, forfeited opportunities, and misallocated resources. A further advantage of rapid-cycle execution lies in its facilitation of incremental enhancement: small, frequent corrections are inherently more sustainable and less disruptive than sweeping reformations.

Refining Enterprise Flow

Entities that adopt value-centric principles as the foundation for workflow design position themselves to achieve superior adaptability, competency, and economic performance. Once the essential architecture—comprising delivery arcs and asset warehouses—is firmly established, the work of optimization begins. Senior leaders, in concert with operational managers, systematically apply core value constructs to refine flow, eliminate impediments, and synchronize execution with strategic priorities.

This refinement is not passive. It demands the active engagement of management in identifying pressure points—val-

ue streams suffering from latency, inefficiencies, or underperformance—and in orchestrating remedial measures. Effective
optimization rests equally on structural coherence and the
timely provisioning of knowledge, ensuring all actors possess
the insight necessary to execute with purpose and precision.

Workforce Knowledge as Leverage

It is unrealistic to expect widespread value contribution in
the absence of rigorous knowledge transfer. Leaders and personnel alike must be immersed in role-specific training that
grounds them in the principles, language, and expectations
of a value-oriented enterprise. This is not a peripheral en-
deavor but a strategic imperative: a fully educated workforce
becomes a reservoir of institutional strength—amplifying creativity, accelerating problem-solving, and elevating individual
and collective performance.

What measurable gains can be expected from a single day
of high-quality, value-focused instruction for every employee
and associate? Empirical observation suggests the benefits are
considerable. While experiential learning yields practical insight, it is the infusion of underlying concepts that deepens
comprehension, enriches contextual understanding, and cultivates enduring expertise.

***

It's late August in Des Moines. The market's been closed
for two hours, but Russ hasn't left his office. When I find him,
he's at the window, not quite staring, not quite thinking. On
his desk sits a single printout—alone on the desk the way bad
news usually is.

"I just got off a call with Rick," he says when I walk in. No greeting. No warm-up.

Rick is the CFO.

"He didn't yell. That's how I knew it was bad."

He turns from the window. "Forty-two million." A beat. "The worst part isn't the loss. It's that three of my desk analysts saw it coming. They had the data. They flagged it internally. And it died somewhere between their screens and a conversation that never happened."

He moves to the desk and slides the paper over to me. Basis shift on September contracts. The warning signs are obvious in retrospect—they always are.

"Why didn't it escalate?" I ask.

He leans back. "Because nobody wanted to be the person who called a false alarm. We've rewarded certainty here. You don't bring a problem to this floor unless you already have the answer. So they waited. And by then it was too late."

That's the mechanism. Not a systems failure. Not bad models. A culture that made speaking up feel more dangerous than staying quiet.

"Rick wants a post-mortem," Russ says. "He used the phrase 'accountability structure.' The CEO wants 'root cause.' Nobody's asking the right question."

"Which is?"

"Why does this keep happening?" He looks again at the printout. "This isn't the first time information sat in the system and went nowhere. It's the first time it cost us forty-two million in one hit. But when these things happened before, we'd call it 'suboptimal forecasting' and move on."

There it is.

"So what do you do with that?" I ask.

He doesn't answer right away. When he does, the resolve I half-expected isn't there. What's there is something closer to exhaustion. "I don't know. I've been running this floor for nine years. I built it for speed and execution."

He pauses. "But maybe I built it wrong, because what we've just experienced is that speed without feedback is just faster ignorance. And it really hurts to say that out loud."

Not a breakthrough—an admission. And admissions, in organizations like this one, are the rarest currency there is.

We talked for another hour about what a functioning feedback loop might look like on a trading floor—post-mortems without blame, analysts with standing to escalate incomplete signals, a CFO brought in not to judge but to understand the gap between what the models show and what the people actually know. None of it is simple. Some of it won't survive the culture he's built.

When I left, Russ was still at his desk with the printout.

He hadn't solved anything yet. But he'd stopped pretending the problem was the models.

That's where it starts—not with the system, but with someone finally willing to say what they've known for a long time. The $42 million didn't create the problem. It just made it too expensive to keep ignoring.

***

Feedback & Learning Best Practices

1: *Establish a disciplined communication cadence to reinforce learning.* The Valorys cadence promotes structured behavior, iterative experimentation, and enterprise-wide learning. Without validated strategic hypotheses, organizations lose opportunities for timely insight and informed adjustment. When feedback is framed in the language of goal-strategy-outcomes (GSOs), it flows naturally through the central cycles, requiring minimal interpretation and enabling coherent, data-driven decision-making across all levels.

2: *Integrate diverse cognitive frameworks to deepen orga-nizational understanding.* Within Valorys, multiple perspec-tives—operational, human, and cultural—combine to form a multidimensional view of the enterprise. Sustaining psychological transformation demands that every member, regardless of role or rank, be educated in the principles and methods of value thinking, ensuring alignment of mindset and behavior.

3: *Pursue continuous improvement within value streams.* Val-ue-based organizations employ a wide range of techniques to uncover and exploit opportunities for operational advancement. Incremental refinements within value streams, compounded over time, generate lasting gains in efficiency, coherence, and strategic performance.

***

Organization Highlight: Adobe

Adobe continues to distinguish itself as a learning orga-nization by institutionalizing listening, reflection, and re-sponsiveness as foundational elements of its strategic iden-tity. Far from treating learning as an episodic exercise or a discrete function, Adobe has embedded continuous devel-opment into the daily rhythms of its operations—reinforcing a culture where curiosity, feedback, and adaptability are not just encouraged but expected.

At the heart of Adobe's differentiation is its deliberate cultivation of input-rich environments. Employees are empowered with tools and structured opportunities to solicit and act upon feedback from both peers and supervisors. This two-way communication model engenders trust, accelerates individual growth, and ensures that evolving employee needs are met with tailored support. Adobe's commitment to nurturing self-directed learning journeys not only elevates workforce capability, but also enhances engagement and retention—key drivers of organizational versatility and long-term success.

What makes Adobe's feedback culture particularly effective is not just its frequency, but its framing. Feedback is treated less as an appraisal and more as an impetus for iteration—mirroring the company's design ethos. Managers are trained not merely to assess, but to coach. Employees are encouraged to view feedback as a means of creative refinement rather than corrective discipline. These subtle cultural distinctions have powerful behavioral implications: they promote psychological safety, cultivate learning dexterity, and encourage experimental problem-solving—core traits of a resilient workforce.

Programs such as Adobe Kickbox exemplify the company's commitment to listening and acting on the intrinsic motivations of its personnel. By equipping employees with tangible tools, mentorship pathways, and executive visibility, Kickbox broadens access to innovation and removes hierarchical barriers to creative contribution. Since 2013, the program has generated over 1,200 ideas globally and has since been open-sourced for other firms to adopt.[7]

The organization also leverages technology to scale its assessment infrastructure. Adobe's Check-In system, which replaced annual performance reviews, enables real-time, informal feedback loops tailored to individual development goals. This shift away from rigid appraisal frameworks aligns production discussions with the dynamic pace of modern activity and reflects Adobe's broader rejection of bureaucratic orthodoxy in favor of adaptive systems. As a result, feedback becomes not an interruption to work, but an integral part of it.

Moreover, Adobe's strategic investment in managerial development—anchored in emotional intelligence, change leadership, and inclusive decision-making—ensures that managers are not just directing but actively listening and facilitating the growth of those they lead. This has produced measurable results: Adobe's voluntary attrition rate in fiscal 2023 stood at 7.4%, substantially below the U.S. technology industry average of 13.2%, highlighting the organizational benefits of its developmental investments.[8]

This reinforces a compounding dynamic: listening informs learning, learning propels innovation, and innovation sustains competitive distinction. In this way, Adobe exemplifies how a learning organization thrives by transforming employee voice into organizational evolution.

---

1. Peter Senge, *The Fifth Discipline: Art and Practice of the Learning Organization* (Doubleday, 1990).

2. The attribution of this sentiment to Henry Ford is widespread but unverified. No reliable primary source—letter, speech, or publication—has been identified connecting the precise formulation to Ford directly. It circulates extensively in management literature as a Ford aphorism but is more accurately described as a principle consistent with his documented philosophy of iterative improvement rather than a confirmed quotation.

3. The quote's most traceable primary source is the General Electric Annual Report, 1996, in which Welch articulated the fuller version: "Our behavior is driven by a fundamental core belief: the desire and the ability of an organization to continuously learn from any source, anywhere, and to rapidly convert this learning into action, is its ultimate competitive advantage." The condensed form cited here is drawn from Janet Lowe, *Jack Welch Speaks: Wit and Wisdom from the World's Greatest Business Leader* (Hoboken, NJ: John Wiley & Sons, 2007).

4. Eric Ries, *The Lean Start-up: How Today's Entrepreneurs Use Continuous Innovation to Create Radically Successful Businesses* (Crown Business, 2011).

5. James Womack and Daniel Jones, *Lean Thinking: Banish Waste and Create Wealth in Your Corporation* (Simon & Schuster, 1996).

6. William Tate, *The Search for Leadership: An Organisational Perspective* (Triarchy Press, 2009).

7. Adobe Inc., "Unlocking Innovation from Within: The Story of Adobe's Kickbox," *Adobe Blog* (May 25, 2021).

8. Adobe Inc., *2023 Corporate Social Responsibility Report* (San Jose: Adobe Inc., 2023).

Value Culture

Experiencing Greatness

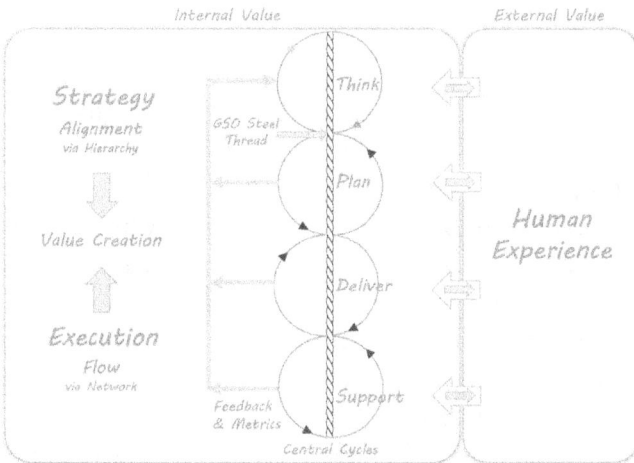

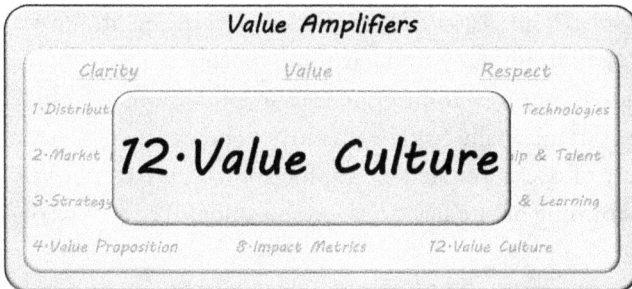

Purpose as Operating Logic

E nduringly effective enterprises distinguish themselves by articulating their organizational purpose with precision and
depth—defining not only a coherent reason for being but also a
refined understanding of the constituencies they intend to serve.
Such clarity is not ornamental; it is structural. It establishes the
cognitive framework through which strategy is crafted, priorities
are synchronized, and results are meaningfully interpreted. Without such definition, organizations risk descending into directional ambiguity, cultural fragmentation, and declining stakeholder
confidence.[1]

An organization's core purpose must function as more than
an aspirational statement. It should serve as a guiding constant—a durable premise against which strategic planning, operational choices, and behavioral expectations are continuously tested. When purpose is authentically embedded within the enterprise, it lends coherence to complexity and informs the deliberate
allocation of financial, human, and intellectual resources.

This integration is neither abstract nor symbolic. It animates
the design of disciplined value-generation systems that transform high-minded ideals into observable and replicable outcomes.
Organizations coherently aligned around purpose consistently
outperform in areas such as workforce engagement, innovation
throughput, and long-term customer fidelity.[2]

In such settings, commitment to mission is not externally imposed but internally cultivated. Purpose becomes the silent architecture of decision-making, shaping conduct across all levels and
transforming habitual actions into meaningful contributions.

Anchoring Intent to Impact

Crucially, purpose does not exist in tension with financial discipline. In commercial enterprises, the imperative of economic return remains central. Strategic efforts that fail to produce verifiable value cannot be rationalized through narrative alone—they must be reexamined, recalibrated, or responsibly concluded. A well-articulated purpose becomes an evaluative lens—ensuring that aspiration remains anchored to execution and that organizational aims reflect both principled intent and economic viability.

A culture grounded in purpose does not sacrifice discipline for inspiration. It cultivates both. In such settings, financial targets and cultural commitments are not in opposition; they are interdependent. The organization becomes not merely a system for executing tasks, but a cohesive instrument for generating meaningful, accountable progress. Value, in this sense, is not academic—it is evidenced through the consistent convergence of strategic clarity, cultural integrity, and economic return.

Thus, the most consequential organizations are those that embed purpose at the core of their operational architecture—those that allow it to shape identity, inform governance, and direct the logic of execution.[3] In doing so, they align passion with execution—ensuring that every decision reinforces both the organization's purpose and its power to deliver sustained, measurable impact.

Advancing Intrinsic Talent

The workforce represents the cornerstone of any value-focused enterprise—its most indispensable asset and the primary engine through which strategic imperatives are realized. In *Drive*, Daniel Pink identifies three innate motivators that elevate the performance of contemporary professionals: autonomy, mastery, and purpose.[4] These dimensions form the scaffolding upon which the understanding and stewardship of today's enabled workforce is constructed.

Contrary to legacy assumptions that posit a direct correlation between financial incentives and elevated performance, modern behavioral science suggests that meaningful engagement arises from purposeful contribution rather than extrinsic reward. While the psychological underpinnings of human motivation extend beyond the scope of this discussion, acknowledging the authentic drivers of worker fulfillment is essential to stimulating a culture oriented toward durable value creation.

One hallmark of mature, value-driven organizations is the deliberate cultivation of multidisciplinary competence. Cross-training initiatives equip personnel to navigate dynamic customer expectations and evolving market conditions with greater fluidity. This adaptability is further reinforced by recruitment strategies that emphasize cultural alignment, a collaborative disposition, and a proven capacity for continual learning.

While technical acumen remains a critical hiring criterion, the most effective organizations also prioritize a candidate's potential to rise above disciplinary silos. In such environments, individuals are encouraged to expand their repertoire beyond specialized functions—developing related or complementary skills that enhance overall team versatility. These multi-skilled professionals are often referred to as *generalizing specialists* or *specializing generalists*, reflecting their ability to both contribute deep expertise and flex across adjacent domains.[5] Through such deliberate workforce development, organizations not only fortify operational resilience but also affirm the intrinsic worth of their employees—elevating both morale and strategic capacity.

Transforming Error into Insight

Organizations truly committed to value creation recognize that errors are not anomalies to be eliminated, but integral elements of the human learning process. Mistakes, while often accompanied by unproductive emotional responses such as shame, fear, or guilt, possess latent instructional value. When properly contextualized, each failure presents an opportunity for reflection, insight, and organizational refinement.

The imperative lies in diagnosing the underlying factors with analytical precision—be they miscommunication, erroneous data, flawed premises, insufficient training, or lapses in supervisory guidance. Addressing these root causes transforms individual errors into institutional improvements, enhancing operational resilience and strategic coherence. It is not the presence of failures that imperils performance, but the tolerance of repeated, unexamined missteps that undermines credibility and effectiveness.

It falls to senior and middle management to cultivate environments in which high-performing employees can thrive—settings marked by communication openness, intellectual rigor, and constructive accountability. Empirical literature consistently affirms the centrality of workplace culture and environmental conditions—ranking them second only to human capital itself in determining sustained organizational performance.

Empowerment, mutual responsibility, operational transparency, and cross-functional collaboration comprise the foundational architecture of value-centric enterprises. Within such cultures, the recontextualization of failure becomes not only permissible but imperative, fueling the ongoing advancement of both individuals and the institution.

Visibility That Builds Trust

Furthering a culture of trust and transparency demands sustained visibility into the continuous flow of value creation across the enterprise. One particularly effective technique involves the use of *information radiators*—prominently positioned visual displays that communicate real-time progress within value streams and functional domains.[6] In physical work settings, these may take the form of wall-mounted dashboards or mobile whiteboards. For virtual environments, their manifestations are varied and depend entirely on the circumstances. In either case, up-to-date real-time displays serve as immediate reference points for operational awareness.

By externalizing key metrics and process states, information radiators provide managers with a tangible means of monitoring activity, deepening their contextual understanding of specific functions. This practice aligns with the leadership principle of direct observation—a posture that calls upon senior executives to engage firsthand with the physical and cognitive spaces where value is generated.[7] Such personal observation cultivates greater empathy, sharper insight, and more effective stewardship.

Integral to this ecosystem are confidence, clarity in communication, and operational visibility—three prerequisites for genuine collaboration in any value-centered enterprise. When disagreements emerge, leaders employ principled conflict resolution strategies that reinforce mutual respect and encourage deliberation, rather than division. Paradoxically, well-managed discord strengthens organizational health by surfacing divergent perspectives that, when reconciled, lead to superior outcomes.

For adaptive leaders committed to continuous advancement, fluency in the mechanics of value flow is indispensable. Key constructs such as synchronized workflow, queue length optimization, and batch size modulation exert significant influence on organizational output. Further refinement may be achieved by investigating related dynamics—cadence stability, transport latency, handoff efficiency, capacity bottlenecks, inventory volatility, multiplexed workloads, and systemic throughput constraints. Though many of these concepts originate in industrial engineering, they possess universal applicability across sectors, manifesting in diverse and nuanced ways throughout both service and knowledge-based organizations.

Culture as Strategic Power

Peter Drucker famously observed that "culture eats strategy for breakfast"—a dictum that remains profoundly relevant in any discussion of sustaining organizational transformation.[8] Recasting the cultural fabric of an enterprise demands unwavering commitment and the fortitude to persist through inevitable resistance. It is not the proclamations of leadership, but their consistent behavior that reveals the true character of a value-centered organization. Senior leaders model this ethos through lived example, maintaining a comprehensive view of how value cultures nurture resilience, creativity, business efficiency, and long-term profitability.

Adaptive leaders who embrace this cultural evolution seek not only operational excellence but institutional learning. They exhibit a genuine desire to cultivate adaptive organizations—those capable of reflection, knowledge integration, and strategic refinement. These leaders equip and entrust a competent workforce with the authority to make decisions aligned with organizational purpose, elevating both performance and morale. In such settings, workers are not merely managed—they are developed, empowered, and entrusted with the stewardship of value.

Enterprise advancement is ultimately a function of deliberate investment: in product innovation, market expansion, mergers and acquisitions, and enhanced operational infrastructure. These capital allocations originate from strategic goals, ensuring that each expenditure aligns with intent and yields quantifiable value. Business unit portfolios are curators of financial resources, balancing growth and transformative imperatives with foundational maintenance. Allocation decisions are guided by their demonstrable alignment with strategic intent.

Within this architecture, delivery arcs are structured as autonomous profit centers, accountable for both the generation and justification of financial returns. Supporting business functions and asset warehouses receive budgets proportionate to their contribution to these value outcomes—achieved through chargebacks, resource-based funding models, or analogous mechanisms. In this paradigm, the prevalence of traditional cost centers diminishes markedly; nearly every unit is evaluated through the lens of value creation. Such economic clarity ensures that fiscal conservancy is integrated with strategic intent, reinforcing the foundational principle that each organizational function must contribute meaningfully to the firm's collective success.

Evaluating Value Beyond Numbers

For-profit, value-oriented enterprises anchor the majority of their decisions in rigorous economic reasoning. But not all variables that influence strategic outcomes can be neatly quantified or monetized. Intangible assets—such as social goodwill, reputational capital, or stakeholder trust—often resist precise financial valuation. In such cases, it becomes essential to adopt a framework of relative evaluation, wherein tradeoffs are assessed not by strict ROI calculus, but by their broader alignment with long-term value creation.

During short-, medium-, and long-range planning cycles, organizations systematically evaluate their GSOs using structured value analyses. This comparative approach enables leadership to craft strategic forecasts and developmental roadmaps that reflect both tangible financial returns and the more nuanced dimensions of institutional purpose.

Instilling a value-centric mindset across the enterprise remains one of the most formidable challenges in organizational transformation. The gravitational pull of entrenched corporate culture often mirrors the inertia of a massive vessel—redirecting it demands extraordinary effort, intention, and sustained leadership. Cultural change of this magnitude cannot be rushed; it requires both intellectual conviction and practical resolve.

One effective point of entry involves convening value-focused workshops for board members and senior executives in settings deliberately removed from daily operations. These sessions help dislodge entrenched thinking and introduce new conceptual frameworks in an environment conducive to reflection and recalibration. Such engagements are ideally followed by facilitated planning events that emphasize transformative strategies—those capable of reshaping the organization's identity, structure, and long-term trajectory. Through these immersive experiences, enterprises begin the disciplined journey toward becoming fully value-aligned institutions.

Rhythms That Accelerate Value

Sustained acceleration in value delivery is most effectively achieved by compressing lead times to their logical minimums. Organizations structured around value streams rely on intentional, rhythmic cycles to orchestrate the flow of development and deployment. However, to preserve the inherent benefits of this model, progression must be aligned with disciplined simplicity. Excessive procedural complexity or entangled interdependencies can erode the efficiency and responsiveness that value stream design inherently fosters.

Regular, face-to-face planning forums—be they physical or virtual—serve as vital instruments for enhancing communication, alignment, and cross-functional cohesion, both within and across value streams. These sessions not only facilitate shared understanding and synchronized execution but also enable enterprises to capitalize on evolving market dynamics, thereby securing early competitive positioning. Using iterative timeboxes to scope and achieve incremental advancements ensures offerings are delivered on reliable timetables, while preserving leadership engagement in outcome realization.

When pivotal delivery milestones are coordinated across the enterprise, they generate coherence—amplifying planning accuracy, feedback frequency, and adaptive learning. This synchronization contributes directly to the production of solutions that are not only of higher quality, but also exhibit greater alignment with the nuanced needs of end users.

Within this architecture, unresolved backlog elements—be they obsolete feature designs, misaligned marketing assets, outdated customer requirements, or dormant software code—represent a form of organizational waste. The phenomenon of multiplexing, wherein individuals are compelled to divide their attention across concurrent tasks, undermines flow continuity. It produces latency, elevates wastefulness, and often degrades output quality.

Paradoxically, one of the most efficient strategies for preserving resource integrity involves deferring critical decisions until the *last responsible moment*. This disciplined delay—far from being indecisive—ensures that actions are taken considering the most accurate and current data, thereby minimizing rework and optimizing the use of organizational capacity.[9]

***

An insightful communication from my telecommunications client to their C-suite follows:

To: Executive Leadership Team
From: Renée M., Head of Human Resources
Subject: Practical Steps for Creating Value
Date: March 27, 20xx

Hello Team,

A few weeks ago, you asked me to help make "value" the foundation of our culture. I took that request seriously and met with a consultant—recommended by the CEO—who has years of experience helping organizations turn value into something real and workable. After talking with him, it became clear to me that this isn't just an HR project. It needs to be a company-wide effort.

We talk about "value" often—in investor updates, leadership meetings, and internal messages. But if we're honest, we haven't always known how to turn that word into something concrete in our day-to-day operations. It's become a phrase we use, but it hasn't been clear what it actually means in practice.

When I brought this up, the consultant explained it in a way that made sense. He said that value is created when our resources—people, money, time, and leadership judgment—come together to produce results that make us more relevant in the market and more helpful to our customers and stakeholders. In other words, value isn't the outcome at the end of a project. It's the principle that should shape everything we do as leaders.

This reframed things for me. Below are the main takeaways and the steps I believe we should focus on next:

1. Value Creation Happens Across the Entire Company

We usually think about value in terms of financial results—like profit margins, revenue growth, or efficiency. But these numbers are the result of something deeper. Real value starts with our people: field techs, engineers, sales teams, customer support, marketing, and everyone else.

When I asked myself who creates value in a telecom company like ours, I first thought of engineering or customer service. But I was missing the bigger picture. Value is created everywhere—from the moment a product is planned, to the installation, to troubleshooting, to ongoing customer support.

When these teams don't work together, value breaks down. We see delays, miscommunication, and wasted effort. Culture, in this sense, is the connection point. It's what keeps all these pieces working toward the same goal.

2. Feedback Is a Source of Real Intelligence

We've all seen processes that were meant to make life easier end up making things harder. For example, our dispatch optimization system recently slowed down one of our field techs, forcing him to override it just to get through his day. That's not just a technical issue—it harms morale.

The answer isn't to throw the system away but to make sure the people doing the work can help shape how our tools evolve. We need to build systems with our teams, not simply hand them systems created for them.

3. Culture Only Matters If It Shows Up in Daily Work

We often reference concepts like autonomy, mastery, and purpose in leadership discussions. They sound great, but if they don't show up in how we run performance reviews, resolve problems, or shape job roles, then they're just talk.

- If contact center reps don't feel safe sharing ideas, we haven't created autonomy.

- If our installation teams don't get updated training, we're not supporting mastery.

- If employees can't see how their work helps customers, we've missed the mark on purpose.

4. Cross-Training Should Build Careers, Not Just Fill Gaps

Our cross-training programs for broadband and wireless support have gone well, but we need to be clear about the real goal. This shouldn't just be about covering staffing shortages. When cross-training is framed as a chance to build skills and advance, people feel invested in—and they show up differently. This strengthens the organization and strengthens our teams.

5. Leadership Sets the Emotional Tone

Many employees still hesitate to raise concerns because they worry it will reflect badly on them. The shift starts with leadership. When executives, VPs, and directors are open about mistakes and learning moments, it sends a powerful message: feedback and growth matter more than looking perfect. This is the only way to build a culture where problems are surfaced early instead of hidden until they become serious.

6. We Need a Clear, Shared Language About Customer Value

During the fiber pilot, one customer rated us poorly because the team arrived ahead of schedule. We saw it as being efficient; the customer saw it as disruptive.

This mismatch shows why we need a consistent way to talk about value—one that reflects what customers actually care about. Metrics alone won't fix this issue. We have to talk with customers directly and let their priorities shape how we measure success.

7. Mistakes Should Lead to Learning, Not Blame

When a technician misses a step, it might not be carelessness. It could be unclear directions, outdated training, or tools that don't work well. In a value-centered culture, mistakes help us figure out what needs to improve. With automation and AI becoming more common in our workflows, this mindset is more important than ever.

8. Value Comes From Iteration, Not Perfection

Value doesn't appear because we planned everything perfectly at the start. It grows when teams are encouraged to try things, learn from them, adjust, and keep going. When people know they're trusted to adapt, they tend to innovate instead of just follow instructions.

I recommend the following next steps:

1. Build Real-Time Feedback Loops

Create simple ways for employees to share what's helping or hurting value creation—starting with issues we already know about like the dispatch system and early arrival concerns. Focus on fast learning instead of complicated reporting.

2. Try Out a Stakeholder-Informed Decision Process

For two or three upcoming strategic decisions, include direct input from customers, employees, and community partners. Let's see how expanding the decision base changes our outcomes and helps us stay relevant.

3. Strengthen Leadership Skills Around Value Creation

Invest in coaching and development programs that help leaders better recognize and support value creation—through judgment, collaboration, and mentoring, not just new frameworks.

Thank you for your continued commitment to building a healthier, more supportive culture. Making value a real part of how we work isn't a box-checking exercise—it's a shift in how we behave every day. If we follow through on these steps, we'll create a workplace where people see themselves as real contributors to our mission and our future.

With appreciation,
Renée

***

Building Value Governance

To institutionalize a culture genuinely anchored in value creation, organizations must move beyond aspirational language and build the structural conditions that make continuous learning, capability development, and principled leadership sustainable over time.

Central to this effort is what I call the Value Realization Office—the VRO. This is not a project management office or a performance reporting function. It is a dedicated enterprise-level governing body responsible for guiding and sustaining the organization's transformation toward value-centricity. Through executive sponsorship and strategic integration, the VRO provides the architectural backbone the transformation requires: structural oversight, operational cohesion, pedagogical infrastructure, and governance frameworks that operate across the full enterprise.

The VRO's most important characteristic is this: it functions not merely as a programmatic operation, but as a cultural engine. Its mandate is to ensure that value realization is embedded in the daily practice of every division, team, and individual—not as a campaign, but as a permanent operating norm. Organizations that establish the VRO with genuine executive commitment and cross-functional authority are the ones that sustain transformation beyond the initial momentum of launch.

Customer-Centric Value Architecture

What separates institutions that achieve enduring, authentic, value-based excellence from those that merely espouse it? In truly value-driven enterprises, there is an unambiguous recognition that consumer value is ultimately defined by those who receive it—the end users. Their opinions, experiences, and outcomes are the final arbiters of organizational relevance and success.[10]

One persistent pattern I have observed across sectors is the misalignment between internal assumptions about value and the perceptions of customers. This disconnect, if left unaddressed, undermines competitive advantage and impedes growth. To bridge this divide, organizations develop refined techniques to capture and interpret the authentic voice of their constituents—processes capable of discerning articulated needs as well as latent aspirations.

Such insights are most effectively realized through carefully constructed value proposition architectures, which serve as both strategic compasses and design blueprints. The disciplined release of minimum viable products not only sustains customer engagement but also promotes co-creative relationships in which solutions are developed in partnership with users, not simply for them. This participatory model shortens feedback loops, accelerates time to market, improves alignment with demand, and conserves institutional resources.

From Silos to Systemic Coherence

In this light, organizations come to see themselves as integrated systems, where individual actions yield cascading effects throughout the whole. Fragmented or siloed optimization often produces counterproductive outcomes when misaligned with broader organizational goals. As W. Edwards Deming observed, a system will not manage itself—left unguided, its components tend toward self-interested, compartmentalized behavior that ultimately destroys the coherence of the whole.[11]

Misaligned incentives and behaviors that prioritize local optimization over enterprise-wide effectiveness undermine systemic coherence. Valorys is positioned as the means by which firms can counteract fragmentation and misalignment by fostering the very entrepreneurial behavior that helps redirect focus from siloed interests to collective progress. Yet entrepreneurship alone is insufficient; it must be balanced with discipline. The VRO is the institution charged with this responsibility, offering the frameworks, behavioral expectations, and operational standards required to support structured creativity within a unified strategic vision.

Expanding the Value Horizon

The adoption of value-centered approaches yields profound effects that reverberate far beyond the immediate boundaries of any single enterprise. These approaches, when earnestly embraced, generate societal benefit through an array of interrelated mechanisms—economic, social, and relational. Recognizing the expansive scope of such influence is essential. In truly value-driven organizations, profitability is not pursued as an end in itself, but emerges as a consequence of delivering excellence to those whom the organization is designed to serve.

Jack Ma, founder of Alibaba, articulated this ethos with striking clarity in his prioritization hierarchy: "customers first, employees second, and shareholders third."[12] This formulation exemplifies the most mature expression of value-driven thinking—placing consumer experience and benefits at the heart of strategic purpose.

The term "customers," in this context, is employed broadly to encompass not only end users but also intermediaries, distributors, and strategic partners—any party essential to the orchestration and fulfillment of the enterprise's extended value streams. Their participation in the delivery dimension of the value network generates synergistic benefits that cascade throughout the organizational ecosystem. Likewise, extending these value streams to include suppliers and vendors enables holistic alignment across the broader value architecture.

Leaders entrusted with value orchestration bear a profound responsibility: to extend and harmonize both ends of the value stream continuum for the shared benefit of all constituencies. While corporate boards are, by design, fiduciaries of shareholder interests, it is increasingly apparent that not all shareholders are singularly focused on stock performance or quarterly dividends. A growing cohort of contemporary investors now views long-term profitability and social benefaction as jointly reinforcing, rather than mutually exclusive. Accordingly, executives must broaden their definition of responsibility to encompass both financial excellence and societal value.

A value-first mindset enhances leadership's sensitivity to opportunities for civic contribution that would remain invisible within a purely fiscal frame. This expanded awareness enables senior officials to identify and act upon initiatives that create enduring benefit not only for customers and employees but also for communities, regions, and the broader world. In doing so, they fulfill a higher standard of leadership—one grounded in the integration of economic success and social responsibility.

Scaling Through Team Architecture

The realization of enterprise goals, as defined by governing boards and executive leadership, depends on the disciplined execution of strategy by senior management. However, for value creation to permeate the organization, middle managers and operational personnel must be empowered with both the conceptual understanding and practical tools necessary to act as agents of productivity and innovation. It is through the deliberate cultivation of workforce intelligence and creativity that organizations attract exceptional talent and sustain high levels of engagement and performance.

Among the most effective structures for delivering superior outcomes at speed is the deployment of small, autonomous teams that are both self-organizing and self-managing.[13] These units operate with substantial local authority, enabling rapid responses to shifting conditions while remaining anchored to overarching strategic priorities.

When multiple teams are aligned with shared objectives, they are aggregated into *teams-of-teams*—meta-structures whose fractal logic extends across the enterprise. Such an architecture allows organizations to mobilize thousands of individuals toward shared objectives without sacrificing coordination or strategic coherence. Its inherent extensibility makes it applicable across diverse domains—including product development, service delivery, customer engagement, and supply chain operations.

This approach draws conceptual lineage from lean manufacturing's use of work cells—modular units of production designed for concentrated efficiency. Yet its application extends far beyond industrial contexts. Small, value-focused teams have been successfully embedded within traditionally hierarchical departments, such as sales, marketing, finance, legal, operations, and human resources—demonstrating the versatility and universality of this model.

Organizing Around Value

Within this evolved organizational archetype, virtual value streams assume primacy as the dominant organizing principle, while traditional business functions are repositioned as enablers rather than centers of authority. These value streams, both delivery arcs and asset warehouses, deliver coherent product and service outcomes and are structured to contain or maintain direct access to all requisite support functions. The number and complexity of these value streams correspond directly to the breadth and diversity of an organization's offerings.

By realigning operational architecture around value streams, enterprises not only enhance their delivery capacity but also elevate the strategic clarity and accountability of their internal constructs. In doing so, they transcend the constraints of fragmented management structures, unlocking a more integrated, responsive, and value-oriented organizational form. A key shift in this model is the reorientation of funding logic: rather than allocating capital to discrete projects or initiatives, assets are directed toward goals. This model enables more adaptive and outcome-driven deployment of capabilities, enhancing strategic responsiveness across the enterprise.

Within value-driven enterprises, the pursuit of economies of scale traditionally associated with functional silos remains both viable and strategically relevant. Some functions may be preserved through asset warehouses where specialized talent is loosely aligned with domain managers and flexibly deployed across business units to meet evolving needs. This dual affiliation ensures continuity of craft, coherence in standards, and functional coordination without sacrificing responsiveness to the timely demands of delivery arcs.

Maturing Flow Systems

The performance of fully resourced cross-functional value streams is tightly correlated with the fidelity of value-based operating principles that inform how work is sequenced, ready assets are allocated, and impact is measured. Achieving optimal throughput requires a multifaceted approach, one that integrates foundational concepts such as batch size calibration, queue length reduction, critical path mapping, and bottleneck elimination.

In parallel, organizations must address synchronization of effort, cycle time compression, minimization of handoffs, and optimization of information flow. Further dimensions include strategic alignment among teams, proactive dependency management, and the identification and removal of redundant work.

While many of these disciplines originate in manufacturing science, their analogs exist in every enterprise, manifesting under different terminologies across diverse domains.

To ignore these principles in non-industrial contexts is to overlook powerful levers of organizational efficiency. When carefully applied, they elevate value creation performance, enhance cross-functional coherence, and enable enterprises to scale both intelligently and sustainably—preserving domain excellence while advancing strategic outcomes.

Value Stream Stewardship

The quality of value stream management—across both delivery arcs and asset warehouses—exerts a decisive influence on the broader landscape of operational performance. Senior executives bear the responsibility not merely for overseeing efficient execution but for ensuring that every value stream is strategically coordinated with the organization's overarching objectives. Achieving such alignment entails rigorous baseline assessments, ongoing comparative benchmarking, and disciplined governance—particularly in illuminating how value streams absorb and manage costs to generate meaningful returns on investment.

Within this architecture, delivery arc managers are entrusted with the orchestration of value as it flows through interconnected processes, while domain managers act as custodians of expertise within asset warehouses. The domain manager's mandate is twofold: to define and maintain the organization's professional standards through the design, dissemination, and periodic refinement of methodologies, tools, and practices; and to oversee the development of human capital by ensuring that personnel receive comprehensive training and are afforded clear, structured pathways for career growth. This model not only sustains technical integrity but also ensures that individual development remains tightly integrated with enterprise imperatives.

At the heart of operational excellence, value stream managers are charged with cultivating the systemic conditions necessary for achieving high throughput, minimal inventory burden, and optimal deployment of resources. These outcomes are not accidental—they result from the disciplined application of a curated set of operational principles, carefully aligned to support both enterprise efficiency and enduring value creation. The following conventions exemplify this disciplined approach:

- Establish the synchronous flow of work across a full delivery arc and the maturation of business capabilities realized within an asset warehouse.

- Implement pull-based systems that regulate work-in-process, optimize resource capacity, and ensure workloads align with group-level constraints.

- Apply prioritization and sequencing techniques grounded in strategic intent to ensure that critical tasks are addressed in the right order and at the right time.

- Reduce cross-boundary handoffs to mitigate the friction and latency associated with material and information transfers between disparate units.

- Eliminate interruptions and inefficiencies, such as context-switching, redundant effort, and other forms of non-value-added activities that dilute performance.

Embedding Quality in Flow

A mature, value-based management system integrates the above elements seamlessly, transcending traditional functional departments and enabling systemic coherence. In the Valorys system, quality is not relegated to a discrete checkpoint or end-stage inspection function; rather, it is embedded in the logic of every activity and decision point throughout each value stream. This mirrors the core philosophy of the Toyota Production System, where quality is inherently "built-in" through the structure and logic of the value stream itself.

Effective stewardship of talent, processes, and enabling technologies remains essential for sustaining continuous improvement and minimizing organizational waste. To accelerate the maturity of each value stream, I recommend embedding at least one seasoned coach within every stream. This individual serves as a change agent for aligning culture, refining operations, and reinforcing desired behaviors—thus advancing VRO objectives and strengthening flow until the stream achieves sustained autonomy.

The architecture of value streams may—and should—vary depending on the maturity and lifecycle stage of its associated offerings. New value flows might emerge in response to novel innovations, or through the aggregation and refinement of existing solutions. An organization's product taxonomy provides guidance in determining the optimal formation and configuration of these streams.

Value Culture Best Practices

1: *Balance autonomy with accountability and trust.* Genuine empowerment requires clear frameworks of responsibility and consequence. High-performance cultures uphold standards of excellence while affirming professional autonomy. When outcomes fall short, responses center on diagnosis and improvement—not blame. By fostering psychological safety, adaptive leaders enable individuals to learn, recalibrate, and contribute with confidence and renewed commitment.

2: *Align empowered decision-making with value creation.* As enhanced workers internalize the principles of value economics, their daily choices naturally reinforce enterprise-wide cost discipline and value generation. Regular, synchronized operational cadences strengthen this alignment, promoting coherent resource planning, dependable delivery, and shared foresight across all organizational levels.

3: *Lead cultural transformation by principled role modeling.* Sustainable change begins when leaders model value-centered behavior rooted in foundation and practice. Establishing a Value Realization Office at the corporate level provides essential structure and governance, guiding the enterprise through its evolution toward a value-driven culture.

4: *Create principled cycles of mutual benefit.* Value-centered organizations generate outcomes that extend beyond operational performance—enriching employees, uplifting customers, and rewarding shareholders. This integrated philosophy transcends competitive strategy; it represents a holistic philosophy dedicated to realizing enduring value and mutually beneficial impact.

***

Organization Highlight: Semco

Semco, the Brazilian industrial conglomerate renowned for its extraordinarily effective management philosophy, offers a compelling blueprint for nurturing corporate cultures where value transcends mere delivery—becoming intrinsically institutionalized. Under Ricardo Semler's visionary leadership, Semco reimagined the traditional enterprise by embedding a value-centric ethos into every organizational stratum, thereby transforming its workforce into active stewards of both purpose and performance.

Semco's transformation was not primarily driven by a reengineering of operations or a shift in market strategy, but by a radical reframing of how value is culturally produced and sustained. At the heart of this redefinition is the conviction that value does not emerge from top-down directives or bureaucratic compliance—but from the distributed intelligence of those closest to the work. This belief challenges one of the most persistent myths in traditional management—that authority correlates with insight.

By systematically decentralizing decision-making, Semco activated latent capabilities within its workforce—encouraging innovation, responsiveness, and strategic alignment from the ground up. Employees ceased to be implementers of policy and became co-authors of organizational success. As of the early 2000s, approximately 75% of all operational and strategic decisions at Semco were made by employee consensus, not management fiat.[14] This model served not only as a mechanism of empowerment but as a feedback loop through which cultural tenets reinforced performance and accountability.

The implications of this philosophy are not abstract doctrines referenced in leadership rhetoric. Semco embedded its values through a suite of progressive structural reforms that executives in other organizations regularly study and adapt to this day. For instance, Semco eliminated its corporate headquarters, replacing it with a series of fluid, satellite office environments. Employees were empowered to choose their workspace based on need, proximity, or team alignment—an approach that presaged today's distributed work models by nearly two decades.

At Semco, value is a lived organizational norm, reinforced through transparent processes, democratic forums, and collaborative planning structures. Employee participation extends to financial transparency as well—workers review company financials every two weeks and help set their own salaries through peer committees, an approach virtually unheard of in traditional firms.

From a theoretical standpoint, Semco represents a living model of organizational sovereignty, anchored in the principles of self-determination theory, emotional well-being, and collective efficacy. By creating environments where individuals experience autonomy, mastery, and purpose, Semco activated intrinsic motivation as a driver of business outcomes.

For executives grappling with disengagement, turnover, or legacy inertia, the Semco model offers actionable insight: cultural transformation must be underpinned by structural congruence. It is insufficient to preach empowerment while maintaining rigid reporting lines and opaque decision rights. Executives should determine where decisions are made and by whom, whether value is defined operationally or philosophically, and how much delegated permission is embedded in their processes.

Semco is not simply a success story from Latin America's industrial sphere—it is a standing provocation to the status quo. It challenges the orthodoxies of hierarchy, exposes the myth that oversight must be unrelenting to be effective, and refutes the premise that coordinated value formulation must originate at the apex of power. The results speak without equivocation: a workforce that is more engaged, more innovative, and more accountable precisely because it has been trusted rather than controlled. For executives conditioned by decades of command-and-control convention, Semco offers an uncomfortable but clarifying truth—that the architecture of authority is often the greatest obstacle to the performance it purports to protect. The company affirms that when every individual assumes ownership for advancing value, innovation ceases to be intermittent and instead becomes an intrinsic, self-sustaining force within an enterprise.

1. Simon Sinek, *Start with Why: How Great Leaders Inspire Everyone to Take Action* (Portfolio-Penguin Group, 2009).

2. *Harvard Business Publishing*, "The Purpose Factor" (November 2022).

3. *MIT Center for Information Systems Research*, "Building Business Value With Employee Experience" (June 2017).

4. Dan Pink, *Drive: The Surprising Truth About What Motivates Us* (Penguin, 2009).

5. Scott Ambler, *Agile Modeling: Effective Practices for eXtreme Programming and the Unified Process* (Wiley, 2002).

6. The term "information radiator" was coined by Alistair Cockburn in 2001, although the concept is rooted in earlier practices. Notably, the Toyota Production System introduced the idea of "visual control" in the 1980s, aiming to make production processes transparent and easily understandable at a glance. Later, Kent Beck popularized the term "Big Visible Chart" (attributed to Martin Fowler) in his book *Extreme Programming Explained*, highlighting the importance of visible progress information.

7. Taiichi Ohno, *Toyota Production System: Beyond Large-Scale Production* (Productivity Press, 1988).

8. Jacob M. Engel, "Why Does Culture 'Eat Strategy for Breakfast'?" *Forbes* (November 20, 2018).

9. Mary and Tom Poppendieck, *Lean Software Development: An Agile Toolkit* (Addison-Wesley, 2003).

10. James Womack and Daniel Jones, *Lean Thinking: Banish Waste and Create Wealth in Your Corporation* (Simon & Schuster, 1996).

11. W. Edwards Deming, *The New Economics for Industry, Government, Education* (Cambridge, MA: MIT Center for Advanced Engineering, 1993).

12. Jack Ma articulated this prioritization principle on multiple occasions. Among the most cited primary instances: a letter to employees written in advance of Alibaba's IPO filing, reported by Reuters (May 13, 2014), and remarks to Charlie Rose, reported by Mashable (September 17, 2014). Duncan Clark's biography *Alibaba: The House That Jack Ma Built* (Ecco, 2016) provides useful context for the philosophy but is a secondary source for the quotation itself.

13. Douglas Smith and Jon Katzenbach, *The Wisdom of Teams: Creating the High-Performance Organization* (Harvard Business Review Press, 2015).

14. Ricardo Semler, *Maverick: The Success Story Behind the World's Most Unusual Workplace* (Warner Books, 1995).

Part Four: Coda

The Valorys Value Creation System

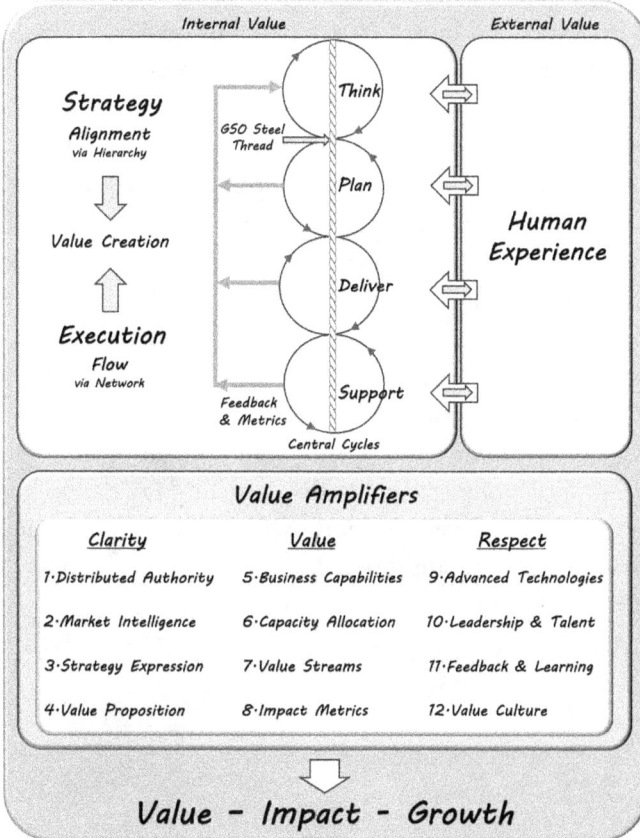

Internal Value | External Value

Strategy
Alignment
via Hierarchy

GSO Steel
Thread

Think

Value Creation

Plan

Human
Experience

Execution
Flow
via Network

Deliver

Feedback
& Metrics

Support

Central Cycles

Value Amplifiers

Clarity	Value	Respect
1·Distributed Authority	5·Business Capabilities	9·Advanced Technologies
2·Market Intelligence	6·Capacity Allocation	10·Leadership & Talent
3·Strategy Expression	7·Value Streams	11·Feedback & Learning
4·Value Proposition	8·Impact Metrics	12·Value Culture

Value – Impact – Growth

Value creation aligns capital, talent, and wisdom toward outcomes that uplift stakeholders, sustain purpose, and shape an organization's legacy. It is my sincere hope that the Valorys system, rooted in the tenets of value, clarity, and respect—and distinguished by its twelve value amplifiers—will exert a transformative influence on organizations, both public and private. Beyond institutional applications, I hold a deeper ambition: that this framework be harnessed to confront some of humanity's most urgent challenges—housing crises, systemic poverty, disaster relief, and countless other imperatives that call for innovative, value-centered solutions.

What excites me most is the prospect of others adapting and advancing this system through their own necessity-driven ingenuity. Its evolutionary potential—tested in diverse contexts and refined by real-world demands—may offer the most powerful testament to its enduring relevance and structural integrity.

This written work reflects the culmination of a lifelong pursuit—an enduring commitment to inquiry, experimentation, and applied service. The opportunity to distill decades of insight into a coherent, actionable system—capable of supporting leaders and organizations across every scale, sector, and geography—has been profoundly meaningful and deeply fulfilling.

As you turn from these pages back to your own work, I thank you for considering this progressive system. May the principles of authentic value creation, purposeful impact, and sustainable growth guide your path forward—serving as both compass and inspiration in your leadership journey.

Acknowledgments

I wish to express my gratitude to the colleagues and collaborators whose unique contributions were instrumental in bringing this work to fruition: Dr. Jody Saltzman, Nishant Sasidharan, Eric Robertson, Phil Reynolds, Jody Frank, Eddie Burns, Dr. Wendy Saltzman, Michael Bauer, Greg Frank, and Dr. Steve Macedo.

Your insight, patience, and support helped shape its direction and brought clarity when I needed it most.

About the Author

Colin O'Neill is a respected entrepreneur, thought leader, and value creation consultant whose career reflects a dedication to redefining how organizations conceive, create, and deliver enduring value. A graduate of the United States Naval Academy, he served as an officer in the U.S. Marine Corps where he developed his leadership instincts and deepened his lifelong commitment to service and principled action.

For over four decades he has guided government and industry leaders toward innovative business and technology solutions beneficial to employees, organizations, and society. Colin is the creator of Valorys, a comprehensive system that enables entities to unlock latent value across all operational levels through adaptive leadership, distributed authority, empowered workers, advanced technologies, and a distinctive constellation of twelve value amplifiers. He co-founded Vterra, an enterprise dedicated to enriching the personal and professional lives of leaders worldwide.

Beyond his consulting work, Colin pursues a diverse array of interests, including Eastern contemplative traditions, cognitive science, conscious capitalism, and the compassionate discipline of nonviolent communication. Residing in San Diego, California, Colin embraces a path of personal and spiritual development enriched by family, friends, and nature's gift of quiet restoration.

www.ingramcontent.com/pod-product-compliance
Lightning Source LLC
Chambersburg PA
CBHW060542200326
41521CB00007B/453